WAKE UP, LAZARUS!

Also by Pierre Hegy:

L'espoir déçu. L'autorité dans l'Église catholique.
Villeurbanne Cedex: Éditions Golias, 2006. (Second
edition of *L'autorité dans le catholicisme contemporain).*

*Equal at the Creation. Sexism, Society, and Christian
Thought.* Joseph Martos and Pierre Hegy, Editors.
Toronto University Press, 1998.

Feminist Voices in Spirituality. Edwin Mellen Press, 1996.

The Church in the Nineties. The Liturgical Press, 1993.

L'autorité dans le catholicisme contemporain. Paris,
Beauchesne, 1975.

Introducción a la sociología religiosa del Perú. Lima,
Studium, 1971.

WAKE UP, LAZARUS!

~

ON CATHOLIC RENEWAL

PIERRE HEGY

iUniverse, Inc.
Bloomington

Wake Up, Lazarus!
On Catholic Renewal

iUniverse books may be ordered through booksellers or by contacting:

iUniverse
1663 Liberty Drive
Bloomington, IN 47403
www.iuniverse.com
1-800-Authors (1-800-288-4677)

Because of the dynamic nature of the Internet, any web addresses or links contained in this book may have changed since publication and may no longer be valid. The views expressed in this work are solely those of the author and do not necessarily reflect the views of the publisher, and the publisher hereby disclaims any responsibility for them.

Any people depicted in stock imagery provided by Thinkstock are models, and such images are being used for illustrative purposes only.

Certain stock imagery © Thinkstock.

ISBN: 978-1-4620-0158-3 (sc)
ISBN: 978-1-4620-0159-0 (ebk)

Printed in the United States of America

iUniverse rev. date: 05/11/2011

To Fr. Pete Chiara

who launched "operation Lazarus" as a wake-up call to his parish

In his words:

One day [in the early 1970s] when we discussed church statistics at a staff meeting, someone said, "It's like the church is dead." I said, "That's it! That's what we must look at."

We then sent out personal letters to all the 6400 families with the mention on the envelope, *"The Church is dead."* In this letter we announced that the church would be closed, and that we would have four evening discussions [called *"operation Lazarus"*] to explore what we should do. About 1,200 showed up at every meeting. One of the things that came up most was the need to learn how to pray: "We go to mass, but we don't know how to pray at mass!"

They wanted to have more input in what we do. So we had twenty people elected to serve as advisory group to the parish. After that, I got sick, and was no longer the pastor of the parish…

Today [2007] this parish is again very low in attendance. The current pastor feels it is less than 17 percent. What we now do is maintenance. People feel we do not approach them enough. We do not address their needs.

Preface
and
Acknowledgments

Crises are times of opportunity. This book was written at the time of two major crises, the clerical sex scandal and a trend of Catholic decline amid evangelical growth. It was a time when nearly every day or week, the Catholic Church was in the news for clerical sexual abuse, while at the same time, national and international research documented evangelical vitality and growth in the United States and abroad. This is not a time for complacency but change, and change usually begins at home, in one's own backyard. Small improvements are not only feasible but also imperative, and small changes are what this book proposes.

The contributors of this book were many. I owe a special debt to the about eighty parish leaders and the fifty theologians I interviewed about parish life and current theological issues. Through their answers to my questions and the questions raised by their answers, they have expanded my sociological imagination. I have also made many friends at the two churches described in chapters 4 and 5. Over several years, I spent many months at both churches, and they became somewhat part of my imagination. In both churches, I have met and befriended scores of members. Their religious behavior and spiritual journeys have enriched me beyond words. Since I do not mention the name of these churches, their members shall also remain anonymous, but not forgotten.

Contents

INTRODUCTION

〜

Catholic decline in the West may be of the magnitude of the decline that happened at the end of the Middle Ages and the Reformation. The digital revolution under way seems as important as that of the printing press; it acts as a powerful force of secularization through its ethic of consumption, leaving the soul empty but the mind full of bits and pieces of noncumulative information. Evangelicals have capitalized on the possibilities of the new media; the Catholic Church has not, or not much. A cultural revolution of discontinuity between generations has evolved as well. For the first time ever, children will not necessarily espouse the religion of their parents. One's religious preference, as well as one's major in college, have become matters of personal choice, and Catholicism is ill prepared for religious individualism. More generally, cultural discontinuity exists to the extent that the new knowledge of the young displaces the knowledge of the old: new knowledge is the driving force in science and business, while tradition is not, and students often display amnesia in their study and understanding of the humanities. In such a context, religious tradition—a major characteristic of Catholic teaching—is less appealing than the apparent creativity of nondenominational and evangelical churches; not surprisingly, the latter are growing while Catholicism is not.

Decline is best documented by numbers. Regular Sunday attendance is down to about single digits in European countries. There is little solace in the view that religious quality (if quality there is!) is better than quantity, because over time, nonpractice leads to religious disaffiliation, and later to nonreligion. In various countries of low religious practice (France, Benelux,

1

Germany, and also in Latin American countries like Brazil), the Catholic Church has lost about one third of its members in one or two generations. If the trend continues, Catholicism will have lost half its members in these countries in another generation or so. This possible loss of up to half the membership is comparable to the loss of half of the Catholic world at the time of the Reformation.

At the global level, membership statistics are not more encouraging. At about the beginning of the third millennium, Catholicism has moved from being the first world religion to the second or even the third. There are now undeniably more Muslims in the world than Catholics, but there may also be as many or more non-Catholic Christians than Catholic Christians[1]—if not today, then in the foreseeable future. The irony is that it is Catholicism (i.e., the papacy) that has rejected and/or excommunicated non-Catholics; hence, it should exhibit indisputable superiority, but this is not the case. Throughout the world, the growth rate of evangelicals and Pentecostals is greater than that of Catholics, as they multiply through conversions rather than population growth. Hence, it is the intrinsic qualities of these churches that attract new conversions; orthopraxis seems increasingly more important than orthodoxy, which has been the hallmark of Catholicism for centuries.

In the United States, evangelicals are now the greatest religious force, counting for 26.3 percent of the population, versus 23.9 percent for Catholics, according to the 2006 Pew Forum. Catholic increase in the United States is due to population growth, not conversions, but 71 percent of that growth since 1960 comes from immigration, especially from Latin America.[2] The proportion of Latinos in the Catholic Church is expected to increase from 33 percent today to 41 percent in the next twenty-five years, according to the 2006 Pew Forum. Latinos are generally more religious than Anglos; hence, they are a blessing for Catholicism. Yet the low ratio of Latino priests to Latino Catholics in the United States (lower than in any other country in the world) is likely to limit their influence and development. US church attendance rates are a matter of debate among specialists, as survey respondents tend to exaggerate their religious participation. I give most credence to the finding of the Center for Applied Research in the Apostolate (CARA) of a stable 30–35 percent

Sunday attendance rate, consisting of 20–25 percent weekly attenders and about 10 percent occasional attenders. More specifically, according to the 2008 CARA research on sacraments, 23 percent of Catholics attend Mass weekly, 21 percent monthly, 24 percent a few times a year, and 32 percent never.[3] Thus more Catholics attend seldom or never (56 percent) than regularly, monthly, or more often (44 percent). The Catholic Church is also the religious body in the United States that most loses members, either to other churches or to the growing number of those with "no religion."

There is nothing new about these statistics. The purpose of quoting them is to draw attention to the seriousness of the situation. What is needed is renewal. There are many vibrant parishes in the United States, and many programs of parish renewal, but they do not seem appropriate to the magnitude of the problem. Exceptional parishes still grow, which is comforting, but they attract members from other parishes rather than converts. They may even lose some of their own members who are not sufficiently engaged—namely the young and the inactive Catholics—as they are unable to address the forces of secularization at work in society and the churches. More radical proposals are needed.

After three short chapters on decline, I come to renewal. Chapter 4 describes a little-known nondenominational church that has grown steadily over the last fifty years from a few hundred members to 2,700 in 2007. The vitality of this church is built on neither doctrinal innovation nor charismatic personalities (although the senior pastor is a remarkable preacher), but on assiduous prayer and a sense of mission. This is a church that looks outward, not inward, to its neighborhood, the nation, and the world. It supports about seventy to eighty full-time missionaries. There is a real sense of community in the happiness people find in seeing each other at church. This congregation employs a simple formula for growth that is easy to imitate.

Chapter 5 describes a vibrant Catholic parish that can best be described as a community of communities, as it consists of scores of small Christian communities meeting weekly. The parish itself is structured as a community of ministries, which are organized as communities. Scripture and prayer are central to its spirituality, following the Vatican II inspiration. The Sunday liturgy is the focus of the week, with music that is attractive to both the old and the young, as it blends traditional hymns with evangelical and avant-garde creations. What is remarkable about this parish of 3,800 families is that it has only one resident priest; hence, all ministries are carried out by the laity. This is a laity-driven parish, where lay initiatives develop within the pastor's grand vision. This is a vibrant parish to be emulated, yet it is not totally adequate to overcome the Catholic downturn, as it is, like most parishes, essentially looking inward.

Before coming to my own proposal, I review various renewal plans in chapter 6. I begin with *Go and Make Disciples: A National Plan and Strategy for Catholic Evangelization in the United States*, adopted by the Catholic Conference of American Bishops in 1992. This is a list of evangelization strategies, not a list of successful parishes or local programs. It offers a total of 32 objectives and 153 strategies, but nothing really new. Over the last fifteen years, this plan has made no significant dent in the ongoing Catholic decline. I turn next to two sociological tools for religious growth: the Gallup parish surveys and the Congregational Life Surveys, which provide invaluable insights into parish needs but provide no strategies; they are tools, nothing more. In Rick Warren's *Purpose-Driven Church* we find strategies but also great sociological wisdom, but no data. This book has inspired and continues to influence numerous churches. Finally, in the Willow Creek surveys, we find both strategies and quantitative data. Among their major findings are the following: many churchgoers are stalled in their religious practice, yet satisfied with the status quo of the parish; it is Christ-centeredness, not church-centeredness, that correlates with spiritual growth; and finally, the needs of beginners are different from those of the more advanced, as the former need more church support and supervision while the latter need less.

Using some of the insights gained in the above, I finally outline a plan for 2030—that is, a long-term plan that may take decades to accomplish. In this organic plan, one level builds on the next. The first and most urgent step is to stop the hemorrhaging of Catholic losses, which comes from the low level of Sunday participation. Many regular Mass attenders seem stalled in their spiritual lives; they may be satisfied with the relative mediocrity of the Sunday liturgy, but their children are not, and will not follow suit. Over time, passive Mass attenders may switch from weekly to monthly to seasonal church attendance, then to no more attendance, and finally to the "no-religion" status. The first move is to strengthen the most vulnerable Catholics, the passive Sunday attenders (as many as 80 percent), who must be brought to a more active church participation. The next step is to help active Sunday members become involved in discipleship through the numerous devotional organizations, especially small Christian communities meeting weekly. Commitment to discipleship requires a weekly involvement besides the Sunday liturgy. Finally, total commitment to discipleship requires daily involvement, in one way or another. Total commitment is one of ministry, not only in service ministries but also in mission ministries, and not only inward but also outward looking. A church is only as strong as its totally committed members, but the latter will only flourish in a parish of many active Sunday worshippers and numerous committed members involved in communities of discipleship. Horizon 2030 may be with us only too soon.

One relative innovation of this study is the use of theological, scriptural, and canonical sources. In sociology, the primacy of scientific objectivity may suggest to some that theological ignorance is a sign of one's religious neutrality, but this was not true of Max Weber and Troeltsch, among others, who are classics of social-scientific scholarship. Theology is the language of Christianity, just as Mandarin was the language of imperial China; any outsider must learn the language of insiders in order to converse with the established authorities. This is particularly necessary in research about church renewal, as any proposal must wrestle with accepted theological, biblical, and canonical views.

We may be at a historical junction when the social sciences of religion may become a new form of theological reflection. Generally speaking, it seems that academic theology reflects on beliefs rather than faith; on doctrine rather than practices; and on theological publications rather than individual and collective experiences. Some of the hallmarks of academic theology are knowledge rather than spiritual growth, along with structural change in the church rather than individual conversion. Yet theology is a mansion with many rooms. Systematic theology represents one end of the continuum of theological studies, while pastoral theology stands at the other end. Pastoral sociology is often like a twin sister of pastoral theology, although the two may flourish in quite different environments. Pastoral sociology may be viewed with suspicion in clerical circles, while pastoral theology may not. But as an outsider to the ecclesiastical establishment, pastoral sociology may be able to take a more radical and prophetic stand than pastoral theology.

According to Lonergan writing in 1968, theology "has largely become an empirical science" as "Scripture and Tradition now provide not premises, but data."[4] Pastoral sociology would go one step further. Going beyond the "two sources" of Scripture and tradition referred to by Lonergan, pastoral sociology can look at lived faith, devotions, popular religiosity, and the *sensus fidelium* as *loci theologici*—that is, objects of theological and pastoral reflection. While pastoral theology may look at these practices from the standpoint of theology and orthodoxy, pastoral sociology may analyze them from the perspective of comparative religions or general sociological theories. As a result, pastoral sociology may be a new form of God-talk or theology. For ordinary parishioners, academic theology, like Mandarin, is a language difficult to master, while the languages of Scripture and pastoral sociology/theology are easier. Most pastoral strategies are blends of biblical and pastoral reflections. This book deals with pastoral strategies; hence, it must use the various languages of theology, Scripture, canon law, and pastoral sociology/theology in addition to statistics and sociological theory. In sum, this book hopes to make a contribution to the growing field of pastoral sociology, as well as to renewal in the Catholic Church.

Why did I write this book? In Chapter 3, I distinguish between insiders and outsiders. Insiders feel a strong sense of identification with the institution; they tend to defend it, even against legitimate criticisms. Outsiders have the opposite feeling: a feeling of abandonment and betrayal; they tend to be critical, even hostile at times. The churchly love of the first may be infatuation; that of the second regrets and disappointment. I identify with neither the insiders nor the outsiders, trying instead to be an insider/outsider.

I learned the role of insider/outsider when preparing for my PhD dissertation. My chosen topic at the University of Paris was authority in the Catholic Church after Vatican II. It was the time of *Humanae Vitae* on birth control (1968), a time of betrayal for the liberals - many of whom became outsiders, and a time of renewed assertiveness for conservatives - many of whom became militant insiders. Facing my thesis was a jury of intellectuals, one a Marxist, another a probable agnostic, and a third a likely cultural Catholic. As an insider/outsider I was able to present the great intuitions of the dogmatic constitutions of the church (*Lumen gentium*) and of the pastoral constitution of the church today (*Gaudium et spes*) because I also exposed the political weakness of the papal conception of authority as God-given from *Mirari Vos* (1832) to the *Syllabus of Errors* (1864); the intellectual obsolescence of neo-scholasticism prevalent in the 19th century; and the rigid authoritarianism of the 1917 code of Canon Law, still in effect at that time. My thesis was cast in light of the structuralist theory of my dissertation mentor (Roland Barthes), and couched in the structuralist language of the time. The jury was satisfied. Their questions and objections were intellectual, not religious. I came out as neither a defender nor an attacker of the Catholic Church. I made *my* points, but I had accepted *their* language and intellectual concerns as legitimate, indeed as enlightening.

Much has changed in the world since the early 1960s, the time of the flower revolution in the U.S. and pre-Vatican II neo-scholasticism in Catholicism, but not much (or not enough) has changed in the Catholic Church. Within two generations or so, the American church has lost about a third of its members, either to other religions or secularism. I felt it was time for me to take my pen again and say, "Wake up, Lazarus" You can't sleep for another generation or two. The time to act is now!"

Finally, one suggestion to the hurried reader who may want to learn quickly about Catholic renewal: I would suggest beginning with the inspiring story of St. Mary Star of Hope on page 113 (without the theoretical introduction of chapter 5). St. Mary's is an example of the renewal that can be achieved according to the approach that I develop in the last chapter, which addresses renewal for Horizon 2030. If you want a quick look at my proposal, start at page 224. The basic principle of renewal is to help the faithful move up from passive to active participation in the liturgy, next from active participation to parish involvement, and finally from involvement to commitment in discipleship. These are lofty goals that may not easily be achieved, even by 2030.

CHAPTER 1

~

INCONVENIENT STATISTICS

We easily accept statistics when they reinforce what we believe; when they do not, they are simply inconvenient. So, let us find out what you believe. Here are four questions that will be answered in the course of this chapter: 1) What is the fastest growing religious body in the United States, and who joins it? 2) Do more Protestants convert to Catholicism or more Catholics to Protestantism? 3) In terms of vitality and spirituality, how do Catholic parishes stand in comparison to Protestant congregations—better, about the same, or worse? 4) What is the main reason Spanish Americans leave the Catholic Church, and what special contribution can Latino Catholics make to the Church? Let us find out.

This chapter offers little new information. So what is its purpose? Many Catholics seem ignorant of the seriousness of the decline; hence, the first step is to go over basic statistics. Causes of decline will be investigated in chapters 2 and 3, and renewal will be the focus of chapters 4 to 7.

Believed Religion Is Losing Influence
in 1957 14%
in 1962 31%
in 1965 45%
in 1967 57%
in 1968 67%
in 2008 67%

In the 1960s, most religious bodies in the United States started to decline, not only in membership and church attendance, but also in religious school enrollments and the building of new churches and schools.[5] As shown by the insert on the left, by 1968 the majority of Americans already believed that religion was losing influence.[6] Where do we stand today, forty years later? I will review basic statistics—first about religious affiliation and church attendance; next about priests and sisters; and finally about Catholic and Protestant parishes. Considering that the proportion of Hispanics in the Catholic Church will increase in the coming decades, we will look at the more encouraging signs of religious vitality in the American Hispanic population at the end of this chapter.

In absolute numbers, the Catholic Church in the United States has changed little over the last forty years (from 24 percent of the US population in 1965 to 21 percent in 2010). These numbers are misleading, however, since the influx of immigrants and the higher birth rate of Hispanics hide actual decline. If the immigration of Hispanics continues as in the past, their proportion in the Catholic Church will increase from about 33 percent today to 41 percent by 2030. Yet the relatively higher religious practice of American Hispanics will not offset the general decline, due to persistent decline in religious practice among the young. Indeed, the mass exodus of the young is the major issue facing the Catholic Church, as will be seen below.

1. Religious Identification and Church Attendance

Membership records vary from church to church, because membership itself may be defined differently. In surveys, interviewees are asked to indicate their religious preference, but these answers are often meaningless, because there are so many ways of being Protestant or Catholic. A more reliable measurement is that of religious change—that is, conversions (e.g., from Protestantism to Catholicism and vice versa); hence, I will use the number of conversions as an indicator of gains and losses within and between churches.

A standard set of national data is found in the General Social Surveys (GSS), taken every year or every other year since 1972. The most recent data available are those of 2008. Beginning in 1973, the data reflect the respondents' religious identification and also the religion in which they were raised. Thus, from 1973 to 2006, out of the 12,240 Catholics in all the samples, 11,029 (or 90 percent) grew up in the Catholic Church, while 10 percent converted from other religions, a 10 percent gain. Similarly, out of the 28,254 Protestants in all the samples, 91.3 percent grew up in a Protestant church, which represents an 8.7 percent gain. Losses are computed in a similar way: out of the 13,964 respondents raised as Catholics, only 79 percent were still Catholic at the time of the survey, a 21 percent loss. Out of the 29,323 raised as Protestants, only 88 percent remained Protestant, an 11 percent loss. Combining gains and losses, we find that Catholics declined by 11.6 percent and Protestants by 3.3 percent. Table 1 gives gains and losses for the various religious bodies.

The first column presents the relative importance of the various religious bodies. The Protestant faith has constituted the majority in the

Table 1
Gains and Losses by Religious Identification
(GSS 1973–2008)

	% in all samples	% losses	% gains	% change
Protestant	58.6	12.4	9.1	−3.3
Catholic	25.9	21.5	9.9	−11.6
Jewish	2.0	16.5	10.7	−5.8
None	10.0	47.8	74.9	27.1
Other	1.8	36.9	57.1	20.2

United States since its foundation, but its position has eroded in recent years. In the 1972–1974 GSS surveys, Protestants accounted for about 62.6 percent of the population, while in 2006–2008, they were only 50.1 percent. The proportions of Protestants and Catholics in the GSS samples are not as accurate as the census data or those from larger samples; from the latter, we know that today Protestants have dropped below 50 percent. While the Jews have always been a very small minority (2 or 3 percent), Americans with no religion jumped from 6.2 percent in 1972–1974 to 16.2 percent in 2006–2008—even 18 percent in a larger survey, as indicated below. The remaining 1.8 percent includes all "other" religious affiliations—that is, Buddhists, Muslims, Hindus, Native Americans, Orthodox, interdenominational Christians, and those self-identified as just Christians.

Looking at the losses and gains in table 1, we see that Catholics suffered enormous losses: 21.5 percent, nearly double that of Protestants (12.4 percent). Both Protestants and Catholics made significant gains from other churches (8.7 percent and 9.9 percent, respectively). The greatest gains and losses are found in the less stable groups, the "none" and the "other." The Jews lost 4.9 percent, but their small numbers in the sample makes this conclusion tentative. Protestants lost a modest 3.3 percent, nearly four times less than Catholics (11.6 percent). The major gains overall are in the "no religion" and "other" categories, with impressive gains of 27.1 and 20.2 percent, respectively. The "no religion" is by far the fastest growing religious group. Today about one adult American in six claims to have no religion; their number is about five times that of American Jews. At the current growth rate, the "no religion" may constitute one third of the American population within a generation.

We can now answer our first question: The fastest growing religious body is that of no religion. Who joins them? Since only 25.3 percent of them were raised without religion, most of them (about 70 percent) are former Protestants and Catholics. A more detailed source of information than the GSS, the 2001 comprehensive survey on religious identity, based on 50,000 replies, found that out of the nine million ex-Catholics, 28 percent now identify themselves as having no religion; conversely, out of the six million respondents identifying with "no religion," as many as 43 percent (or 2.5 million) are ex-Catholics.[7]

Have gains and losses increased over the years? For the purpose of simplicity, the data in table 2 are grouped in five-year categories (surveys have been taken every other year since 1994; no survey was taken in 1979 and 1981).

Table 2
**Catholic and Protestant Losses and Gains in Religious
Identification over the Years (GSS data)**

	% Losses		% Gains		% Change	
	Prot.	Cath.	Prot.	Cath.	Prot.	Cath.
1973–1978	9.7	15.9	6.2	9.9	−3.5	−6.0
1980–1985	9.1	17.2	6.8	10.7	−2.3	−6.5
1986–1989	10.7	19.1	8.1	11.2	−2.6	−7.9
1990–1996	11.7	22.3	9.3	9.8	−2.4	−12.5
1998–2002	16.9	25.6	11.1	10.3	−5.8	−15.3
2004–2008	18.2	27.3	14.4	7.6	−3.8	−19.7
Avg. (73–08)	12.4	21.5	9.1	9.9	−3.3	−11.6

For both Catholics and Protestants, the losses have increased over time. Protestant gains have increased; Catholic gains have not. On average from 1973 to 2008, Protestants lost 12.4 percent of their members, while Catholics lost 21.5 percent. Protestants losses rose from about 9.7 percent in 1973–1978 to 18.2 in 2004–2008, while Catholic losses rose from 15.9 percent to 27.3 percent, an increase of about 42–45 percent in both cases. By combining gains and losses, we get the growth/decline rates. From 1973 to 2008, Protestant membership declined on average by a modest 3.3 percent and Catholic membership by 11.6 percent, or nearly four times the Protestant decline; the decline in 2004–2008 was a catastrophic 19.7 percent.

What happened to the dropouts? In the 1973–2008 data, out of the 14,716 respondents in the sample raised as Catholics, 10.7 percent on average became Protestant (13.7 percent in 2008) while out of the 30,304 raised as Protestants, 3.4 percent on average joined the Catholic Church (2.5 percent in 2008). The differences between Catholics and Protestants have been increasing: in the 1972–1979 period, 7.8 percent of raised Catholics joined the various forms of Protestantism, while in 2000–2008, 12.3 percent became Protestant. On the other hand, in 1972–1979, 3.3 percent of Protestants became Catholic, while in 2000–2008, 3 percent became Catholic: not much change.

In reference to our second question, have you been told that many Protestants converted to Catholicism? This was true in the past, in the pre-Vatican II days under Pope Pius XII. Today nearly three times more Catholics join Protestant churches than Protestants the Catholic Church. The Pew Forum Report of April 2009 presents similar findings. On average, 3 percent of those raised in Protestantism joined the Catholic Church, while 15 percent of those raised as Catholics are now Protestant, mostly evangelicals.[8] Let us first look at church attendance.

Since Sunday Mass attendance is mandatory by canon law, one would expect to find very high Catholic attendance rates. In the 1950s and 1960s, attendance was equally high among the young and the old, percentagewise. According to Fichter, 92.8 percent of Catholics under the age of 20 and 90.9 percent of those 60 and over 65 attended Mass every Sunday in a Southern urban parish in the 1950s.[9] The parents made it their duty to take their children to church, enforcing the law of mandatory attendance. This situation still prevailed in 1963, when weekly attendance was equally strong in all age groups: 79 percent for the 20–29, 78 percent for the 30–39, 80 percent for the 40–49, and 79 percent for the 50–59.[10] The only acceptable excuses for nonattendance were illnesses or other emergencies.

Weekly Mass Attendance by Age (Fichter, 1954)	
10–19	92.8%
20–29	77.6
30–39	69.3
40–49	74.3
50–59	77.2
60 and over	90.9
Average 78.6	

It is commonly believed among researchers that survey answers about church attendance tend to be exaggerated, due to prestige bias. But because we are interested in growth and/or decline rather than attendance per se—in attendance *changes* rather than their actual *rates*—we do not have to consider the recent issue of attendance inflation. The change in attendance is clearly shown in the Gallup surveys taken every year, even if the rates are inflated.

In 1955, Catholics of all ages attended church at very high rates.[11] At that time, an enormous gap of 30 percent separated Catholics and Protestants in church attendance. But from then on, the Catholic attendance levels dropped for all age categories, even among older Catholics. Among the young, the drop has been catastrophic: within one generation, their attendance level fell below the average of Protestants (see graph 1). On the other hand, Protestant church attendance has not changed over the last fifty years.

According to the Gallup polls, weekly Mass attendance peaked around 1958 at 74 percent for all Catholics. It dropped to 33 percent in 2003, according to CARA research. This research also found great generational differences: 38 percent among those over 60, as opposed to 21 percent among the 18- to 30-year-olds.[12] Weekly Mass attendance nationwide is now found to hover around 20 to 25 percent; the latter percentage is based on head counts and self-administered questionnaires, compared to the 30–35 percent found in face-to-face interviews.[13] More specifically, on an average Sunday, Mass attendance is likely to be in the 30–35 percent range; out of these, about 20–25 percent are weekly attenders (as found in head counts), and the others are seasonal attenders. These percentages have remained stable over the last few years.[14]

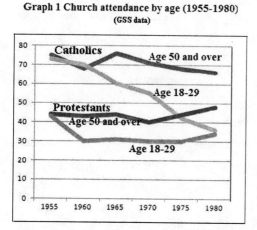

Graph 1 Church attendance by age (1955-1980) (GSS data)

Attendance among the young has consistently been about 20 percent lower than among adults. This difference also exists among Protestants, but it is smaller. Hence, the difference in church attendance between Protestants and Catholics will increase over the years. Weekly church attendance among Protestant is now higher, on average, than that of Catholics, as seen in graph 2. This is a historically significant event, since it makes mandatory attendance questionable: if attendance is higher among those not required to do so than among those required to attend, something must be wrong with the attendance requirement—more specifically, with the system of government setting the requirement. Today, all over the world, democratic governments elicit more citizen participation than authoritarian ones.

Why is attendance lower among the young? The trend began in the 1960s, when religious beliefs and practices dropped abruptly, as documented in a study in the San Francisco Bay area. In that study, most of the decline could be explained by involvement in the counterculture.[15] Since then, the "flower revolution" has faded away, but the decline continues: each generation begins its spiritual journey with lower rates of

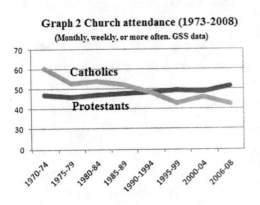

Graph 2 Church attendance (1973-2008)
(Monthly, weekly, or more often. GSS data)

church attendance. This pattern of further decline with each generation (as seen in graph 3) has been documented in England for the last hundred years. Hence, the cause is to be sought in the cultural environment (e.g., consumerism), rather than in individual characteristics or historical events (e.g., the Vietnam or Iraq wars).[16]

It is generally accepted today that young people tend to drop out of religion. In the United States, this is true for mainline Protestants and Catholics but not for black and evangelical Protestants. Among the latter, regular church attendance has actually increased in the last thirty years. Moreover, among the 18- to 25-year-old Protestants, the proportion of those who feel "strongly" that they are part of their churches has steadily increased, while among Catholics, a general decline has occurred.[17] This trend is ominous for the

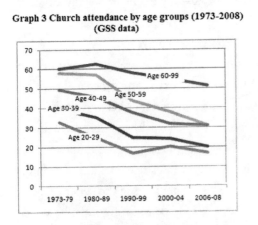

Graph 3 Church attendance by age groups (1973-2008)
(GSS data)

future: as the young generation enters adult life, the attendance rate among Catholics will continue to decline. Moreover, as the proportion of evangelicals who feel strongly about their church is about double that of

Catholics (about 55 percent versus 25 percent), the polarization and gap between the two will increase, with a likely increase in the rate of Catholic conversions to Protestantism.

Why is the decline among young Catholics more abrupt than among young Protestants? An answer can be found in the National Study of Youth and Religion of 2001. The general finding about Catholics is that "On most measures of religious faith, belief, and practice, Catholic teens as a whole show up as fairly weak."[18] Here are a few examples[19] comparing teen replies of Roman Catholic (RC) with those of mainline Protestants (MP) and conservative Protestants (CP). The large number of young Catholics who never attended religious education (40 percent, as opposed to 13 percent among Conservative Protestants) suggests that a major factor of decline is to be found in the Catholic culture discussed in chapter 3.

National Study of Youth and Religion of 2001

	RC	MP	CP
Religious faith is extremely important	10%	20%	29%
Has experienced a moving spiritual worship	37%	64%	70%
Was ever involved in a religious youth group	67%	84%	86%
Has never attended CCD or Sunday school	40%	19%	13%

2) Institutional Decline: Sisters, Priests, and Church Leadership

The strength of an institution comes not only from its members, but also from its staff and leadership. Attendance and membership are declining, but so is the number of priests and sisters. The decline is sharpest among religious sisters, whose number dropped from 179,954 in 1965 to 59,601 in 2009, a 66.7 percent decline.[20] The decline of the total number of priests, by contrast, is less than half (30.6 percent).

It has been suggested that one major factor for the decline of priests and sisters is the Vatican II vision of the whole church as a community of holiness in which all share in the priesthood of Christ.[21] Lumen Gentium (no. 44) and canon law (canons 207 and 208) emphasize the universal call to holiness, rooted in the one priesthood of Christ, which leaves no special mission for the religious. Sisters are laypeople, not clerics, but before Vatican II, vowed

17

religious had a *de facto* special status, at least in the eyes of the laity. The council's universal call to holiness tends to level out these differences, making it less attractive to enter religious life. Furthermore, as work in Catholic schools and hospitals can equally be performed by lay professionals, religious vocations to educational and charitable work are likely to decline.

The decline of Catholic schools parallels that of sisters. The number of students in Catholic elementary schools declined from 4.4 million in 1960 to 1.7 million in 2006, a 61 percent decline that parallels the 66 percent decline of sisters.[22] Obviously part of the decline in Catholic schools is due to the withdrawal of sisters from these schools, but the decline may continue for other reasons. If anyone with the proper professional credentials can work in Catholic schools and hospitals, the Catholic identity of these institutions will progressively be weakened. The same trend is at work in Catholic universities and colleges.

The decline of the number of priests is less precipitous than that of sisters. In 2009 it had declined by only 30.6 percent from the 1965 level, as opposed to 66.7 percent for sisters. This statistic, however, is misleading, since the Catholic population increased from 45.6 million in 1965 to 65.2 million in 2009. The ratio of priests to faithful has passed from one priest for 767 Catholics in 1965 to one for 1,603 Catholics in 2009, double that of 1965. In five dioceses, the priest ratio is one to over 5,000 Catholics, up to one for every 10,000 in Las Vegas, Nevada.[23] Moreover, priests are older today, which makes them less attuned to the needs of the young. Increasingly, foreign priests are invited to fill the gaps, leading to language and cultural barriers. One direct effect of the priestly decline is the increasing number of parishes without priests—or worse, the closing of parishes. The number of priestless parishes has jumped from 549 in 1965 to 3400 in 2009, a 500 percent increase.[24] In five dioceses, more than half the parishes are without a priest, up to a high of 71 percent of parishes in Rapid City, South Dakota.[25] As can be seen in graph 4, the number of priestless parishes is now outpacing the number of seminarians. Since it takes at least five or more years to train a seminarian for the priesthood, by knowing the number of students in seminaries, we can estimate the number of ordinations five years hence. Based on the number of seminarians in 2005, one can expect, by 2010, a 12 percent decline in the number of diocesan priests, which will lead to more priestless parishes.[26]

The decline in the number of priests is happening in most Western nations. In the 1985–2002 period, the decline was only 16 percent in the United States but 42 percent in the Netherlands, 35 percent in France, and 34 percent in Belgium.[27] Priestly decline is often symptomatic of a general religious decline. Thus 45.2 percent of the people interviewed do not believe in life after death in the Netherlands, 47.6 percent in France, and 49 percent in Belgium, according to the 1999–2004 World Survey of Values. The ratio of priests to faithful is also worse in the rest of the world than in the United States: in 2007 there was only one priest for every 7,139 South American Catholics, one for every 6,918 Central American Catholics, and one for every 4,470 African Catholics.[28]

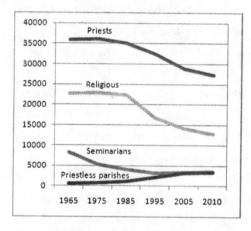

Graph 4 Clergy Decline

If the priestly decline is so widespread, is it due to outside factors, or is it special to the Catholic Church? To find out, Davidson checked the clergy supply in all major denominations in the United States from 1981 to 2001. He found that in all churches, "including denominations in which membership has declined (e.g. the Episcopal and evangelical Lutheran churches), the total number of clergy has increased." The increase was 29 percent and 11 percent for the Episcopal and evangelical Lutheran churches, 27 percent for the American Baptists, and 35 percent for the Assemblies of God. According to Davidson, "The Catholic Church is unique in several areas: the dwindling number of priests, the increasing number of laypeople per priest, the declining number of priests per parish, the increasing number of priestless parishes and the declining number of priests in nonparish ministries." Hence, the causes of priestly decline are to be sought, at least in part, in the church structure and belief system, rather than its social and cultural environment.[29]

The strength of an institution depends not only on its personnel but also on its authority—that is, its ability to make people abide by its leadership. Confidence in all major institutions has declined nationwide since the 1960s, and so has confidence in the churches. The 2007 Gallup poll found that confidence in religion is at an all-time low, but more so among Catholics than among Protestants. "Confidence in the church or organized religion has dropped from 53 percent in 2004 to 39 percent today among Catholics. Among Protestants, confidence increased from 60 percent in 2004 to 63 percent in 2006 and then dropped to 57 percent today [2007]."[30]

Confidence in the authority of the church can be measured by asking Catholics, "Who should have the final say about moral issues? The church leaders? Individuals? Or a combination of both?" This question was asked in a series of five surveys about five basic moral problems widely discussed under the papacy of John Paul II: divorce and remarriage, contraception, abortion, homosexuality, and nonmarital sexuality. Table 3 gives the replies from the 2005 survey—for the whole sample first, and the pre- and post-Vatican II generations in the next two columns.[31]

As can be seen in table 3, only one Catholic in four or five trusts the moral authority of the church on these specific issues. This is less than the percentage of regular Sunday Mass attenders. On the other hand, nearly half would trust themselves rather than the church; (not shown in the table are those who trust both).

Table 3
Locus of Authority by Generation[32]

	Whole sample	Pre-Vatican II	Post-Vatican II
Locus of authority in Church leaders:			
—divorce and remarriage	22%	22%	21%
—contraception	13	20	11
—abortion	25	33	19
—homosexuality	24	33	19
—nonmarital sexuality	22	30	21
Locus of authority in individuals:			
—divorce and remarriage	42%	33%	42%
—contraception	61	46	63
—abortion	44	31	50
—homosexuality	46	30	50
—nonmarital sexuality	47	38	49

Attitudes change with the generations. People born before 1941 (the pre-Vatican II generation) grew up under the pontificate of Pius XII when confidence in the church's authority was nearly absolute. This generation was raised with total confidence in the church, but has lost most of this confidence, since only one in three would locate the moral authority in the church leaders in 2005. These people are not individualists: they tend to locate moral authority in both church leaders and individuals. The influence of this pre-Vatican II generation is waning; there are only 17 percent of them in the sample.

Today's church is dominated by the post-Vatican II generation (born between 1961 and 1978); they have grown up under the aegis of John Paul II and have no firsthand knowledge of preconciliar forms of piety. Being the majority (40 percent of the sample in 2005), they set the agenda of the church for the coming decades. The "Millennials" (born between 1979 and 1987) are a small minority (9 percent in the sample). Not enough is known about them, except that their religiosity is substantially lower than that of the previous generation. If attendance is any indication (as seen in graph 4), their acceptance of moral authority of the church is likely to be only half that of the post-Vatican II generation, which would bring acceptance of the moral leadership of the magisterium down to about 10 percent.

It seems that renewal is not likely to come from today's leadership, as most Catholics do not have great confidence in their leaders, as seen in table 3; hence, let us look at parishes as possible centers of renewal.

3. Principles of Parish Dynamics

American parishes were studied extensively twenty years ago in the Notre Dame Study of Catholic Parish Life, with fifteen reports published from 1984 to 1989. Unfortunately these data do not make possible comparisons with non-Catholics. Such comparisons are possible, however, in the 2001 US Congregational Life Survey, replicated in 2008. For this survey, over 300,000 worshippers in over 2,000 congregations filled out a questionnaire in their church during the weekend of April 29, 2001; hence, this survey only gives us information about churchgoing members. From these data, we learn that 37.6 percent of Catholics strongly agree that their spiritual needs are met in their parish, but so do 42 percent of evangelicals, 49.5 percent of Pentecostals, and only 34.4 percent of liberal Protestants. Similarly, 51.6 percent of Catholics always experience a sense of God's presence during worship services, as opposed to 46.7 percent of evangelicals, 55.7 percent of Pentecostals, and 32.6 percent of liberals.

Comparing Catholics and non-Catholics on various scales is more meaningful than comparing single variables. Cynthia Woolever and Deborah Bruce have constructed ten scales of congregational strengths that illustrate the dynamics of parish life. Thus their index of church participation includes five categories : weekly attendance, involvement in parish activities, leadership, decision making, and financial contribution. Church participation is important, because it predicts membership growth, individual spiritual growth, and parish growth in its various activities. On average, 60 percent of all worshippers answered positively to these five categories: 44 percent of Catholics, 55 percent of mainline Protestants, and 69 percent of conservative Protestants.[33] In reference to financial contributions, 14.5 percent of Catholics tithe—a surprisingly high number—along with 42.7 percent of evangelicals, 64.8 percent of Pentecostals, and only 12.8 percent of liberal Protestants. Obviously when half the church members give 10 percent of their income, a church can finance many more ministries. The same can be said about frequency of church attendance: when members attend more than weekly, they experience more spiritual growth. Thus 10 percent of Catholics attend church more than weekly; 27.1 percent of evangelicals and 47 percent of Pentecostals do so as well; but only 7.9 percent of liberals attend more than weekly. On the index of spiritual growth based on the five questions, Catholics rank lowest, with 38 percent answering positively the five questions, as opposed to 41 percent of mainline and 55 percent of Conservative Protestants.[34]

Two other factors of parish growth are outreach to new members and vitality of youth ministry. Any congregation must attract new members to compensate for those leaving or retiring. Obviously the success of this outreach depends on the amount of time and manpower invested in this ministry. In a typical congregation, one third of the members are newcomers (members who have joined during the five previous years). In comparison to this average of 33 percent for all churches, Catholics parishes are less successful, with only 27 percent of newcomers, as opposed to 29 percent in mainline churches and 39 percent in Conservative Protestantism.[35] This outreach effort explains part of the Catholic decline and Protestant growth. Equally important for church growth is youth ministry. This index is measured by three questions, resulting in an average acceptance score of 50 percent for all congregations. Catholics are again below average, with a score of 46 percent, as opposed to 49 percent in mainline and 53 percent in conservative Protestantism.[36]

Another very important factor of spiritual and organizational growth is a congregation's vision for the future. A church with a clear vision about its mission, goals, and ministries is more likely to shape the future according to its plans. This index consists of four questions, yielding an overall score of 41 percent of positive replies. Catholics rank lowest with a score of 34 percent, and Conservative Protestants highest with 47 percent.[37] This index is important, because it correlates with five other strengths: strong lay participation, vital youth ministry, successful outreach to newcomers, a sense of belonging among members, and empowering leadership.

What we have gleaned from the Congregational Life Survey is a set of principles about congregational dynamics that allow for growth and development. Participation in church life is very important. It includes not only weekly attendance but also involvement in study groups, faith-sharing meetings, charity work, and so on. Not least important for parish stewardship are the financial contributions. A vibrant outreach ministry is important to attract newcomers, and no less important is youth ministry to prevent the exodus of the young. All the various ministries must be seen as part of a global vision for the present and the future. It is this vision that can revitalize a parish. On most of these measurements Catholics rank lowest—an unpleasant and inconvenient statistic. At least now, they may know what direction to go.

Prospective Conclusion:
"Evangelical Catholics"

It is well-known that evangelical churches are growing, while mainline churches are not. Between 1990 and 2000, six major evangelical denominations grew by 16.2 percent, while seven major mainline denominations declined by 6.7 percent. The fastest growing churches—by more than 18 percent each—are the Assemblies of God, the Christian Churches, and the Churches of Christ.[38] Today there are more evangelical Christians in the United States than Catholics, according to the 2008 American Religious Identification Survey.[39]

In the US Congregational Life Survey, respondents could identify themselves as Catholic, charismatic, evangelical, or liberal. Of the more than 45,000 respondents, 192 identified themselves as both Catholic and charismatic. To the extent that the latter are similar to evangelical Protestants, we would expect some of their religious behaviors to be similar to those of evangelicals, and indeed they are. Here are comparisons about topics mentioned above: 37.6 percent of Catholics (but 46 percent of Catholic charismatics and 42 percent of evangelicals) strongly agree that their spiritual needs are met in their parish; 51.6 percent of Catholics (but 57.3 percent of Catholic charismatics and 46.7 of evangelicals) always experience a sense of God's presence during worship services; 14.5 percent of Catholics (but 28.7 percent of Catholic charismatics and 42.7 percent of evangelicals) say they tithe; and 10 percent of Catholics (but 34.6 percent of charismatics and 27.1 percent of evangelicals) attend church more than weekly. In many respects, these Catholic charismatics can be seen as more evangelical (i.e., Gospel-minded) than ordinary Catholics.

Evangelical and Pentecostal Christians are the fastest growing movement within Christianity, numbering about one-fourth all Christians worldwide and possibly outnumbering Catholics in the world within a generation or two. According to the Pew 2006 US Religion Survey, 39 percent of US Latino *Christians* describe themselves as "born again" or "evangelical." Surprisingly, 28 percent of US Latino *Catholics* also describe themselves in these terms. The 2006 Pew survey found that "A majority of Latino Catholics [54%] describe themselves either as charismatic or

Pentecostal," while only 1 in 10 non-Latino Catholics does.[40] For purpose of clarity, the Pew report distinguishes between Pentecostals—that is, members of a Pentecostal Church—Catholic charismatics, and Protestant charismatics (that is, those who see themselves as either charismatic or Pentecostal, but do not belong to a Pentecostal church).

A significant number of Latino charismatic Catholics attend small group meetings, where people pray for healing or deliverance (35 percent of them), prophesize (28 percent), or speak in tongues (30 percent). At Mass they may raise their hands (27 percent usually; 38 percent occasionally) or speak in tongues (21 percent usually; 35 percent occasionally). They also attend church and go to confession more often than noncharismatic Catholics. Catholic charismatics exhibit some behaviors and beliefs that are characteristic of the evangelicals and Pentecostals. Here are the percentages of those who read the Bible, evangelize, and speak in tongues on a weekly basis.[41]

	Read the Bible	Evangelize	Speak in tongues
Among US Hispanics:			
Noncharismatic Catholics	23%	16%	26%
Catholic charismatics	32	27	33
Protestant charismatics	66	56	27
Protestant Pentecostals	80	70	36

To the extent that Latino Catholics are more devout and renewal oriented, they are a blessing for the church. Today they constitute an estimated 33 percent of the US Catholic population, and their numeric importance will continue to grow. Assuming that the immigration flow and the rate of conversion of Catholics to Protestantism will remain constant, the proportion of US Hispanics will grow from 33 percent to 41 percent of the Catholic Church in 2030.[42]

Today about 68 percent of the American Hispanics are Catholic, but if the rate of conversions remains constant, the latter will constitute only 61 percent in 2030. Half of Hispanic evangelicals are converts, and more than four-fifths are former Catholics. Why are most of them leaving? Surprisingly not because they disagree with some church teaching (although many do), but because 90 percent of these converts desire a more direct personal experience of God, and because 42 percent of them found inspiration in an evangelical pastor.[43] Put differently, 90 percent did not find a personal God in their former parish, and 42 percent were not inspired by their former priest. What can we conclude from this?

Catholic renewal is not likely to come from church leaders, because their moral authority is not high enough to inspire enthusiasm and evangelistic fervor. Renewal is not likely to come from the ministerial priesthood, either; given the shortage of priests, their function is increasingly restricted to the administration of the sacraments. Hence, renewal is likely to come from the common priesthood of all. All Christians belong to this common priesthood, from the pope down to the people in the pews, not just the laity. This priesthood is one of holiness, which is exactly what a renewal is about.

There is one church order that traditionally made its special mission to strive for holiness: that of the religious. These religious may not be holier than others, but they serve as reminders—in words and deeds—of the universal call to holiness. The postconciliar decline of the religious is a great loss for the Catholic Church. Because sisters were present in nearly all parishes and heavily involved in the education of the young, their decline has affected both Catholic education and parish life. Their rebirth or the development of highly committed Catholics should be a high priority.

Renewal is much more than the reformation of church structures and changes in priestly ordinations. A few mainline Protestant churches are more democratic than the Catholic Church (the Episcopal Church and the Southern Baptists, for instance), and many ordain women to the priesthood, yet they are still declining in membership. To the extent that the post-Vatican II liberal agenda concentrated on these two items, it failed and has little future—which does not make the reform of church structures any less desirable. Clearly what is needed is spiritual (i.e., evangelical) renewal, not just structural reform. It is to this goal that this book wants to contribute.

CHAPTER 2

~

THREE FACTORS OF SPIRITUAL DECLINE

Because you are lukewarm,
neither hot nor cold,
I will spit you out of my mouth.
—Revelation 3:16

The data presented in the previous chapter can be summarized in two conclusions: 1) Catholic decline is similar to that of mainline Protestantism, which suggests the presence of common contextual factors, and 2) on many measurements (retention, financial contributions, evangelization, etc.), Catholics score lower than Protestants generally, and lower than evangelicals in particular, which suggests the presence of typically Catholic factors. In this chapter I will analyze the contextual factors of decline that apply to all religious institutions. In the next chapter, I will look at institutional factors special to Catholicism.

The purpose of this chapter is theoretical; hence, we must move from the level of variables of the previous chapter to the level of concepts. Low church attendance, clergy decline, religious schooling decline, and so on are variables; what are the concepts behind these measurements? If we say they measure religious decline, what is religion? I would suggest that, at the most general level, they measure spiritual decline ... but what is spirituality?

A point of departure is the tension between nature and culture, social expectations, and personal growth, as in Maslow's pyramid of needs (shown below). At the bottom of the pyramid are physiological and psychological needs; at the intermediate level are social and esteem needs; and at the top are growth needs inspired by self-actualization. Maslow's pyramid is a map of self-transcendence for spiritual growth.[44] It is this drive toward self-transcendence that I would define as spirituality broadly understood.

Self-transcendence is social and institutional, not just individual. Thus the impulses toward instant (as opposed to postponed) gratification are fostered by consumerism, the availability of mass-produced consumer goods, pervasive advertising, and the easy availability of credit. Postponed gratification can equally be socially encouraged (e.g., at home, school, or work). Self-transcendence is also institutionalized in customs and rules (e.g., in professional forms of work spirituality, in education, the arts, sports, tourism, and so on, and the various schools of religious growth).

The strategy of this chapter is to find in the secularization literature factors of *spiritual* decline, both religious and secular.

Secularization refers to a body of theories that try to explain *religious* decline, yet some aspects may apply to *spiritual* decline as well. No single theory has been met with widespread acceptance. Secularization was taken for granted in sociological circles in the 1970s but has been seen as questionable in the last decade(s). In spite of its lack of unity (it was labeled "a hodge-podge of loosely employed ideas"[45]), in my view, it is correct in its main assertions.

The term "secularization" was coined by Max Weber in his analysis of Western capitalism. He described the latter as having developed through inner-worldly asceticism, the rational domination of the world, and "disenchantment"—that is, the progressive elimination of transcendence.

"The technical and economic conditions of machine-production," he wrote, "determine the lives of all the individuals ... with irresistible force" to the point that the social order has become "an iron cage."[46] Such a world order is likely to be a spiritual desert in which religion only survives in isolated pockets. This description, however, is too brief and too general to be easily applicable to concrete situations.

Many factors have contributed to secularization. Bruce[47] mentions structural and social differentiation; individualism; societalization; rationality; industrial capitalism; science and technology; religious diversity; relativism; compartmentalization and privatization; and so on. I will consider briefly three: at the macro level, social differentiation, and at the individual level, privatization and individualism.

1. Macro Level: Social Differentiation and Consumerism

Secularization can be seen as a consequence of social differentiation. As societies become more complex, religion loses its primacy in society to become one subsystem among others. Secularization is then seen as "a process by which the overarching and transcendent religious system of old is being reduced in modern functionally differentiated society as a subsystem alongside other subsystems." As a consequence, "the *societal* significance of religion is greatly diminished."[48]

There are two major problems with this view. First, this theory explains very little of the religious decline since the 1960s. While social differentiation is a slow process that started in the United States with the separation of church and state, among other events, the recent religious decline has been abrupt and unexpected. Social differentiation does not explain why church attendance has sharply declined from about 80 percent in the 1950s to about 30 percent today among US Catholics—a decline that is equally sharp in Canada, Western Europe, and Australia, but not among Protestants. It does not explain the various rates of decline (e.g., of Canadian French Catholics who dropped from 80 percent in 1980 to 67 percent in 1994 and 51 percent in 2007; of Austrian Catholics who dropped from near 100 percent a generation ago to 63 percent today; or of Brazilian Catholics who dropped from 90 percent in 1980 to 64 percent today).[49]

Moreover, this theory is blind to a major social transformation that has taken place in the Western world over the last generation—namely the increasing primacy of the economy at the expense of religion, education, and government. While the United States has been a world economic power since WWII, moneymaking and consumerism have become the prevalent social ideology only in recent times, with the spread of globalization, worldwide communication through digital technology, the mass production of goods in third-world countries, and obsessive advertisement in the ever-expanding mass media. By claiming that progressive differentiation leads to an ever greater number of subsystems, all equal among themselves, this theory demonstrates its blindness to the prominence of business-mindedness and consumerism in modern societies: education is increasingly run like a business; government is often subservient to business interests (the Pentagon is the biggest business in the world); and religion often presents itself as a shopping mall of religious goods. Weber's vision of an economic iron cage is increasingly more appropriate for our age.

By "consumerism," I mean the primacy of consumption in one's life. To the extent that consumerism favors consumption rather than production, spending rather than saving, leisure enjoyment rather than productive work, instant gratification rather than future orientation, and individual benefits rather than community

> Consumerism is a generalized form of shopping addiction, or e-mail addiction, or internet addiction. It is the enjoyment of consumption as the ultimate value of life.

gains, it tends to be destructive of most forms of spirituality. Nowhere is this effect more obvious than in education, with the steady increase of television screens, e-mails, cell phones, and iPods, and the concomitant decline of students' knowledge, skills, effort on assignments, and interest in learning. Today the iron cage is that of a six-year-old watching TV alone in an empty house. Consumerism chokes the spirit. It is unfriendly to both education and religion.

Consumerism starts at an early age. Children spend an average of four hours a day watching television, DVDs, and videos. They spend about 900 hours a year in school (or 26 weeks at 7 hours a day, 5 days a week), but 1500 hours in front of a screen (or 43 weeks watching 7 hours straight per day, 5 days a week). They will be exposed to about 20,000 TV commercials per year, mainly for food. By age 65, the average person has seen about 2 million ads.[50] Now the stage is set for the dance of the fools.

A man said to his wife, "Let's take it easy and eat, drink, and be merry. The value of the typical house has increased by 124 percent between 1997 and 2006. Let's buy a house, as big as possible, at subprime rate, with little or no down payment, and soon we'll be rich!" The banker said to himself, "I will take a loan ten times bigger than my assets and sell mortgage-backed securities for a bright future." The investment manager said: "I'll buy derivatives. What are they? I don't know, but they're a sure kill!" The dance of fools goes on: derivatives are bought and sold ($100 trillion in 2002) and bought and sold again (up to $516 trillion by 2007).[51]

You fool, don't you know that the annual GDP of the United States is only 15 trillion and the GDP for the whole world is only about 50 trillion? You fool, don't you know that a mere decline of about 2 percent will ignite this $516 trillion into a weapon of mass destruction?[52] "You fool! This very night you will have to give an accurate account [of investments]." (Luke:12:20) In March 2008, AIG (American International Group) reported losses of $11.1 billion. The meltdown had begun. The Lehman Brothers went under. Merrill Lynch sold itself. About 1.3 million US homes became subject to foreclosure. The major banks that had invested heavily in MBS (mortgage-backed securities) reported losses of $435 billion in July of 2008.[53] Credit became unavailable: there was no money and/or no assurance to allow borrowers to make back payments. The whole economy had come to standstill—not just in the United States, but worldwide: most derivatives are sold in London, not in the United States, and many heavy buyers are investors from the Middle and the Far Eastern tiger economies. In short, it was a worldwide crisis.

What has been learned? With a $700 billion rescue package and similar packages in other parts of the world, the implicit goal is to go back to the *status quo ante*: more growth, more pollution, more inequality, and the rich getting richer. Consumerism is with us to stay.

Although I know of no research associating consumerism with religious decline, there is strong empirical evidence that denominational growth is associated with high personal expectations rather than self-gratification; asceticism rather than pleasure; church participation rather than leisure activities; church giving (e.g., tithing) rather than personal spending; social justice and community interests rather than personal enrichment; and beliefs defined by church rather than individual preferences. In church-sect research, it is commonly accepted that growing churches are those that reject some major features of their cultural environment. Rejection of consumerism seems necessary to avoid the cultural assimilation that characterizes many mainline churches. Evangelicals tend to be critical of the prevailing culture—they often condemn drinking, smoking, secularism, and materialism while promoting their own entertainment industry—while mainline churches are much more accommodating.

Finke and Stark found that in the nineteenth and early twentieth centuries, denominations declined when their clergy adopted secular lifestyles—that is, academic knowledge rather than piety; careers rather than service; good salaries rather than nonpaid contributions; urban residence rather than frontier life; and social and cultural assimilation rather than high demands for themselves and their congregations.[54] The same factors of decline apply to the Catholic Church today, in their view.[55] Wealth may be sweet, but it kills the soul.

2. Privatization: Sheilaism and the Nontransmission of Values

According to Luckman[56] and Berger,[57] modern societies have become secularized because religion is seen as belonging to the private, not the public, sphere. This theory has little explanatory power in reference to *recent* decline. Moreover, it is inaccurate in reference to institutional religion, as all institutions exhibit a great deal of overlap between the private and the public. There is no reason to consider religion any more private than education or health. Birth, marriage, and death rituals are matters of public record; they are as public as school ceremonies. Obviously, confessions to priests are private, but so are votes in general elections. Religious weddings and funerals are no less public than civil ones. Most institutions have a public and a private dimension. Thus, AIDS, lung cancer, and obesity have a clearly public dimension, besides the personal one. According to Dobbelaere, the opposition of private and public is of little theoretical significance in sociology.[58]

Privatization applies less to institutional religion than to individual and personal religion—that is, one's relationship with God. Privatization of the God-self relationship pushes the Protestant vision of religion to its utter limits: no one (no government, no church, not even parents and family members) can or should interfere with this personal relationship. This is Sheilaism pushed to an extreme. Sheila is famous for having said in an interview that she had her own religion, which she called Sheilaism.[59] Because she grew up in an oppressively religious family, Sheila rejected most religious beliefs and practices. When first described in the 1980s, Sheilaism was seen as an extreme form of individualism cut off from institutional religion.[60] Now, in the light of the increased privatization of religious beliefs, we realize that Sheila cannot impart Sheilaism to her children without contradicting herself. As a religion of one, Sheilaism cannot be transmitted; Sheilaists are isolated monads who cannot propagate their own values.

This form of Sheilaism seems more prevalent among liberals, especially Catholics and Jews. Increasingly parents do not want to impose their religious beliefs on their children and want to allow them to choose their religion at an early age, usually at confirmation or bar mitzvah. In practical terms, since this choice at the time of confirmation is one of staying or exiting, many young people opt for leaving. Judaism and Catholicism have the greatest dropout rates. In the American Religious Identification Survey of 2001, based on 51,470 telephone interviews, it was found that 43 percent of those of "no religion" are former Catholics.[61] If the dropout rate were similar across churches, the Catholic rate should be about 22–24 percent, not double that amount.

Sheilaism is also present in the clergy: church leaders may be reluctant to speak out publicly on controversial church positions. As stated by a priest, "Of course I don't say anything publicly [on controversial issues].

If I would say anything publicly, I would get my head chopped off. Privately, yes, but what I say privately remains private." Similar attitudes are found in megachurches that use a contemporary style and message to "accommodate modernity in order to remain 'relevant' or to reduce the cognitive dissonance with the prevailing rationalism of modern life." These preachers make little or no demands on the faithful. This attitude will not inculcate and transmit Christian values, merely reinforce existing secular ones.[62]

The nontransmission of values—except purely academic ones—also characterizes public education, even in matters of public health. According to the 2007 Columbia University report on student substance abuse half of all full-time students binge drink, abuse prescription drugs, and/or use illegal drugs; on a yearly basis, more than 1,700 students die from alcohol abuse and nearly 100,000 students are victims of alcohol-related assaults. What can administrators do? Nothing! It is a private matter—as long as the police are not involved.[63] When religious and many secular values are considered a matter of personal conscience, society may be "wasting the best and the brightest" of its young (which is the title of the Columbia report on student substance abuse).

3. Political Individualism and Religious Identity

For P. Berger, one major factor of religious decline is individualism—that is, the "individualization" of religion: "Privatized religion is a matter of the 'choice' or 'preference' of the individual or the nuclear family, ipso facto lacking in common, binding quality."[64] Liberal Protestantism illustrates the destructive effect of individualism, according to Berger. Under the influence of Schleiermacher at the beginning of the nineteenth century, liberal theologians progressively came to deny objective forms of truth, thus weakening of church authority and institutional cohesion. Religious beliefs progressively became a question of personal "opinions" and "religious preference." According to Berger,[65] "the Protestant development is prototypical": all churches are likely to follow the same path of individualization, religious liberalism, and decline.

Individualism seems, indeed, a major factor of secularization. The roots of individualism are not to be sought mainly in liberal Protestantism,

> The fear of imposing our values impedes the transmission of values and creates a society without strong common values.

but rather in the kind of liberalism that conceives *freedom as choice*, in the tradition of the Bill of Rights.

The development of religious individualism is widely documented. The opposition of individualism versus autonomy is central in the study *American Catholics,* of D'Antonio and colleagues, which analyzes data on a continuum of conformity versus autonomy in matters of faith and morals. In conformity, "the emphasis is on complying with church norms … individuals subordinate themselves to Church rules and regulations." In autonomy, on the other hand, "individuals put their own experiences first and Church norms second. They believe … the Church's norms and values should reflect their experiences."[66] Four surveys over twenty years document the increase of religious individualism in the United States.

The Anglican Communion illustrates the drama of individualism and autonomy in religion. In this communion of thirty-eight autonomous national and local churches, matters of faith and morals are discussed and often decided democratically, at local or national synods, with input from the laity, the clergy, and the bishops. There has been no problem with artificial birth control since the Lambeth conference of 1930 settled the issue. There is no problem with sexual morality, divorce and remarriage, clerical celibacy, and the ordination of women, lesbians, and gays. What makes this possible is the freedom of choice at all levels. This freedom includes, for adolescents at confirmation, the freedom to leave. Individuals and whole parishes started leaving after the ordination of women. The 2003 ordination of gay bishop Robinson threatened to break the communion apart. The Anglican Communion was at a crossroads. Either they hold church autonomy and democratic procedures as their ultimate values (Bishop Robinson was selected democratically) and the Communion is no more than a loose administrative organization of churches, or they put their spiritual unity in Christ as top priority, in which case local autonomy cannot be an absolute. In 2008 nine groups of American conservatives defected from the Episcopal Church to form the Anglican Church of North America. What happened to the spiritual unity of the Anglican Communion?

Democracy is based on freedom without coercion in matters of polity, as established by an agreed-upon list of rights. The American Bill of Rights guarantees freedom of speech, assembly, and conscience against possible abuses by local or federal governments. Political individualism as foundation of government through the participation of free individuals has been an outstanding factor of democratization throughout the world. Today it remains a major force of social liberation of minorities in most countries. Although most productive in its own sphere, political liberalism proves destructive in religion and education when the latter become cafeteria-style institutions. When freedom of choice is seen as a major right in education, students want the option of dropping out of courses when they do not expect to receive a high grade (an increasingly common practice), in which case education becomes a high-grades certification agency. Similarly, when religion becomes a mall of endless religious goods—or more commonly, when a church condones among its members a cafeteria selection of beliefs and practices—such a church loses its identity and thus loses its appeal to members in the long run. Strong and growing churches, on the contrary, are those that offer specific programs of spiritual growth and strongly encourage their members to engage in spiritual practices toward this growth. Strong churches have an identity—namely, their special programs of spiritual growth. Strong churches impart an identity on their members based on individuality, individuation, self-actualization, and self-differentiation—not individualism, as commonly understood.

The importance of today's religious individualism raises the question of religious identity. While only one or two generations ago, children inherited their parents' religion and usually remained faithful to it throughout life, today one's religion is a personal choice to about the same extent as one's major

> Religious individualism leads to a cafeteria of values and beliefs; religious individuality does not.

in college. While one may easily find an advisor about what major to choose, little help is offered to teenagers to select their religious "preference," often for life. In the absence of strong denominational identities (as a consequence of internal liberalization and secularization) and the decline of religious knowledge in adults, teenagers are often left to forge their own religious identities, for the better or for the worse. Today there are many ways of being a Protestant, a Catholic, or a Jew. Hence, sociological research cannot focus exclusively on denominational identification; it must also look into personal religious identity. The former is usually ascribed, the latter achieved. In light of this ongoing shift, we must briefly look at theories of identity.

All theories of identity and individual development (e.g., psychoanalysis, object relations theory, cognitive development as in Piaget, family-systems theory, cognitive therapy, faith development theory as in Fowler, and so on) describe growth as development from a low level to a higher level of individuality, as in Maslow: from self-gratification to self-actualization. At the lowest levels, the development of religion or education is pursued for extrinsic reasons (such as personal gains and self-gratification), while at higher levels, the motivation becomes intrinsic (learning for the sake of knowledge, and religiosity for the love of God and neighbors).

It is Erikson[67] who first described identity formation as a stage of human development. At adolescence, "ego identity" requires a synthesis between past, present, and future—that is, the development of the ego out of the superego inherited from the family and the social environment. Building on this work and also that of Piaget, Kohlberg, and Erikson, Fowler constructed six stages of faith development, four of which span the adult life. In Fowler's stage 3 (synthetic-conventional faith), the adolescent makes a commitment, moving out of the mythic-literal faith of childhood. By committing to a freely chosen community, the adolescent will be able to draw his or her identity from it. This new identity, however, is "conventional," because it tends to accept the norms and values of the group, while the individual is convinced that they are actually his or her own. The sources of authority in stage 3 are external; they are those of

> Religious identity is achieved individuality, not individualism. Identity comes with growth and development, not just the freedom to pick and choose.

the peer group, the church, or the Bible as commonly interpreted in one's congregation. "A considerable number of adults we have interviewed— both men and women—can best be described by the patterns of Stage 3 Synthetic-Conventional faith."[68] Many churchgoers seem to have a stage 3 identity for life.

There is more to religious development than stage 3. In the subsequent stage (individuative-reflective faith), the believer tends to relocate authority from the group to the self and engage into a systematic critique of the implicit value system held previously. For Fowler, it is only in that stage that the believer develops an authentically personal self. Yet stage 4 must be outgrown in favor of a higher level: that of conjunctive faith, characterized by the rejection of the excessively ideological positions of the previous stage in favor of a new synthesis, a "second naïveté," open to irreconcilable differences. And this stage, too, may lead to a higher form of religiosity, the stage of universalizing faith.

There is more to individualism than freedom of choice. *Individuality* requires the rejection of conformity—that is, the rejection of the prevailing individualism as cafeteria selection. Individuality implies growth beyond conformity. It is called self-actualization in Maslow, individuation in Jung, and self-differentiation in family systems theory. Individuality requires one to move beyond the conventionality of stage 3.

We may now see why the prevalence of political liberalism is likely to be a recipe for decline in education and religion. When a government becomes a theocracy, education a business, the military a democracy on the battlefield, and religion a democracy of beliefs and values, these institutions tend to lose their proper identities and purposes. Business is not a charity, but may gain from being more socially responsible; education is not a business, but must remain solvent; and religion is not a democracy of beliefs, although authoritarian churches may gain much credibility in greater transparency and accountability. We can also see now that the continuum from obedience in the pre-Vatican II church to individualism today is no real opposition: uncritical individualism today is as much a form of conformity as uncritical obedience in the past. What is needed, in the study of a religious institution, is the examination of its level of religious growth or salience. Strong and growing churches are precisely those that are characterized by high levels of spiritual growth, and the declining churches by the opposite.

If freedom is the essence of democracy (as suggested by Tocqueville), profit the essence of business, and knowledge the purpose of education, this would indicate that spiritual growth, rather than freedom of conscience, is the essence of religion. Indeed, there cannot be much spiritual growth without freedom, yet it is the God-man relationship that is the essence of Christian religion, not the freedom of beliefs embodied by cafeteria religion.

In summary, I see three major factors involved in spiritual and religious decline. First, the retreat of religion from social prominence negatively affects stage 3 believers who depend on their environment for personal reinforcement. Today, however, the prevailing consumerism is a much more potent factor of decline, my second factor. I expect most people to agree. Finally, the nontransmission of values is a much more frightening prospect, because the liberalism of cafeteria religion is a factor of decline for both individuals and institutions. A personal religion is more than one's religious preference—the only one usually studied by sociologists—and it is more than a personal "religious orientation"; it is achieved, rather than ascribed, on a continuum from low to high, as in Maslow or Fowler. Similarly, the identity of religious institutions is more than their ideological orientation, from conservative to liberal; it is *also*, if not mainly, defined by the salience of their religious icons (e.g., Jesus Christ or Buddha) and the intensity of their spiritual growth.

Let us now turn to the factors of *Catholic* decline.

CHAPTER 3

~

THREE FACTORS OF CATHOLIC DECLINE
THE OUTSIDER CATHOLICS' PERSPECTIVE

Let me begin with the image of a Catholic solemn Mass. There are about ten to fifteen acolytes, twenty to thirty candles burning around the altar, lots of incense, and the ringing of the bells at the Elevation of the Host. There is beautiful, polyphonic singing by the choir, all in Latin. The faithful are silent; they do not participate in the Latin singing. Even the Our Father is recited in Latin. The sermon or homily lasts about half an hour. The solemn Mass ends with the exposition of the Blessed Sacrament and the singing of the Te Deum. The Blessed Sacrament will be removed at midnight, with the singing of the Tantum Ergo.

Was this a solemn Mass of fifty years ago? No. Is this the solemn Mass of integrists who have rejected Vatican II? No. Is it a solemn Mass in a monastery or retreat house? No. It was the 6:00 p.m. solemn Mass of December 31, 2007, in the basilica of Santa Maria Maggiore in Rome, under the presidency of Cardinal Law, former archbishop of Boston (who was later compelled to resign

---

An Insider's View of the Church

"The church is not an organization, but a community of disciples in love with the Lord. We are not just an organization held together by some kind of structure, we are the bride of Christ reaching out to the Lord.... Pope John Paul II, Pope Benedict, these are holy men; but even if they weren't, it wouldn't matter. Popes come and go. Bishops come and go. *It is Christ* that rules the church."

—Archbishop Collins, Canada, WYD 2008

because of his management of clergy sex scandals). Is this an image of Catholic permanence, or is it an image of Catholic obsolescence?

The answer to this question depends on one's perspective—whether one is an insider or an outsider Catholic. Any institution depends on the loyalty of its core members. In the Catholic Church, the core members are those who espouse the goals of the church on a daily basis—that is, the priests, the members of religious congregations, and dedicated laypeople. It is these core members who constitute the most dedicated *insiders* of the church today. When, in the 1960s, Sunday attendance was about 80 percent, Catholic outsiders were called apostates, heretics, or atheists. At that time, the voice of the "Teaching Church or simply the Church" was nearly unanimously accepted by the "believing Church or simply the faithful."[69] There was no room for dissent in the pre-Vatican II ghetto church.

Totally different is the situation today. With the clergy declining and the weekly attendance dropping to about 30 percent, *the outsiders constitute the majority in the church.* Among the outsiders, about 30 percent are indifferent or alienated from the church and never attend; another 15–20 percent are inactive or disengaged, attending only seasonally; and another 15–20 percent attend irregularly. Not included but still present in society are former Catholics who have dropped out of religion or switched to another church. This typology suggests that, today, regular Catholics are likely to be much more influenced by outsiders than by core members when it comes to controversial issues. Yet the teaching church continues as if nothing has changed, as indicated by the solemn Mass described above. This chapter will look at the church from the outsiders' perspective, which is often different from that of insiders, especially core members.

An Outsider's View

"When I came back to the Church, I was appalled how backward the structure of the institution was. This is an organization that doesn't change. Like any structure, when threatened, it will do whatever it can to survive, and at times, it will deny reality. People deny reality; organizations deny reality and the need to change, simply because it's not their way of doing business."

—Interview

Among US Protestants, church attendance has not dropped significantly over the last fifty years (see graphs 1 and 2 in chapter 1), but among

Catholics, the drop has been drastic (from about 75 percent to about 30 percent). Moreover, between 1973 and 2008, Protestant churches lost 12.4 percent of their members while gaining 9.1 percent of converts. Catholics, on the other hand, lost 21.5 percent but only gained 9.9 percent. What explains these losses?

Several studies, one in the Archdiocese of Philadelphia and three in Australia, inquired into the reasons why nonpracticing Catholics have stopped attending Sunday Mass. The alleged reasons for nonattendance are divided into two categories: church-centered and participant-centered. The first (22 percent of all reasons in Philadelphia) constitutes a list of grievances about the Mass, the parish, or the Church; the second (49 percent of the reasons, with 27 percent classified as "other") are more serious: they state, directly or indirectly, that the Mass is not a priority anymore.[70] The 1996 Australian study has even more damaging findings: 54 percent "No longer feel that being a committed Catholic requires going to Mass every week," 43 percent disagree with Church teachings, and 18 percent "No longer accept many Catholic beliefs." (Due to multiple choices, the percentage does not add to 100 percent.)[71] The 1998 Australian Community Survey presents the following typology: 16 percent are no longer Catholic (the dropout category); 31 percent never attended Mass as adults (the indifferent or alienated); 22 percent have stopped attending (the inactive); 15 percent attend weekly (the Sunday regulars); and the remaining 16 percent consist of irregular and marginal or seasonal Catholics.[72] With about 85 percent of Catholics as outsiders, it is very unlikely that the Australian core Catholics (priests and committed Catholics) will be able to hold the tide of secularization among the remaining 13 percent of Sunday regulars—actually only 7 or 8 percent among the young. Hence, there is a need to look at the Catholic Church from the perspective of outsiders, rather than that of insiders or core members.

There are many factors of decline. Here are a few.

1. The American Church has become so assimilated into society that very little differentiates Catholics from non-Catholics in our consumer society (the effect of consumerism is described in the previous chapter).

2. The church itself—including its administration, academic theology, and religious schools—has become secularized to the point of having greatly lost its religious identity (see discussion of the nontransmission of values and lack of identity in the previous chapter).

3. In comparison to evangelical churches, biblical literacy is low in the Catholic Church to the point of having little vital contact with the evangelical ideals.

4. With the disappearance of traditional devotions, there seems to be less of an intense prayer life, thus leading to routinized liturgies and sacrament.

5. Although there is much talk about community in Catholic circles, large parishes served by few and aging priests rarely invoke a sense of community.

6. Youth ministries are not a high priority, in spite of the vast exodus of young Catholics.

7. Religious education is often experienced as ineffective.

8. There is not much left of the traditional Catholic subculture to provide an intellectual, social, and cultural environment favorable to the sustenance of Christian religious life.

> **10 Percent of Americans Are Former Catholics**
>
> "Catholicism has experienced the greatest net losses as a result of affiliation changes. While nearly one in three Americans (31%) were raised in the Catholic faith, today fewer than one in four (24%) describe themselves as Catholic. Roughly 10% of all Americans are former Catholics. One third of American born Catholics have left the church of their baptism. Almost half of these former Catholics joined Protestant denominations."
> —The 2008 US Religious Landscape Survey, based on more than 35,000 interviews. http://religions.pewforum.org/reports

9. There is little emphasis on evangelization, and often little or no spirit of evangelism.

10. For all practical purposes, the Catholic Church still identifies itself as the only true church, thus leaving little room for growth through ecumenical cross-fertilization.

Not much conflict occurs between insiders and outsiders about these factors of decline, some of which will be discussed in the coming chapters.

Totally different are the next three, about which insiders and outsiders may be in violent opposition.

1. The Catholic Church is more church-centered than Christ-centered. As an institution of power and wealth, it often becomes a screen hiding the face of God and the Gospel message. This has been the Protestant criticism for the last four centuries—a view that is increasingly shared by outsider Catholics.

2. The sacramental theology and practice are not convincing anymore. This is not the Protestant rejection of sacraments, but the Catholic outsiders' view that sacraments are not important, since one can be a good Catholic without attending Mass regularly.

3. Catholic moral teaching is seen as fuzzy and vague, except about traditional sexual matters. On matters of sexual behavior, birth control, and abortion, church teaching appears ironclad, while on social issues, the teaching offers flexibility and understanding. The result is a vague morality with a few absolute rules and a rhetoric of social justice, both of which relate very little to everyday concerns.

The discussion of these three factors of decline may be difficult, because it confronts readers who are insider Catholics with an unpleasant reality. Insiders and outsiders may be tempted to shout at one another in disagreement. Because there is likely to be much antagonism in the first section on church-centeredness versus Christ-centeredness, I will act as moderator, allowing both parties to speak. I will also act as the speaker for the outsider Catholics, since their opinion is the focus of this chapter.

1. Church-Centeredness Versus Christ-Centeredness

As the speaker, let me introduce a few witnesses. Here are excerpts from personal interviews in reply to my question "Are you ever angry at church or God?"

> Angry? Oh! All the time. Vatican II opened up so much and called for collaboration and collegiality, but at the present time, that's being reversed. And with the shortage of clergy, they seem to be holding on

more tightly to the reins, being fearful of laypeople who are as qualified or more qualified.

—Married female, 55, religious education director

Angry? At the church? You better believe it. I'm a woman in the church; it's very hard. Even though we've come light-years, we still don't really appreciate, as a church, the role of women in leadership positions.

— Sister, 57, diocesan staff, PhD

I get angry at the church leaders, specifically the lack of dedication and knowledge of the clergy. I have almost *no* use for the Roman hierarchy. I respect the Pope but do not believe that he is a true leader of the global church.

—Single male, 36, pastoral associate, MA

In the postmodern culture, there is no authority. There is no truth, something along those lines. Infallibility is a very difficult concept even to raise in a postmodern era. I don't know what it could possibly mean, even.

—Married male, 55, religious education director, PhD

Infallibility? No, I don't believe in that, but I can't say that publicly.

—Single female, 45, religious education director, PhD candidate

A bishop: Objection! This is scandalous. These people should not be in leadership position in the church!

Religious education director (angrily): You can fire us, but those who will replace us will probably think the same … so you better listen for once!

Speaker (placatingly): Let us try to understand. Here is a brief historical review.

Until Vatican II, for nearly two thousand years, the Catholic Church considered itself the full realization of the kingdom of God. The Council of Florence of 1442 taught that there is no salvation outside the Catholic Church: pagans, Jews, and heretics "will go to the eternal fire prepared for the devil and his angels."[73] Moreover, only the Catholic Church—so it was claimed—holds the plenitude of the Christian truth to which all other churches must return. Finally, the magisterium has always been seen as the sole authentic interpreter of natural law, since "No member of the faithful could possibly deny that the Church is competent in her Magisterium to interpret the natural moral law."[74] Then came Vatican II …

Outsider Catholic: Objection! People under fifty have no knowledge of Vatican II. And as far as I know, nothing has changed: for most people, the church is its hierarchy. Even the witnesses quoted above say "church" when they mean "the hierarchy!"

Speaker: Let us move on and look at church structures in canon law, beginning with the top. "The bishop of the Church of Rome … enjoys supreme, full, immediate and universal ordinary power in the Church, which he can always freely exercise" (canon 331).[75] Nearly every word of this canon ("supreme," "full," "immediate," "universal," "always," "freely") emphasizes the supremacy of the pope's power. Vatican II introduced the notion of collegiality in the church, but this principle does not apply to the pope, who "has the right, according to the needs of the Church, to determine the manner, either personal or collegial, of exercising this function" (canon 333 § 2). The authority of the pope is above collegiality. "There is neither appeal nor recourse against a decision or decree of the Roman Pontiff" (canon 333 § 3).

The Church as IBM

"I have been working at the diaconate office for twenty years. I was the director. I was responsible for the men that are ordained. I was the intermediary between the deacons and the hierarchical agencies. Then the bishop decided to put a priest in charge of all his agencies. I was demoted to assistant director. Then the new director told me, 'You know, as of June, we're reorganizing. I don't think you're going to fit in.' Now I am removed. 'But what happened to our Christian charity?' I complained to the bishop. 'I don't work for IBM—I work for the church!' I was very angry."

—Interview

Canon lawyer: Objection! You should start from the bottom up and begin with the people of God.

Catholic outsider: To me, that's exactly the way it is. It's full power from the top down.

Speaker: On behalf of the outsiders, let us look at local power and next the laity.

The "legislative, executive and judicial" power of bishops within their dioceses is nearly as absolute as that of the pope (canon 391). They can make laws and execute them as they see fit. In a diocesan trial, they are both the prosecutor and the judge. The possibility of an appeal to the pope against a bishop's decision is neither mentioned nor excluded, but would have little chance of success. Collegiality within dioceses is not mentioned; a bishop is only required to "listen to [his priests] as his assistants and advisors" (canon 384). There is no mention of priests' councils, which bishops may ignore. "The Supreme Pontiff freely appoints bishops." Before taking office, a bishop takes "an oath of fidelity to the Apostolic See" (canon 380). Moreover, a diocesan bishop "is bound to present a report to the Supreme Pontiff every five years concerning the state of the diocese committed to him" (canon 399) and, on the occasion of this report, "to appear before the Roman Pontiff" (canon 400). Because of their special oath and their accountability to the pope and not to their people, bishops are very unlikely to publicly disagree with papal decisions and wishes. Heads of states take an oath of fidelity to the Constitution; heads of dioceses take an oath, not of fidelity to the Gospel, but to the pope, because the latter is seen as "representing" Jesus Christ as his "vicar."

Canon lawyer: Objection! This is an unacceptably biased selection of canons!

Catholic outsider: No, that's the way it looks! If these canons are biased, abolish or change them!

Doubt God, but Not the Pope

"I find it strange that, if I were to tell a cardinal in the Vatican that I was struggling with doubts about the existence of God, I would receive sympathy and support. But if I were to tell the same cardinal that I had doubts about papal teaching on contraception and the ordination of women, I would receive a stern lecture on loyalty to the pope."

—Bishop Geoffrey Robinson in "Confronting Power and Sex in the Catholic Church" (in *America*, March 17, 2008)

Speaker (soothingly): Let us turn to the laity, or "listening church." "The Christian faithful ... are bound by Christian obedience to follow what the sacred pastors, as representatives of Christ, declare as teachers of the faith" (canon 212). This principle is clarified thus: "A religious respect (*religiosum obsequium*) of intellect and will ... is to be paid to the teaching which the Roman Pontiff or the college of bishops enunciate ... even if they do not intend to proclaim it with a definitive act" (canon 752). When public dissent became rampant in the 1980s and 1990s, John Paul II issued an apostolic letter titled "To Protect the Faith," which condemned all forms of dissent.[76] He rewrote canon 752, dividing it into two parts. The first stated that doctrines considered *de fide* "must be believed with divine and Catholic faith." The second concerns what is often called the noninfallible teachings—that is, "propositions required for the sacred preservation and faithful explanation of the same deposit of the faith." These "must also be firmly embraced and maintained; anyone, therefore, who rejects those propositions ... is opposed to the doctrine of the Catholic Church." The pope quotes canon 1436.1: "One who denies a truth which must be believed with divine and Catholic faith ... is to be punished as a heretic or an apostate with major excommunication." The implication is that public dissent is heresy and/or apostasy and hence subject to public condemnation. In this letter, faith is to be "protected" (according to the title of the letter) by greater centralization, control, and condemnations, rather than a closer relationship with Jesus Christ.

> **The Freedom of Loyalty to Christ**
> "In small groups, people talk about faith and connect it to their lives. With that they come to a certain freedom—a freedom that they never had before. People now have a deep sense that the Church is not the absolute conduit for the presence of God. Their loyalty is to Christ; that's what I mean by freedom. I don't think our leaders see that. They still think that the institution is the be-all and end-all of faith, and it isn't."
> —Interview

Catholic outsider: I can't believe it! This is nineteenth-century thinking dating before Vatican II!

Speaker: Let's avoid another confrontation and look at what bishops actually do in their annual meetings. Collectively, American bishops act as legislators, adopting laws, rules, and guidelines to be followed by all Catholics, and these rules and guidelines are mainly church-centered, rather than Christ-centered. In the fall of 2006, the bishops approved two documents. One deals with "Married Love and the Gift of Life." It restates that "Suppressing fertility by using contraception denies part of the inherent meaning of married sexuality and does harm to the couple's unity."[77] This is probably the most "Catholic" of all church teachings, not upheld by any other major Christian church.

An educated outsider (quoting the *National Catholic Reporter*): "There is a reason 96 percent of Catholics has ignored the birth control teaching for decades. We doubt that the new document will significantly change that percentage."[78]

Speaker: This is a good example of how the insider and outsider Catholics are unable to listen to one another. If only 4 percent follow church teachings on birth control, that means that 96 percent of Catholics follow the lead of outsiders. It is really time for the teaching church to listen.

The same can be said about the other document adopted in 2006, "Ministry to Persons with a Homosexual Inclination." There, the bishops reassert that "The homosexual inclination is objectively disordered."[79] For whom are the bishops writing? For their Roman overseers, whom they try to appease, or for the homosexuals in the church, whom they once considered "always our children"? In either case, is ministry to people with a homosexual inclination the most pressing issue of Christ-centeredness in a declining church? In the fall of 2007, the US bishops again adopted two major documents. In "Faithful Citizenship," they give guidelines for the 2008 elections. They offer seven key themes to be considered when voting for a candidate, the first of which is "The Right to Life and the Dignity of the Human Person." Under that heading, they state that "In our society, human life is especially under direct attack from abortion."[80] This view may be shared by Protestant evangelicals and conservatives, but to make it the first criterion for the election of political candidates is a very church-centered agenda.

Catholic outsider: Nothing on sex scandals? Is it over?

Speaker: Not totally. In 2007 various dioceses in California settled sex-abuse reparations for 1.8 billion. The San Diego and the San Bernardino diocese agreed to pay 198.1 million; the diocese of Davenport, OH, settled for 37 million;[81] several dioceses went into deep debt or bankruptcy because of sex-abuse trials. This is why the American bishops proposed a new law, to be approved by the Vatican, demanding that bishops receive consent from their finance councils for, among other things, going into debt for more than $1 million or going into bankruptcy.

Catholic outsider: Does that mean that a bishop can move around up to $1 million without accounting for it?

Canon lawyer: A diocese is a corporation sole, with a single incorporated office—that of the bishop. The canon law sets no clear limits on what he can do.

Outsider (sarcastically): Is it surprising that 85 percent of US dioceses report embezzlement?[82]

Speaker: Irony and sarcasm do not help! It only shows the level we are at in our dialogue. What we have here are opposite views of the church. Outsider Catholics see it as no different from IBM or Microsoft. Insiders disagree. Outsiders describe what they see—namely, the church as a power structure. Insiders describe it in theological terms, as it should be, as sacrament of God. In this debate, the burden of the proof rests with insiders, who have to convince outsiders that bishops act differently from CEOs and that the church is more than its structure of power.

In summary, many Catholic Sunday regulars (not just outsiders!) have come to believe that the power structure of the church itself is the main obstacle to church renewal, as asserted repeatedly by Protestants. Instead of drawing believers to Christ, the teaching church tends to bind them too tightly to its own rules and regulations—thus, in effect, becoming a screen rather than a sacrament. What can be done? Every parish priest can be the living counter-proof of such an assertion. Thus, the Catholic bishops would gain in credibility if they were to meet in a seminary, retreat house, or university, lodging in student dorms or retreat cells rather than in Hilton hotels like CEOs.

2. Catholic Sacramentality

Catholics do not reject the sacraments, since 80 percent in 1999 and 76 percent in 2005 considered them very important in church life. Yet weekly Mass attendance is increasingly seen as optional. In a 2005 survey, 76 percent of Catholics agreed that one can be a good Catholic without going to church every Sunday.[83] This position is, of course, unacceptable to the core members of the church; yet the insiders' view is losing ground rapidly. While as many as 57 percent of the Vatican II Catholics saw Sunday Mass as optional in 1987, the percentage is as high as 95 percent among the millennials (ages 18 to 26) in 2005.[84] Even among Catholic students at Catholic universities, 88 percent think so.[85] The practice follows these beliefs: only 15 percent of the millennials said they attend Sunday Mass regularly in the 2005 survey, and only 22 percent of Catholic students in Catholic universities do so. I will try to explain these trends by sociological as well as theological factors.

A. Sociohistorical factors.

1. Overemphasis on the objective dimension of Christian life (objectivism).

Any human behavior has an objective or external dimension, which can be controlled, and a subjective personal dimension, which usually escapes human power. The more institutionalized and the more centralized a church, the more likely it is to emphasize the objective dimension at the expense of the subjective one.

In official Catholic documents, faith is essentially defined as creed, with little emphasis on faith as personal trust in God. Over the centuries, many councils have defined disputed beliefs and declared opponents "anathema." The emphasis on faith as trust was left to parish core members, parents, and priests, while the magisterium emphasized creeds. In Scripture, the objective dimension is the text in its literal (though not fundamentalist) meaning. Academic exegesis and parish homilies tend to emphasize the literary or historical meaning, while the spiritual dimension is best appropriated individually, in prayer and *lectio divina*—not a common practice among Catholics. Revelation has an objective dimension (the deposit of faith) which, according to official teaching, came to an end with the death of the apostles (a teaching not upheld anymore by Vatican II); it is the mission of the teaching church to transmit and interpret this objective revelation. But there is also a personal dimension that continues over the centuries: all believers learn about or experience the self-revelation of God through parents, role models, and their personal appropriation of Scripture. Catholic official teaching emphasizes the objective, rather than the personal, dimension of revelation and salvation. The official teaching tends to adopt exclusively the "penal substitution" or restitutive view of salvation (Christ "paid" for our sins), usually called "redemption," which is not very attractive today (except among some conservative Protestants as described in the next chapter), with little emphasis on personal healing, which is more common in the Gospels.

Sacraments, too, have a personal as well as an objective aspect. They are "visible signs" and thus can be controlled and recorded. The subjective dimension of the recipients does not affect the sacramental validity. For administrative purposes or for the recording of sacramental reception, only the external dimension is important. Thus Sunday Mass is to be "attended," something that can be required and controlled. Mass participation is encouraged but cannot be enforced. Thus, at the Santa Maria Maggiore solemn Mass described above, attendance was high, but participation was minimal, except by the choir. Certain days of the year are called "days of obligation," a reminder that is counterproductive in our antiauthoritarian age.

2. Decrease of devotional practices.

A church can emphasize both the objective at the corporate level and the subjective at the personal level. Thus fundamentalist and conservative churches often require strict submission to their teachings—as much or even more than the Catholic Church—but this emphasis is often compensated by a strong personal relationship with God. The objective and the subjective dimensions may have been well balanced in the Catholic Church when personal devotions were high. The hierarchy required religious assent—the submission of intellect and will (*religiosum obsequium*)—but parish priests, local congregations, and devout parents encouraged religious piety as a counterweight to objectivism.

Among the devotions of the pre-Vatican II church, none was more popular than the recitation of the family rosary. This devotion was brought to new heights in 1943 by the Rosary Crusade. "The crusade achieved an extraordinary success, with mass rallies across the United States and Canada."[86] Other Marian devotions were novenas; the use of medals and scapulars; and May Day celebrations. Devotion of the Sacred Heart was also very popular. A picture of the Sacred Heart was to be "enthroned" by the parish priest in a prominent place in the homes in order to elicit "a permanent state of devotedness and love" of the Sacred Heart. Associated with this devotion were the communion and confession on the First Friday of the month; a holy hour on Thursday nights; and prayers of reparation and expiation. In the Archdiocese of Chicago, by 1946, "Almost 500,000 enthronements had taken place, with 13,465 registered night adorers, and about 40,000 youngsters pledged to spread the devotion in their homes."[87] A simple form of prayer was the daily "morning offering" of the Apostleship of Prayer, usually at the intention of the Holy Father. The Eucharist has always been central to Catholics, with the paraliturgical devotions of the Forty Hours, nocturnal adoration, the benediction of the Blessed Sacrament, and Eucharistic congresses. When personal religion was intense, as often was the case in the pre-Vatican II church, the objective dimension emphasized by the hierarchy could easily be accepted. But once these devotions fade away, official church teaching comes to be seen as an unacceptable imposition.

3. Ritualism.

The decline of personal piety is one obvious factor fostering ritualism. Another is the mere ritualistic performance of the liturgy.

Church-Centeredness Versus Christ-Centeredness

"The old Church attitude was "Don't ask questions; just obey and submit. Believe in the church, do the things they tell you to do, and if you're good enough, you'll get in." That's a big turnoff to a lot of people.

"Catholics who are alive in their faith have a real personal relationship with Christ, whether it comes in an instant or over a lifetime. Christ says you're not going to be part of the Kingdom unless you're born again, so you have to be born again in some sense."

—Interview

Generally speaking, little invitation to personal prayer is provided by the liturgy, and little innovation is often shown by the celebrant. A typical example is the priest's invitation of "Let us pray": without praying himself or giving anyone a chance to do so, he continues by *reading* a stereotypical prayer that is supposed to reflect everyone's personal, but often nonexistent, prayer. The faithful *attend* Mass, with little opportunity for personal participation. The Mass may begin with a song, followed by "Lord have Mercy—Christ have mercy" and the Gloria. Then comes another song, followed by the Sanctus, the Eucharistic prayer recited by the priest; the common recitation of Our Father; another song; communion; the dismissal; and a final song.

Ritualism comes from both the rigidity of the liturgy and the absence of prayerful innovation in its celebration. The Sunday liturgies are planned as rigidly as an astronomical calendar: one can know in advance the prayers to be recited and the readings to be read in the next decades or even centuries, if no change is introduced. Often there is also little creative or personal prayerfulness, as the liturgy is more performance than adoration: for the Sunday Mass, the priest, the sacristan, and the music director arrive and leave at about the same time, as if their personal participation were about the same. Cradle Catholics who have been accustomed to ritualism for many years may find it comfortable; young people and outsiders do not. Ritualism was not absent among irregular and outside Catholics in the pre-Vatican II church, but at that time, the outsider Catholics were the minority, and clerical and parental authority in religious matters was pervasive. This is not the case anymore. In the preconciliar church of the 1950s, Mass often included intense private prayer, especially at communion. This type of private prayer is somewhat out of place in the more communal celebrations of today, and ritualism may creep in easily.

4. The tide toward personal religion.

It is probably false to oppose Protestantism as personal religion and Catholicism as external observances. Luther opposed faith to works (e.g., indulgences) as developed in the letter to the Romans, not faith as trust in God versus

> **The Trend of the Times**
> "The trend is towards more personal religion, and Evangelicals offer that. Those losing out are those offering impersonal religion."
> —*New York Times*, February 26, 2008.

creed. Faith as personal and/or emotional experience was not a common concept at the time of the Reformation among either Catholics or Protestants. It is John Wesley who, having experienced a warming of his heart in 1738, is said to be the father or grandfather of the born-again experience. According to Hadaway and Marler in their study of American mainline churches, "For much of American history, almost all denominations were evangelical, including those that are now called the mainline."[88] It is only after the evangelical-mainline split in the 1920s that the born-again experience and personal religiosity became prominent among American evangelicals. The emphasis on subjective religiosity is also part of a general trend toward individualism and personal growth in all areas of life since the 1960s. The selection of one's religious preference is no less important than the choice of one's career. While, as a concept, having a personal relationship with God was absent in pre-Vatican II days yet present among devout Catholics, today the language of a personal relation with God is common even among nonpracticing Catholics, who usually continue to pray.

Today the tide has turned toward a personal religion. Surveying the religious landscape of the 1990s, Wade Clark Roof found that a third of the baby boomers could be classified as born-again: half the conservative Protestants, a fourth of Catholics, and 20 percent of mainline Protestants.[89]

Growing and Declining Churches

"Members of evangelical Protestant churches are slightly more numerous (26.3 percent) than Catholics (23.9 percent).

"Out of 100 Catholics, 89 are cradle Catholics and 11 are converts. Among members of Evangelical churches, 51 are cradle Evangelicals and 49 are converts (31 from other Protestant denominations, 11 from Catholicism, and 8 from other faiths/sources)."

—The US Religious Landscape Survey, chapter 2

Similarly, among American teenagers, Smith found that "about half of U.S. teenagers report in their survey answers strong subjective importance and experiences of religious faith in their own lives, measured as importance of faith, closeness to God, commitment of life to God, experience of powerful worship."[90] It is symptomatic that churches emphasizing personal religiosity are growing, while those emphasizing objective religious practices are not. As outlined in the previous chapter, liberal individualism and a religion of obligations are a destructive mix. A religion of commandments and obligations is generally rejected by the young today. While in the past, the submission to the rules and regulation of the teaching church was seen by many as a practical or even comfortable way of gaining salvation, today any salvation based on obligations is seen as suspect. The Sabbath (salvation) is for man (and woman), not man for salvation.

B. *Theological factors*

If the majority of Catholics stop attending church, something about Catholic sacramentality must not be working, the way a machine is not working when one or several parts are deficient. I will present here a functional analysis of theological concepts and indicate the "parts" that do not seem to be working. I see three.

1. Original sin, and salvation as "Redemption."

Few doctrines have been stated more clearly, more authoritatively, and more enduringly than that of original sin. It was first affirmed by the Council of Carthage in 418, restated by the second Council of Orange in 529, and reaffirmed by the Council of Trent in 1546.[91] Pius XII reaffirmed it in *Humani Generis*.[92] The *Catechism of the Catholic Church* affirms it (no. 390, "a primeval event, a deed that took place *at the beginning of history of man*" [emphasis in text], and no. 419, "transmitted with human nature 'by propagation'"). Finally Pope John Paul II felt the need to expand the original-sin doctrine in four weekly public audiences from September 10 to October 8, 1986.[93] According to the pope, the original sin is "a primordial event" (II, 1),[94] an "infection" (III, 4) having taken place "at the beginning" (II, 9), at "the very dawn of history" (III, 1), something "hereditary ... which everyone receives at the moment of conception from one's parents" (IV, 4). The first parents lost the original holiness "in which they were 'constituted' from the beginning, drawing upon themselves the anger of God" (IV, 5). This original sin "contains the original 'model' of every sin of which man is capable," namely "disobedience to God" (II, 9). Finally, "the consequence of this sin was death as we know it" (IV, 5). On the issues of original sin, Adam and Eve, and evolution, there seems to be a disconnect between church teaching and science. Although there is ample material that discusses the relationship between Genesis 1–2 and the findings of science, the official teaching lacks the nerve to engage the debate.

Because humanity lost its "original holiness" and was deserving of the "anger of God" (physical death and eternal damnation), salvation will be understood, from Augustine to Anselm, Luther, and Trent, as "redemption"—that is, buying back. Here is a summary of Augustine theology of sin and redemption according to Haight: "Because of sin, on the basis of God's justice, human beings are, as it were, given over to the power of Satan … Christ's death was a ransom which was paid to Satan. Jesus is a redeemer, one who buys back something that is in captivity."[95] Anselm's version is based on the medieval conception of justice and honor: at the sovereign's court, "satisfaction [requires] something greater than the amount of that obligation" in his relationship to God, and "what man took from God by his sin, he has no power to repay."[96] Hence, salvation is only possible through the "satisfaction" of God made man. This conception of sin and salvation as redemption has been transmitted to us through the Council of Trent, which restated it. There are other conceptions of salvation (as in Thomism), but because of magisterial objectivism and the absence of theological pluralism after Trent, this position has remained central in Catholic official teaching to this day.

But if Adam and Eve are not historical individuals, the original sin cannot be imputed to the first couple, and it remains unexplained. Moreover, in traditional teaching, salvation cannot occur without baptism, because the latter washes away original sin (you are "anathema" if you deny this).[97] But if there is no first couple's original sin, baptism thus understood is not absolutely necessary. Are sacraments necessary for salvation? Most theologians I interviewed said no. Is salvation through Jesus Christ necessary? In light of *Dominus Jesus*, let us recognize that this is a difficult question. Core members with a solid theological background may have some answers, because either they have internalized official teaching or, thanks to the relative theological pluralism in academia, they are cognizant of alternate interpretations.[98] Those outsiders with only remnants of catechism teaching are likely to be puzzled. For 95 percent of the millennials interviewed in 2005, regular Mass attendance is not a necessary part of being a good Catholic; are any sacraments necessary? Outsiders may not be able to answer this question, but they may have entirely dropped out of sacramental practice.

2. General and specific sacramentality.

According to McBrien, sacraments are, generally speaking, visible signs of the invisible God—and, more specifically, the signs through which the church manifests its faith.[99] From Augustine to Hugh of St. Victor, these two aspects in Christian sacramentality—the general and the specific, the subjective and the objective—have been in balance. Since Trent, however, church teaching has mainly emphasized the second, while the faithful relate mostly to the first. Let us look at these two dimensions.

First, general sacramentality. According to tradition (and the theologians I interviewed), anything can be seen as a sign of the invisible God. The subjective revelation of the self-revealing God (revelation to individual *subjects*) continues through the ages. What are the most common forms of subjective revelation? The first sacrament of Jesus Christ is Scripture, as seen in the lives and sermons of the church fathers and as experienced daily by evangelicals. Moreover, during the first millennium until the end of the Middle Ages, the book of nature, of life and death, was seen as another source of revelation (as suggested in Romans 1:19–2:15, regarding God's law written in man's heart). Nearly none of the people I interviewed, when asked about important religious marker events in their lives, mentioned sacraments as important, but death, suffering, and failure were often cited as gifts from God. In Alcoholics Anonymous, probably the greatest mass spiritual movement of the twentieth century, people come to experience God through addiction. Parents and parish core members are the primary vehicle of God's revelation for children. For adults, God is found in prayer, both public and private.

Official teaching does not deny the importance of general sacramentality. The *Catechism* recognizes this wider use, but very church-centeredly concludes, "The Church both contains and communicates the invisible grace she signifies. It is in this analogical sense, that the Church is called a 'sacrament'" (no. 774). For theologically trained insiders, the church is clearly seen as a sacrament of the invisible God. For outsiders, however, the church is a sacrament or sign of "eh … power, wealth, and sex scandals." This sarcasm may be unjustified, but the church as power is, willy-nilly, a central perception of outsiders.

According to the traditional definition inherited from Trent and adopted by the *Catechism*, "The sacraments are efficacious signs of grace, instituted by Christ" (no. 1131). Instituted by Christ? Questionable. They are said to be efficacious in the sense of working *ex opere operato* (no. 1128). Will outsiders understand this? Do even insiders understand it? In the sociological perspective, they are "efficacious" in the sense that, in the case of baptism, confirmation, and marriage, they will automatically be recorded; they are also efficacious in the sense that baptism and confirmation are seldom refused, even if they have little meaning to the petitioners.

According to constant Church teaching, "The fruits of the sacraments also depend on the disposition of the one who receives them" (no. 1128). Many parishes have preparation classes, even retreats, before the major sacraments of baptism, confirmation, and marriage. Without the daily reinforcement of general sacramentality—that is, private Scripture reading and prayer; the examples of core members; the support of family and friends to help one read the book of life as gift; and the sustaining celebration of the Eucharist—these preparation classes may be a two-week crash language course one might take before embarking on a journey toward a foreign country. Private dispositions are important, but so is the support of the religious environment. How supportive, for both insiders and outsiders, is the celebration of the Eucharist?

3. The Eucharist as sacrifice versus community celebration.

The sixteenth and seventeenth centuries saw the development of new religious orders: the Jesuits, the Oratory, the Company of Saint Sulpice, the Congregation of Jesus and Mary, and many others, all of which were congregations of priests. According to the theology of the time, the church is divided into two parts: "One is the people, and the other is the clergy. One receives holiness, and the other brings it about." In the past, according to Bérulle (1575–1629), in his Letter on the Priesthood, "holiness dwelt in the clergy as in its fortress."[100] For Bérulle, this fervor was lost at the end of the Middle Ages. It would be regained through a spirituality of abnegation, sacrifice, and adoration, which culminates in the sacrifice of the Mass. At their daily silent Masses, priests were to participate in the sacrifice of the cross and experience the presence of Jesus suffering. Over the following centuries, this spirituality emphasized frequent communion and confession, benediction of the Blessed Sacrament, nocturnal adoration, and the devotions associated with the Sacred Heart. It was a spirituality of abnegation to which suffering people could relate (still popular in Latin America), a spirituality of adoration and expiation for which the Sunday Mass was central. Today it may appear as clerical, with little appeal in an age of instant gratification. But has it been effectively replaced?

An alternate theology is found in the Constitution of the Sacred Liturgy on the presence of Christ in the church in various forms. "He is present in his word ... he is present when the church prays and sings ... He is present ... most of all in the Eucharistic species."[101] This new spirituality is concomitantly leading to involvement in parish ministries and a new sense of community. An example of this new spirituality will be presented in chapter 5. Today it is the parish ministers who are the core members of the local church. The question is whether the local church can generate new practices ("devotions") that will reach regular and irregular Catholics the way the devotions to the Blessed Sacrament did in the spirituality of the Mass as sacrifice. The question is whether the parish community is truly a community, not merely an aggregate, when the faithful sit in the church the way readers do in the reading rooms of public libraries—that is, as far as possible from one another. Clearly we are in a state of transition from one spirituality to another. In the meantime, 95 percent of the young believe that attending Sunday Mass is not necessary to being a good Catholic, and they have stopped attending.

3. The Vacuum of Moral Teaching

Let me begin with a few testimonies from college students. Numerous are the examples I could give about religious and moral emptiness. Let me just quote two, both rather vague in their vagueness.

> My family's ethnic or religious background is Italian and Portuguese. We are not very religious. Some distinctive beliefs and practices of my family is that we believe that there is a God and that everyone is forgiven for their sins. Our practices consist of going to church together on special occasions, such as Christmas and Thanksgiving.

> My family celebrates the traditional Catholic holidays, but does not have any distinctive beliefs or practices. I attended religious education, as did my sisters. I do believe in God and in my religion, but not in a strict sense. I look to it more for inspiration and guidance than for rules on how to live my life.

More specific are examples of rejection of what is perceived as an empty, church-centered religion:

> Although we call ourselves Catholics, I have not been to church since my little brother's confirmation. I believe in God, but I don't think that religion should be forced upon anyone. I think religion should be a choice. Both of my parents grew up in Catholic households, and both of them attended Catholic school for a great portion of their lives. For them religion was never a choice. It was what they knew and what they had to obey. I am grateful that my parents did not impose religion on my brother or me as it was imposed on them.

> After being in Catholic school for my whole life, I felt that [the schools] were pushing their religion onto you, and whatever they said went. I just got tired of hearing the same stuff over and over again, especially in church.

After my brother died, I lost all faith in organized religion. Although I no longer had faith in Catholicism, I completed religious education until I made my confirmation. I have completed every holy sacrament with the exception of marriage, holy orders, and anointing of the sick. Religion isn't something I incorporate in my everyday life. I do not plan to marry in the church.

In each of these testimonies, no one mentions Jesus Christ.

In the survey data presented below,[102] the reasons for stopping church attendance are not theological, but moral and spiritual; people seem to object most to the traditional moral positions of the teaching church. This traditional moral theology is rooted in nineteenth-century neoscholasticism and the manualist school (to be considered next). This traditional moral theology was also central to the teachings of John Paul II, as will be seen below.

On the topic of moral vacuum, I will proceed in three steps: first a review of the manualist tradition of moral theology; next the teachings of Pope Paul II; and finally the current situation.

1. Neoscholastic moral theology dominated Catholic thought until Vatican II. Because its major works were published in the form of manuals (usually written in Latin and often published in Rome or some major Catholic universities), this tradition is called the manualist school. Most of these manuals follow the same outline and are based on the same presuppositions. According to this tradition, there are "objective norms of morality"—that is, "rules by which men must regulate their conduct."[103] How are these norms established? To quote the same authors, "Catholic Moral Theology is based on the dogmatic teaching of the one true Church. Protestant ethics rests on arbitrary doctrinal assumptions." This statement is both dogmatic and polemical: Catholic moral theology is based on true dogmatic teaching, while Protestant morality is arbitrary. Why is this so? According to the same source, "Catholics acknowledge an infallible authority in questions of both dogma and morals, whereas Protestants

possess no objective rule for either, but are buffeted to and fro by the winds of subjectivism and error."[104] The implication is clear: in order to be saved from subjectivism and error, one must submit to the sound teachings of the "one true church." The emphasis was on obedience and submission to authority. As seen above, for John Paul II, original sin was the "original 'model' of every sin of which man is capable," namely "disobedience to God." In one way or another, sin is disobedience to God, the church, and society. According to Koch-Press, "The terms sin, transgression, iniquity, offense, and disobedience are synonymously employed by Holy Scripture to designate a willful transgression of the law of God."[105] Obedience is seen as the greatest virtue, and disobedience the root of all evil.

According to the revised code of canon law (canon 212), all Christians, Catholic or not, owe obedience to the pastors (from the pope to the local pastor) in matters of faith and morals. The main reason for this

---

Reasons for ceasing to attend church
(Telephone survey in England; N=1,604)

—The church has lost its meaning for me:
61% Catholic; 47% Anglican; 49% Free Church
—The church did not allow people to discuss or disagree with its views:
47% Catholic; 23% Anglican; 17% Free Church
—I disagreed with the Church's stance on key moral issues:
48% Catholic; 29% Anglican; 22% Free Church
—The church was not meeting my spiritual needs:
47% Catholic; 36% Anglican; 31% Free Church
—I was disillusioned by the church's lack of response to social injustice:
45% Catholic; 26% Anglican; 28% Free Church
—I was disillusioned by churchgoers' attitudes toward homosexuals:
35% Catholic; 21% Anglican; 21% Free Church
—Sermons were irrelevant to my everyday life:
47% Catholic; 36% Anglican; 35% Free Church
—The church failed to connect with the rest of my life:
57% Catholic; 44% Anglican; 47% Free Church
—The leadership style of the church was too authoritarian
40% Catholic; 20% Anglican; 11% Free Church
—I was tired of being told what to believe by the church:
49% Catholic; 28% Anglican; 32% Free Church
—The church's approach to morality was too black-and-white:
63% Catholic; 34% Anglican; 28% Free Church

---

submission is the belief that the church teaches with certainty and authority. According to traditional moral theology, "the moral law of nature is absolute and unchangeable, that is to say, not even God can change it or dispense from its precepts."[106] Because church teaching is absolute and certain, once the Supreme Pontiff "purposely pass[ed] judgment on a matter under dispute, it is obvious that that matter ... cannot be any longer considered a question open to discussion among theologians" (*Humani Generis*, 20).[107]

The superiority of Catholic morality was quite universally accepted until the 1960s. Catholic moral teaching was believed to be objectively true and unchangeable, and secular morality subjective and unstable. Vatican II and Rahner raised the issue of theological pluralism, and the birth-control controversy brought forth the issue of public dissent in the church. It is Joseph Fuchs who first questioned the foundational claim that Catholic morality based on natural law is superior to all other forms of morality. "Is there a distinctively Christian morality?" he asked.[108] "It does not make sense to distinguish between the precepts of Christian morality and those of human morality."[109] He believed that there is no Christian "system of moral norms" inherited from Christ, Paul, or John.[110] As a professor of moral theology at a Roman university, Fuchs had accepted the claim that the magisterium can decide all questions of natural law, but in a subsequent book,[111] he rejected it. He also resigned from his chair. The issue became settled in the public's mind by the argument that there is no reason to think that "there is a Christian morality any more than a Christian logic."[112]

2. John Paul II followed the neoscholastic tradition in questions of personal morality, but not in issues of social justice. Hence, taken as a whole, his moral teaching is controversial: it is conservative in some areas and reform-minded in others. His polemical encyclical on "Certain Fundamental Questions of the Church's Moral Teaching" is based on a conservative statement of the Constitution on Divine Revelation, "the task of authentically interpreting the word of God, whether written or handed on, has been entrusted *exclusively* to the living teaching office of the church [emphasis added]."[113] Who is excluded in John Paul II's view?

In general, theologians (although in the distant past, the magisterium of theologians was as important as that of the hierarchy), and in particular, those who disagree with him. The motto of theology is "truth seeking understanding." How do theologians and popes come to understand truth? For theologians the answer is obvious: through scholarship, public debate, and prayer. Can popes know the truth without public debate? For the manualists and John Paul II, the answer is equally obvious: as quoted above, "Catholics acknowledge an infallible authority in questions of both dogma and morals"; papal teaching is infallible under certain conditions, and the theologians' teaching is not.

John Paul II developed the notion of intrinsically evil acts by stretching the meaning of a passage of Gaudium et Spes about acts that "are opposed to life itself" like homicide, genocide, abortion, euthanasia, suicide, mutilation, torture, arbitrary imprisonment, deportation, slavery, prostitution, degrading working conditions, and, of course, contraception.[114] It is not said that all of these acts are intrinsically evil; it would even be difficult to argue that deportation and degrading working conditions are always intrinsically evil. John Paul II quotes this passage as if these examples were all acts that "by their nature [were] 'incapable of being ordered' to God, because they radically contradict the good of the person made in his image." These acts are always "seriously wrong," "*per se* and in themselves, independently of circumstances."[115] The conclusion is that there are norms that "oblige *semper et pro semper*, that is, without any exception."[116] We have reached the ultimate conclusion of magisterial objectivism—namely, the denial of the subjective dimension of morality "without any exception." Objectivism is a major issue in both sacramentality and moral teaching, and both are related to the tendency of the institutional church to "govern" through control, laws, and rules. On the other hand, John Paul II's positive teaching on social justice and his saintly way of life made him many friends among the masses, especially among the young who may actually be quite ignorant of his teaching. Yet the overall effect of his teaching was divisive: he alienated many liberals while gaining the admiration of many. Even today Catholics are divided about his teaching. Outsider Catholics may simply ignore it while admiring him as a person.

3.   What are the alternatives? One is Charles Curran's model of relationality-responsibility, but he was removed from his chair as unfit to teach at a Catholic university. "In general this model sees the human person in multiple relationships with God, neighbor, world, and self." The model can be seen as strongly rooted in Catholic tradition: "Scriptural, theological, and philosophical arguments can be made to show the centrality of a relationality-responsibility model."[117] One could begin with the relational covenant between Yahweh and Israel; or the relationship between God and Abraham; or even further back, the relationship between man and his creator; but this is not our purpose here. What can average Catholics learn from such a model?

Here is a list of classes offered at a local church, all of which are thirteen weeks long unless otherwise noted: a class for couples; parenting teens; inner healing (long weekend); free marriage counseling (on a one-to-one basis); how to manage one's finances (a ten-week course); special issues for men and women (ongoing biweekly meetings); issues that Christians face in the workplace; crossroads for 18- to 25-year-olds; divorce care; grief care; great relationships: parents, teens, and God; and the Bible, Christianity, and the American government. These courses (not all are offered at the same time) seem inspired by the relationality-responsibility model, so where is the moral vacuum? All of the above offerings were given in one Protestant church, which offers about fifteen different thirteen-week courses twice a year—or thirty a year—all taught by competent volunteers. I could not find something equivalent in Catholic parishes. For outsider Catholics, the Catholic moral vacuum is real. Insiders may disagree, and here is why: for theologians and church officials, morality is a set of abstract rules, while for most people, it is a concrete way of living—a set of habits of the heart. In the first case, morality is defined philosophically and theologically; in the second, it is part of one's subculture.

Morality *as habits of the heart,* as *the ethic of eating, drinking, working, and relating,* is the *core of any culture.* Without a Catholic morality thus understood, there can be no Catholic subculture. What is different about Catholic schools if their morality is not different from that of their environment? Sociological analysis reveals the existence of a Baptist morality and a Baptist subculture, an evangelical morality and an evangelical subculture. Most sociologists would agree that there is practically no more Catholic subculture. The aim of Catholic enculturation is not just to indigenize Christianity in local customs; it is to transform that local culture according to Christian values. When Christians do not Christianize their environment, they themselves become secularized; they will have no subculture of their own—that is, among other things, no moral culture, or only a fuzzy one.

Conclusion

In this chapter, we have seen that Catholic decline comprises three major factors: objectivism in sacraments, objectivism in moral teaching, and hierarchy as power. The first two may be a consequence of the third: the church as power tends to impose objectivism in both sacraments and moral teaching. All three were put in place by the Council of Trent (1545–1563). Since then, there has been little or no pluralism in the church, either in the official theology or in sacramentality (yet pluralism survived in spirituality, which escapes the control of the hierarchy). Since then, little has changed in the institutional structure of the Catholic Church, while most Western nations have broken away from the absolute forms of government of their past. The American and French Revolutions rejected the absolutism of kings. Gone are the governments of emperors, kaisers, tzars, führers, duces, and generalissimos. The papal powers remain imperial; the triple crown remains the emblem of the papacy. Nothing short of an ecumenical council of the stature of Trent (which dwarfs Vatican II) can undo and redo the structure of the Catholic Church.

The need for *reform* has been obvious since the time when three popes quarreled for the tiara and produced the Great Schism of Western Christianity (1378–1417). Then (as today in the eyes of outsiders), reform needed (and still needs) to begin with the papacy. Several councils (Basel, Florence, and Constance) could not stop the decline of Western Christianity. Then came the Reformation. The papacy excommunicated the Reformers. They left and took with them half of Europe. Then came the Counter-Reformation. Those who had left did not return. Will the same happen again? Today the losses of the Catholic Church are of the magnitude of those of the time of the Reformation.

The need for *renewal* has also been with us for centuries. In terms of renewal, the sky is the limit. During all past centuries, evangelizers and saints were able to advance the kingdom of God in spite of the limitations of the ecclesiastical governments. In reference to the three points mentioned in this chapter, parish priests can champion collegiality, subsidiarity, and clerical modesty. They can also—or rather, they should—promote a profound spirituality of prayer and sacramentality. Finally, they can promote a morality inspired by both the book of God and the book of life, a morality that fosters responsibility and strengthens relationships.

The first three chapters were dedicated to the study of decline; it is time to turn to renewal with the description of two lively churches.

CHAPTER 4

~

THE MISSIONARY CHURCH OF BAYVILLE

> They were all filled with the Holy Spirit. They were
> given the Word and voice. They began to speak in
> their own voices, and every man understood them in
> his own language.
> —Paraphrase of Acts 2:4–6

The growth and decline in attendance studied in previous chapters represent measurements, not explanations. In this chapter, I will try to *explain* growth from a theoretical perspective—namely, social movement theory at the macro level and interaction theory at the micro level. Social movement theory can explain growth in terms of mass participation and resource mobilization. The best known recent social movement is that of civil rights in the 1960s and 1970s, which generated mass marches involving blacks and whites, students and clergymen, and CEOs and blue-collar workers. A social movement may involve a charismatic leader like Martin Luther King or a loose core group like NOW (National Organization for Women) of the feminist movement. It always tends to involve some mass mobilization, an organizational structure, and some cultural innovation. There are also religious social movements like Protestant evangelicalism and the Catholic charismatic movement. There is church growth, in this perspective, when a given church has generated a religious movement—

that is, mass mobilization, organization, and cultural innovation at the national and/or the parish level.

What generates social movements? According to interaction theory, a social movement at the macro level of society may be created when at the micro level, the intensity of emotions and symbols is great enough to generate effervescence and a collective consciousness, which then may spread to the macro level. Following Durkheim, Randall Collins outlined a model of "interaction ritual" that can be applied to both secular and religious phenomena.[118] In short, any interaction ritual produces group solidarity, emotional energy in individuals, and greater participation in collective symbols and values (this is the output) if there is feedback intensification (the input). Thus a birthday party will lead to greater family cohesion if there are many forms of feedback intensification—for instance, a surprise party, the presence of many family members and friends, a huge cake, a valuable gift, champagne, dancing, and so on.

I have adapted Collins's interaction ritual to religious interaction using some of Turner's concepts. The first step is liminality, or what Collins calls "barriers to outsiders." As a precondition, members of a group must be open to the ritual happening, as in a rite of passage. They must be open-minded, as in a "threshold situation" (the literal meaning of liminality). They must be in a state of "spiritual denudation,"[119] as in a retreat or other forms of separation from the secular world. They must be open to spiritual conversion, ready to move beyond past achievements. There must also be "barriers to outsiders" to keep out nonactive members and "free riders." The main phase of the interaction ritual is "collective effervescence" —that is, a great intensity of emotions and shared symbols. This state is characterized by "feedback intensification" or "rhythmic entrainment," which happen when the emotional intensity of one participant leads to a greater emotional involvement of others, and the emotions of one member feed the emotions of others. This process leads to greater "group solidarity." In religious interaction rituals, participants come to see one another in a new light: not just as a group, but as *communitas*, or a spiritual community of believers. Through the process of feedback intensification, they also reinforce, reinterpret, and often transform their shared values and symbols. As *communitas*, they see themselves not only as a spiritual community but also as the bearers of a message with "symbols of social relationship" and new "standards of morality," in Collins's terms. Having acquired "emotional energy" (another of Collins's terms), the members are now ready to march out and "spread the word." They are ready, together, to start a social movement, albeit at a very small scale. In summary, I would distinguish five overlapping phases in the interaction ritual leading to a social movement: 1. liminality, a state of openness; 2. feedback intensification leading to high intensity of emotions and shared symbols; 3. the creation of *communitas*; 4. emotional energy leading to evangelism and proselytism; and 5. a "chain" of interaction, as when interaction rituals are repeated, they lead to ever increased (or decreased) liminality, feedback intensification, *communitas*, and emotional energy. In this chain, the various steps overlap: liminality is already *communitas*, both contain emotional energy, all three may increase throughout the ritual process, and the multiplication of interaction creates a chain of ever greater (or lesser) intensity that can be channeled into a social movement.

To briefly illustrate the emergence of a social movement, one could recall the narrative of the Pentecost (Acts 1:12–14; 2:1–4). After the Ascension, the apostles came together in the upper room to pray. They were in a state of expectation (liminality), having been told by Jesus to "wait for the gift my Father promised." These days of expectation must have brought back the memory of sayings, parables, miracles, and scenes from the passion and resurrection, with one story leading to another and one person's recollection being amplified by the memories of another in a crescendo of intensification. We know from Pentecostal churches what this effervescence looks like in the days and moments before and after a baptism in the Holy Spirit, which is usually a highly emotional event, often leading to speaking in tongues. With the descent of the Holy Spirit, the collective consciousness of the apostles made them see their group as a spiritual community, as *communitas*, with a message to the outside world. Their message spread quickly as a social movement, with the active participation of all, using an embryonic structure (the twelve) and an identity (as "followers of the way"). One important dimension of this inner transformation was, for all participants, the gift of speech or voice. They were transformed from passive and silent followers into active and vocal actors. Not only did they find voice, but they each found *their* individual voices in a personal relationship with God and Jesus involving their special and unique personal talents in their mission.

In the analysis of two cases of lively church life that follow (Bayville in this chapter and St. Mary's in the next), I will point out the various steps leading to a religious movement, beginning with liminality; feedback intensification of emotions and symbols; the sense of *communitas*; and discovery by each participant of his or her personal voice.

Let me begin by defining a few terms. I will use "evangelical" in the traditional and European sense: in Spanish, French, and Italian, "evangelical" is an adjective referring to a life according to the Gospel (from the Latin *evangelium*, or Greek *evangelion*, good news), while in the United States, the Protestant majority has monopolized this term for some of its members (e.g., the evangelical churches), and Catholics have often adopted this Protestant usage. I will use "evangelism" as the spreading of the good news and "evangelization" as an organized form of evangelism. Hence, in my usage, both Catholics and Protestants can be evangelical; both are to be inspired by evangelism, and both have structures of evangelization. Of course, Protestants are stronger on evangelism, as we will see in Bayville below, and often weaker on common structures of evangelization, while the opposite often holds for Catholics.

The Bayville Community Church

The Bayville Community Church (not the real name) is an independent suburban church with little local notoriety. Not being affiliated with a Protestant denomination, it does not receive any publicity or recognition from other denominational congregations. It is tucked away in a dead-end street and cannot be seen when driving by. Visitors usually come at the invitation of friends. I happened to go there by accident.

The Bayville church started in 1955 as a nondenominational home church that grew rapidly. It acquired a corner lot in a residential area in 1955 and dedicated its new sanctuary six years later. Continuing to grow, it purchased a vacant public school in 1978. It opened a Christian school there and a sanctuary in 1983. The current pastor was hired in 2000.

The Bayville church is part of the Fellowship of Christian Assemblies. Each of the affiliated churches is independent, like an independent denomination. The Bayville church does not identify itself as evangelical or reformed, because it aims at transcending all labels. There is a holiness and Pentecostal dimension, but it is muted. There is an ecumenical dimension: at all Sunday services, the pastor prays for all local churches, north, south, east, and west;[120] yet this church is not actively involved in ecumenism. The main emphasis is biblical and evangelical (as defined above). Being an independent church, it has no denominational past: Luther and the Reformers are seldom or never mentioned. The Bible is read as if nothing had happened in the last two thousand years, which is both an asset and a liability.

2008 MISSIONS CONVENTION

SATURDAY, APRIL 12
Missions Modules
This is your opportunity to participate in two modules presented by our guest teachers / missionaries.
Each topic will be offered twice as follows:
• First Session - 9:00 to 10:15 a.m.
• Second Session - 10:30 to 11:45 a.m.
MISSIONS BANQUET
6 p.m. - SGT Fellowship Center
Cost: $20 per person
SUNDAY, APRIL 13
Worship Services
• 8:30 & 10:15 a.m. and 12:15 p.m.
  Speakers: STEVE & SANDI YOUNGREN
• 2:00 p.m., Invite a missionary to lunch
  (at your home or a restaurant)
• Evening Service - 6 p.m.
  Speakers: STEVE & SANDI YOUNGREN
Followed by International Lite Bites

MONDAY, APRIL 14
Missionary visits to SCS
• 9:30 a.m. -1:30 p.m.
MISSIONS FILM
• 7:30 p.m. - SGT Sanctuary
TUESDAY, APRIL 15
Missions Workshops
• 10:00 & 11:30 a.m., 1:30 & 3:00 p.m.
  Everyone welcome!
Prayer Partner Dessert
• 7:30 p.m. with Missionaries
Questions and Answers
  SGT Fellowship Center, Everyone invited
WEDNESDAY, APRIL 16
• 10:00 a.m., **PRAYER MEETING with all**
MISSIONARIES
• 1:30 p.m., **MISSIONARY-TO-MISSIONARY**
INTERACTION
• 5:00 p.m., Invite a missionary home
  to dinner
• 7:30 p.m., **Missions Challenge**
  Speakers: STEVE & SANDI YOUNGREN

By the end of 2007, weekly church attendance was about 2,700, out of which around 800 were members. The distinction between the two categories is not emphasized and is not noticeable in any way. To become a member, one has to have attended this church for six months, taken a thirteen-week course, and be baptized as the expression of one's public commitment. Only members can vote at church meetings; only members can be in leadership positions. This church has grown substantially since its small beginning in 1955 and continues to grow. My interest in this church stems from the fact that its activities have created a social movement of missionary zeal locally, nationally, and abroad. To give an overview of these missionary endeavors, let us look at the program of the five-day Missions Convention, which takes place twice a year. On that occasion, about twenty to twenty-five missionaries come back from the fields, usually abroad, to report back about their work and incite further involvement from the members of the congregation. Not only is there interaction between the missionaries, the congregation, and various small groups or classes of students, but church members are invited to take the missionaries for lunch at home or a restaurant, or even invite them to stay in their homes for the time of their visit. The Sunday banquet is attended by about 400 people. This convention will be described more in details below (pages 97-98). The program of the 2008 convention can be seen above.

This church attracts and caters mainly to the "unsaved"—that is, the unchurched and the religious dropouts. According to the pastor in charge of admissions, "in the last two membership classes [of 2007], we had a total of 110–120; out of these, probably 75 percent to 80 percent are first-generation Christians, never been Christian before." Most of these, based on my interviews, are fall-away or unchurched Catholics, because Bayville is located in a predominantly Catholic area.

The church's mission statement describes its triple commitment: to "magnify Jesus through worship"; help members grow through Word, ministries, and fellowship; and "obey the Great Commission to reach the world." I will divide my presentation into three parts: worship, ministries and fellowship, and mission. Although presented separately, all three are interrelated.

Sunday Worship

The church offers three Sunday services, each an hour and a half long. An in-house survey revealed why people come to this church. According to an associate pastor, "Number one, people enjoy the worship service. Number two, they enjoy the teaching of our senior pastor. Number three, they enjoy and like the activities, which involve adults, youth, and children." The Sunday service consists of two parts: worship (about 20–30 minutes) and the sermon (about 30–40 minutes), followed by a short final prayer (5–10 minutes).

1. *Singing and worship* are the responsibility of one of the pastors on staff. His task is much more than that of a music director. "I'm the pastor of the choir, the orchestra, all the technical areas involving light, sound, or video in the sanctuary, as well as the recording of the services. I'm also the pastor of anyone involved in drama" —that is, the two yearly performances, the Passion play and the Glory of Christmas play. There are about 70 to 80 people in the choir, and around 40 in the orchestra; there is also a band of 7 musicians. "If you include their families, you're talking probably about 300 to 400 people. Pastoring them means trying to stay up to the challenges of their lives. I'm the one that hears about their health issues, or weddings, or funerals. And of course, when they have individual needs, they contact me." There are weekly rehearsals from 7:00 to 9:00 p.m. on Thursdays. On Sundays, members of the choir and the orchestra are on duty from 8:30 to 11:30 a.m. The small band plays at the third service, at 12:30 p.m. Singing in the choir and playing an instrument is a ministry for which one must qualify through a formal application and a forty-five-minute interview.

Advanced technology is widely used. Two big screens in front of the sanctuary allow for the projection of the text of the songs, but also for PowerPoint presentations. Because the projections are perfectly synchronized with the worship service, the presence of the screen is nonobtrusive. The audio version of the sermon is available on the Internet. A bookstore makes available CDs and printed material.

The pastor of worship and music leads the assembly into prayer. This is done through prayer itself. The choir's singing in front of the assembly is prayer, not performance. The choir members do not have pulpits and music sheets in front of them; they have memorized the songs. Their singing is prayerful, often with closed eyed and raising hands. The pastor leads people into prayer by praying aloud in inspirational praying, not by reading or reciting rote prayers. The prayerfulness of the singing comes through in the repetition of a given verse over and over, at the prompting of the pastor (like, "Lord, I'm amazed by you; I'm amazed by you; I'm amazed by you; how you love me!"). The singing may increase to a forte in a crescendo and then fade away into silence.

At no time is the choir louder than the singing assembly. Never does the orchestra overpower either the choir or the assembly, except in a few short fortes; on the contrary, the voices of the choir and the sounds of the orchestra blend together with those of the assembly. It appears as if the choir and the orchestra (together about 100 people strong) are part of the assembly, rather than leading it. The pastor of music does not seem to direct the choir and the orchestra; they seem to sing and play on their own, only prompted by his raising hand at the beginning of a new song. Freed from directing, the pastor can dedicate himself to what seems his main role: leading the assembly in prayer and song. At this point, the service seems like a duet involving him on the one hand and the assembly, the choir, and the musicians on the other. His voice, spoken into a microphone, is always louder than that of the assembly, but not to the point that one cannot also hear one's neighbors singing right and left. He may be praying in voice-over, paraphrasing the song, or singing in voice-over a variation of the lines of the song—or, more commonly, singing a few words to invite the assembly to repeat a line or two. This line may be repeated numerous times, at the end of which his voice may end in a prayer summarizing the song and/or introducing another.

After about twenty minutes of singing, it is the senior pastor's turn to lead the assembly into prayer. Since no rote prayers are used at any time, praying must come from the bottom of one's heart. An improvised prayer, like one before a meal, would be inadequate, because usually such a prayer is stereotypical; hence, it dries up very quickly. The inspirational praying that is needed must be intense enough and imaginative enough to inspire others to pray likewise. At Sunday services, the assembly usually interjects "Yes, Lord" or "Amen" in a soft voice, or people pray aloud on their own, along with the pastor. At prayer meetings, this process may go on for half an hour, or an hour, or more. This deep awakening of the emotions and the firing of the religious imagination are often said to be the result of the baptism in the Holy Spirit, but it may also be learned and developed over time. If worship is viewed as a social behavior, there is always some role-playing involved. In either case, such an awakening requires a keen awareness of one's deep emotions and a broadening of the imagination beyond common stereotypes. Such praying is found in all prayer meetings here at one time or another. It always leads to intense religious emotionality.

After about half an hour of singing and praying, one would expect an answer from God. This often comes in the form of a prophecy—that is, a word of encouragement, exhortation, or admonition. Prophecies, like inspirational prayers, are usually expressed with great intensity, flowing effortlessly in long sentences. Their content is usually as simple as most biblical messages: "Have courage, I am with you," or "Don't be afraid, I have overcome the world." The speaker of a prophecy could have said, summarizing it in prosaic terms for outsiders, "I think the Lord wants us to have courage," or "The Lord does not want us to be afraid," which are low-intensity and reflexive utterances. It is not individual reflection that inspires a prophecy, but the biblical tradition—its content, imagery, and speech pattern. Thus Jesus did not say, as a suggestion, "God does not want you to be afraid," but, authoritatively, "Do not be afraid, little flock, for your Father has chosen gladly to give you the kingdom" (Luke 12:32). Utterances of comfort or encouragement usually follow the prophetic literary form; this is why they are called prophecies. These utterances are usually said to be inspired by the Holy Spirit. Whether this "inspiration" is to be taken literally or figuratively is left to the listener. The same can be said about Bible quotations, thoughts, and prayers "received from the Lord." In this church, prophecies are seen as normal: as faith is a relationship with God, it necessarily involves both requests and replies. At a prayer meeting, a participant may refer to Luke 12:32 and say, "The Lord put on my heart not to be afraid, because our Father will give us to partake in his kingdom," and then elaborate on this theme with numerous biblical images, references, and quotations. This would not be a prophecy, yet it is a "word from God." Prophecies speak from God's perspective, which is the prophetic perspective. The priestly perspective, which is that of teachers and preachers, also speaks from God's perspective but involves more personal interpretation of God's message. At Bayville's church, sermons, the interpretation of God's message, are seen as a vital part of the Sunday service. Both prophecies and the sermons are emotional "highs."

2. *The sermon*. The senior pastor's sermons get high marks of appreciation. They are experienced by many as messages to be meditated on throughout the week. Sermons are carefully prepared: on Thursdays the pastor does not go to his office and does not conduct church business, so that the whole day can be dedicated to sermon preparation. Exactly the same sermon is given at all three services, which indicates that the text has been memorized. It is posted weekly on the church's website.

At church services as well as fellowship meetings, all speakers begin by asking the audience for prayer. Zechariah's famous line "Not by might nor by power, but by my Spirit, says the Lord" (Zechariah 4:6) is often quoted as the motto for all speakers: a preacher may be mightily prepared and his sermon powerfully delivered, but only the Spirit can touch the hearts of the congregants. Usually an associate pastor prays over the senior pastor before his sermon while people in the pews raise their hands in their direction.

Sermons speak from Scripture *as lived faith*, not as learned knowledge for theological or historical instruction. The pastor often begins by saying, "The Lord has put on my heart to speak to you about the following passage." The assembly is then invited to find the passage in their own Bible (many people, maybe the majority, bring their Bible to church, especially if they attend Bible-centered classes afterward). The assembly may read the passage aloud or simply repeat key words after the pastor.

"We are mostly literalists in our Biblical teaching," an associate pastor said. "What we are is middle of the road." The church's statement of faith consists of fourteen articles, the first of which declares, "We believe that the Scriptures of the Old and New Testament are inspired by God; that they are the revelation of God to man and are the supreme and final authority in both faith and practice (II Timothy 3:16,17; II Peter 1:21)." It is not stated that Scripture is to be taken literally, although this is the general tendency. Scripture is the "supreme" authority in faith and morals, a principle that is taken very seriously, making the Bible the ultimate source of wisdom in prayer, family life, business, and all aspects of private and public life. Yet Scripture cannot, realistically, be the "final authority" unless there is an authority structure to interpret the Bible authoritatively and impose its teaching as the only true one. This is not the case here. It may be safe to say, then, that at Bayville, church teaching is biblical and somewhat literal, but not fundamentalist, if by fundamentalism one means a set of "fundamental" dogmas imposed on all. Significantly, the statement of faith states "We believe that …" not "You must believe that …"

The emphasis on Scripture comes with a lack of emphasis upon, or at times even contempt at and rejection of, traditions. In practical terms, this means that the Bible is interpreted as if nothing has happened in the last two thousand years. This has the advantage of allowing one to invest all of one's heart and mind into Scripture and contemporary commentaries; Catholics, on the other hand, may invest much more energy into the wisdom of tradition, but often at the expense of biblical knowledge. Ideally, of course, there should be a perfect balance. A literal interpretation also has advantages. Since Scripture is the "ultimate authority" for *faith and practice*, and *not* for dogmatic teaching (since there is no dogmatic authority structure here), its interpretation is thoroughly if not exclusively spiritual. The enormous scholarship about the historical interpretation of the Bible over the last 150 years is simply ignored in favor of a purely spiritual understanding. Mainline churches, on the other hand, often invest so much energy into the understanding of the historical context and the exact historical meaning of biblical texts that the spiritual dimension may be lost.

In practical terms, the biblical text is taken literally in the Greek and Hebrew originals (the senior pastor seems to be knowledgeable in both). Key terms are explored in various translations, in reference to the context, and in similar passages. The purpose of this literal analysis is to be "moved and touched by the Spirit." The controversial issues of the literal approach (e.g., the creation in seven days) are avoided as fruitless in favor of the spiritual content (e.g., "We believe man was created in the image of God …" in the statement of faith, with no reference to the creation in seven days). This type of interpretation is the basis of biblical *lectio divina*: people are encouraged to read several chapters of the Bible until, in a given passage, they are "touched by the Holy Spirit," at which time Bible reading turns into prayer.

Biblical interpretations are seldom theological and dogmatic. This lack of attempt to create a systematic theology, taken together with the absence of an authority structure to enforce beliefs, renders any teaching to be only optative, or optional, like a suggestion. On several occasions, I inquired about the basic requirements or basic expectations at this church, but I was always been given evasive answers. Even in the thirteen-week preparation class for baptism, the church does not outline any specific expectations, I was told, except for one: be faithful to God's voice. Though tithing is a clear biblical teaching, it is not enforced; yet about 80 percent of the members tithe regularly. Bible reading and prayer are not top-down expectations; yet the majority do so on a daily basis. Bayville's approach is effective for the same reason that Catholics who have been told they do not have to attend Sunday Mass are more likely to show up in order to be faithful to God. With this principle in mind, let us look at a Sunday sermon titled "Immersed into Christ: Discovering Our True Identity," based on Romans 6:1–11. Here is a rough summary.

"Baptism answers the question of who you are and what you are capable of doing. If you listen to the answer of others, you will have ups and downs. Baptism tells us where our identity comes from—namely, Jesus Christ. I know who I am: not my title, not my profession, not what other people say about me. Look up Romans 6: 1–11 in your Bible, or the one that is in your pew. Baptism is a prophetic act; it declares our future by immersing us in Christ. I am not a slave; I am liberated by the work of Christ. I know where I am going; it happens by following the will of God in my life. Baptism into death with Christ is separation. The Greek word for death, *thanatos*, means separation—in this case, separation from bondage, from what binds you, what chains you … like bitterness, unforgiveness, anxiety, arrogance, lust, jealousy. … Self-denial is giving up what produces slavery and bondage, what impedes my ability to move forward. Death to self [in loud voice] *is for freedom; Christ sets you free*! Where the Spirit of the Lord is, *there is liberty!* It sets you *free* from the lies of our culture that say that if you are committed to God, it takes all the fun out of life. Are you kidding? It takes all the bondage out! When we are baptized in Christ, we are immersed in Christ. Are you immersed in your possessions? Your car? Your house? Your money? What you are immersed in tells you what you are. 'You who have been baptized into Christ have put on Christ' (Galatians 3:27). To 'put on Christ' is like putting on a coat: cultural Christians put on their Christian coat just in church; in a secular environment, they take it off. To put on Christ is to know whom to follow. It is going down into death from slavery with him and going up into the newness of freedom in him. The water of the Word keeps you immersed in him. When you are crucified or baptized in him, you are resurrected in him." The sermon is followed by an inspirational prayer asking for the power to put on the coat of Christ.

Missions Are Foundational

"The whole church should be involved in missions, which is not in competition with other ministries. For example, you could have sixty or seventy ministries in a church, but missions and evangelism are not really another ministry in that church; missions and evangelism are foundational.

"What's on my heart for missions is that they become foundational in everyone's life, regardless of what ministry people are involved in. They should be sharing their faith; that's what missions and evangelism are about. Missions should be foundational to all the ministries, not in competition. You could be involved in a nursing ministry; then sharing the gospel would be a natural thing to do."
—Interview with an elder

This sermon is thoroughly scriptural. It quotes the Greek text on several occasions. It avoids controversial topics traditionally associated with baptism, like original sin. It integrates a prophecy given just prior to the sermon: "'Move forward,' says the Lord, 'do not look back.'" At times it uses a populist language ("Are you kidding?") and props to lend life to the message. It looks at Scripture as *lived faith* to be appropriated, not as an occasion for theologizing or historical research. In reference to the previous chapters on decline, we find here a strong rejection of consumerism and the practice of identifying with one's possessions. It defines Christian identity as individuation, not liberal individualism. It is Christ-centered, not church-centered. It begins and ends with inspirational prayer, not ritualism. It is sacramental in the broadest sense.

Let me now summarize the Sunday worship in terms of the various steps of the interaction ritual. 1) There is liminality from the beginning: the worshippers come in a state of expectation of a good sermon, good music and singing, and a high spiritual energy. 2) Then comes feedback intensification—that is, the feedback loop of intensification of emotions, beginning with an emotional high: from the first song, the sounds of the choir and orchestra are forte, nearly shouting, and the assembly is immediately involved in this loud singing. After about ten minutes, there are a few announcements, the offering, and often the greeting of one's neighbors. Then the loud singing picks up again in a decrescendo when the pastor takes over. By the end of the services, emotionality is high. The voice of the pastor may have been emotional at times. Occasionally, there is some crying or sobbing in the assembly. During the final prayer, people may be asked to pray for their neighbors, right and left, holding hands, at the end of which many people have visibly been moved: deep emotions are displayed on their faces, and the room becomes rife with a feeling of bonding with one another. 3) Now there is *communitas*, the feeling of one spiritual community in Christ. The stage is set for mass involvement in a social movement, to be described below.

Ministries and Fellowship

Although there is no liturgical calendar at this church, not all Sunday services are the same. Every month, there is a communion Sunday, a family Sunday, and a missions Sunday. The priorities are missions, family, and youth. There are two associate pastors for children and youth ministries; another for marriage and counseling; one more for missions and evangelization; one for hospitality and assimilation; an administrator of church ministries; and the associate pastor for music. Each of these pastors supervises several teams, who in turn work with scores of volunteers.

The authority structure of the church is congregational and decentralized. The ultimate authority rests with the "combined board," which consists of the board of deacons, the board of trustees, and the board of elders, with up to nine votes each. The trustees take care of finances and maintenance; the deacons and deaconesses visit the sick and do some teaching; and the elders hold the senior pastor accountable in the spiritual realm. In 2008 there were 6 elders, about 18 deacons, 8–10 trustees, and about 15 deaconesses. Trustees and deacons are elected for three-year terms by the assembly of all members. Elders are selected by the pastor among former or current members of the combined board. All are sometimes called "pastors," since their role is to "pastor" others. There is no distinction between the ordained and the nonordained, as ministries are defined by their spiritual mission, not their power of jurisdiction and ordination.

There are about 70–90 different ministries, depending on what is included. The *Ministry Index for 2007–2008* lists 13 children ministries; 9 missions and evangelism ministries; 10 hospitality ministries; 14 marriage and family ministries; 10 in music, art and drama; 5 for youth and the Christian school; and about 30 specialty ministries. I will exclude youth and Christian education, because those categories need special treatment. I have previously introduced the pastor of music, who is also in charge of two theater productions, the Passion play and the Joy of Christmas play, both of high religious intensity. The hospitality ministries include the very useful parking-lot ministers; the ushers and receptionists; and, for newcomers, a four-week informational class ("New Friends") and a weekly spiritual formation, "Renovation of the Heart." Rather than present cursively all ministries, I will concentrate on prayer, which is basic in all ministries. I will present the missions ministries in the next section.

1. *The primacy of prayer.* Feedback intensification or rhythmic entrainment can be visualized occurring among a team in training whose members lead (entrain) others to ever higher achievements. The success of a team depends not only on the intensity but also on the duration and frequency

of its training. A half-hour church service once a week would be weak feedback intensification or entrainment. At Bayville, church services, prayer meetings, business meetings, special concerts, Saturday church breakfast, and so on all last about an hour and a half or more. The frequency depends on an individual's involvement. Daily prayer and Bible reading are common. There are weekly classes of an hour and a half each for thirteen weeks; weekly prayer meetings at 6:00 a.m. on Wednesdays and Fridays and 10 a.m. on Wednesdays; a women's fellowship meeting weekly for two hours; and a men's fellowship meeting twice a month. Other prayer ministries listed in the *Ministry Index* include intercessory prayer meetings, prayer walking, evangelism explosion prayer, missions prayer partners, missions prayer points, short-term missions prayer, unreached people's prayer group, moms' international prayer meetings, Christian school PTF prayer meetings, Christian school moms' prayer meetings, and a prayer request phone line to be answered by a group of intercessors.

No purely secular activities are offered at Bayville. The Passion play and the Joy of Christmas are religious performances taking place in the sanctuary; they are not mainly entertainment. The week before the 2007 Christmas play, the pastor requested a special day of fasting and prayer for its spiritual success. The Passion play was performed six times, with an audience of over a thousand on the day I attended. It was a musical, rather than a play, with a cast of about 150, all from the congregation, with the participation of the choir and orchestra for the music. The pastor spoke four times: an inspirational prayer at the beginning; a spiritual commentary at the end of the first act; a short sermon after crucifixion and resurrection; and an invitation to come forward for prayer at the end. The religious participation of the audience was obvious, as people applauded at strongly religious moments.

The combined men and women's breakfast is not mainly a social event. After socializing with others around a table, attendees are led in song by the pastor of prayer and music, they share with one another on the theme of the day (e.g., Ephesians 4:32, "Be kind and compassionate to one another"). At the January 2008 breakfast, after a brief sharing among couples in the audience, it was the turn of the pastor and his wife to do so. Then followed, for about thirty minutes, a homily by the pastor and another by his wife.

The morning ended in inspirational praying and singing. People knew what to expect, since this is a regular event occurring three or four times per year. About 400 people attended that day. The special "event-celebration" with Rick Warren as guest speaker (author of *The Purpose-Driven Life*) was similarly not what outsiders would expect. It was not a lecture by a guest speaker but a two-hour service of singing and preaching starting at 7:00 p.m. for a packed audience that may already have spent three hours in church in the morning. The "Concert of Praise for an Audience of One" is similarly not a concert to listen to, but a musical of prayer and praise. "You will experience the presence of the Lord," said the pastor in church to advertise it. This concert of singing and praise was most powerful: when invited to do so at the end, about fifty to sixty people came forward to be prayed over, about three times the number on an average Sunday service. There are four to six such concerts per year.

2. *Men's fellowship and prayer group.* The Wednesday and Friday 6:00 a.m. prayer meetings attract mainly men on their way to work. The Wednesday 10 a.m. prayer group attracts more women by a ratio as high as three to one. The men's fellowship and prayer group, which meets on Monday evenings twice a month, is attended by about twenty to thirty men, the majority of whom are regulars, the others being visitors or irregular attenders.

Prayer meetings usually follow the same patterns. The men's fellowship begins with praise and worship. The singing is led by two guitar players. The lyrics of the songs are projected on a screen, so everyone can participate. As the songs are known to most participants, everybody sings, often raising hands and clapping rhythmically with the beat of the music. This singing lasts about twenty minutes; it is followed by a few announcements and the introduction of the main speaker of the evening, either a regular member of the group or an invited guest (usually a layperson, seldom a pastor). Before his talk, the speaker is prayed over, since he is to speak "not by might, nor by power, but by my Spirit." At the beginning and end of his speech, he will start and end in prayer.

Although there is no prescribed type of presentation, most are in the form of testimonies (e.g., regarding one's conversion, family conflict and resolution, missionary work, preparation for missionary work, or one's understanding of biblical themes). All tend to be Bible-centered, quoting biblical texts to show the harmony between faith and practice in the speaker's life. All are well prepared, usually in writing. Here are two examples that stand out as most significant.

One speaker spoke eloquently about trust in God throughout the Bible and his personal life. He spoke for an hour, uninterrupted. It was a good example of the biblical literacy that is common among evangelicals. It was not biblical scholarship. After consulting a concordance, a dictionary of biblical theology, and a few commentaries, a biblical scholar could speak at length about nearly any topic, summarizing the material read and making comments about published comments. The Bayville church does not foster biblical scholarship but personal knowledge of the biblical text. Nearly every page of this speaker's Bible has underlined passages. In a personal interview, I learned that this particular speaker had reads the Bible from cover to cover in about fourteen months; he may have read it a dozen times or more. He spent about two hours in the morning in prayer and Bible reading. He grew up a Catholic, attending a Catholic high school and a Catholic college. So, for him, Bible literacy was a learned process achieved over the years. He has no theological background and currently holds no formal leadership position, but is very much listened to. He exemplifies what common laypeople can achieve: both biblical knowledge and personal experience of trust in God.

Another typical presentation is a conversion story, a story themed around God's grace. Joe came to the United States when he was seventeen or eighteen and at once espoused the American dream of moving up the social ladder. After nine years of marriage, his wife asked for a divorce, citing his overinvolvement in moneymaking and underinvolvement in the family. Joe had to move out of the family home. While he continued his business ventures, a friend witnessed to him about the power of God to bring peace, upon which Joe came to accept Jesus as his Lord and Savior. So did his wife, some time later. They were reconciled, and Joe returned home. That is not the end of his story, as his two children turned to drugs. For many years, Joe prayed every day for their return. They finally have come back to God and are now actively involved in ministries. Joe has told his story a few times, and each time it generates comments about conversion, healing, and the power of prayer.

That night, one participant described how his adopted son had turned to drugs and was now serving a long prison sentence. He had always prayed for him. Recently he learned that while in prison, his prodigal son had returned to the Lord and was using his exceptional musical talents for ministry. Other common stories described the reconciliation of father and son after years of estrangement. The 2007 weekend retreat made the healing of the father-son relationship its main theme. As a result, many experienced dramatic improvements in their relationship with their fathers. Grace-themed stories always have a strong impact. They do not have to be totally accurate, because what they reveal is about religious hope: grace is stronger than failure.

The last part of prayer group meeting is intercessory prayer. This is often the most touching part, as individuals—visitors and regulars alike—come to share their sorrows and ask for comfort, guidance, and supernatural help. One young man broke into prolonged sobbing as he explained that his wife had left him, sued for divorce, and requested sole custody of their two children as an act of rejection and estrangement. What was needed was a miracle of reconciliation that counselors, lawyers, and judges could not deliver. Only the power of prayer could achieve such miracle. Within weeks, reconciliation came out of the blue, at which the young man was elated, but the same week, he lost his job and had no savings.

Pain, suffering, and sorrows come in many ways. A poignant example is that of a father whose son of fifteen was diagnosed with a rare kind of cancer. Out of fifteen cases worldwide per year, only two survived on average. In January 1991, the boy's father had come to the men's fellowship asking for prayer and had attended faithfully ever since. "I have been faithful to attend, because in my heart, God was faithful to me and my son, and he spared my son's life," he said in an interview. The son improved only slowly; in 1999 he got his first job, and a few years later, he got married. End of story? No. Most recently, this father's daughter of forty-seven was diagnosed with breast cancer. He was devastated. His trust was shattered. He needed prayer more than ever.

Requests of prayer for cancer or other life-threatening diseases are common, and so are the testimonies of "miracles," with medical records as testimonies. Some prayer requests are trivial, but they are not rebuffed: even trivial pain is pain, and needs soothing. Other requests ask for supernatural help, not personal comfort, as in the case of a team flying out to Kiev, the capital of Ukraine, to deliver goods galore to an orphanage and seek conversions, or the case of a visiting young pastor going to found a new church in Arizona where none exists with only one year's salary from his mother church. In all of these cases (and many more), the petitioner is prayed for aloud by one member of the group, and all join in inspirational prayer.

Speaking in tongues is muted in men's fellowship. Prophesies are rare. The same cannot be said about the Wednesday prayer group, attended mainly by women. There, emotionality is high, and the leaders tend to encourage it. There, singing is loud, even very loud, and singing and praying in tongues naturally follows. So do prophesies. Do such prophesies only emerge in an emotionally charged atmosphere? If so, why? Speaking in tongues had disappeared in Christianity for nearly twenty centuries when it re-emerged in Los Angeles at the Azusa Street Revival in 1906. It took place in a Methodist Episcopal church and spread years later into mainline charismatic Protestantism and Catholicism. Not much is known about the relationship between emotions and rationality in religious practice, as most theologians in mainline Christianity tend to value free will and rationality over and against emotionality. (Emotions will be discussed in more detail shortly.)

3. *Daily prayer.* In the absence of a survey, it is difficult to know the frequency and length of daily prayer. About 400 prayer partners have committed themselves to pray daily for missions; there are also prayer partners for other intentions. No particular time for prayer and Bible reading is suggested: "Obviously, you should start your day with God, but you can't really tell somebody about their prayer life; that's between them and God."

The problem of lack of time is easily solved; one has only to get up earlier, like 5:00 or 6:00 a.m., which is a common practice. How much time

Daily Scripture Reading

"I don't have a reading plan. I've probably read through the New Testament about fifteen to twenty times, and the Old Testament maybe seven or eight times. I try to read a little from the Old Testament, a little from the New Testament, until the Lord lays something on my heart. At the beginning, I used to read ten to fifteen chapters at a time, but more recently, sometimes I don't get past one before something jumps out at me. Many times, as you begin to meditate on what the Lord is speaking to you in the Scripture, other Scriptures will come to mind, and you'll be motivated to look those up. Then the Holy Spirit will have a whole teaching for you.

"It's very easy and enjoyable. It's the best time of the day, really. I get up between 5:30 and 6:00. It's really the best time of the day."
—Interview

should be devoted to prayer? According to an associate pastor, "Among evangelical Christians, there's frequently a standard of spending an hour in prayer. That comes from Scripture, when in the Garden of Gethsemane, Jesus found his disciples asleep and said 'Could you not spend one hour with me?' So that tends to be one of our goals." Quite a few people I interviewed (not just pastors) pray about an hour a day with variations according to job demands and personal circumstances. Time spent in prayer cannot easily be measured, since it often includes Bible reading. Can prayer time be measured at all? When I asked the pastor quoted above if he prays for one hour a day according to the evangelical norm, he replied, "I wouldn't even want to characterize it that way. Honestly, the more mature you get in the Lord, it's not about numbers and times; it's more about where you are with Christ, and what he's doing in your life. So, I will say, I try to make sure that I pray." He does not count Bible reading for the purpose of preparing for a ministry as personal prayer, he added.

How much time? According to another interviewee, "It's kind of praying without ceasing. There will be focused times in the evening, sure. But in morning, before I start work. How much time? It could be a lot … You could say fifteen minutes at work, a half hour in the car, a half hour before, at home." Praying without ceasing cannot be measured in hours. Several people mentioned praying in the car. "I have the Bible on tape. I listen to that in the car. I listen to Christian radio or Christian music. I don't particularly care for anything other than Christian music, because

I just like Christian music playing in my head all the time, and not the worldly stuff."

In summary, even without survey data, it is clear that prayer is of paramount importance, not only collectively, in numerous prayer groups and in all the ministries, but also individually, in people's lives. In this church, some people practice "prayer-walking" around neighborhoods, alone or in groups, with the hopes that today, as three thousand years ago, the walls of Jericho will fall because of the power of prayer. Praying without ceasing is both a goal and a reality, and prayer is power.

4. *Communitas*. In the social sciences, it is traditional to distinguish between community (*Gemeinschaft*) and society (*Gesellschaft*); the former is conceived as a family, and the latter as an organization. This neat dichotomy does not work well in practice. In common parlance, we call our neighborhood a community, although we may know only a few people. We also call our hometown a community, although a suburb of 5,000 to 10,000 can hardly be seen as a family. I would define a community by the sense of belonging that we feel about it. We feel we belong to our neighborhood, and that our neighborhood belongs to us. We feel the same about our hometown, with its shops, restaurants, and movie theater. And we feel the same way about our church because of our sense of belonging.

A church community is hardly a family, since most of its people do not know one another. Most churches are communities of faith only ideally, but not much in reality. Most local churches are communities of a wider religious culture (e.g., Catholicism, Lutheranism, or Orthodox Judaism). Many churches are ethnic religious communities (e.g., the Irish Catholic or Scandinavian Lutheran cultures). Most church communities are mainly secular, not religious: when two members of a congregation meet in the street, they interact in secular terms, and when they greet one another inside the church, their greetings may still be totally secular. Can a church ever be a real community of faith?

There is often a sense of a religious community when people in a church pray together holding hands, or when they pray specifically for their neighbors right and left, or when they exchange the kiss of peace. At that time, the sense of community may be essentially religious, without reference to ethnicity, culture, race, age, or clerical status. This kind of community is different: it invokes not just the feeling of belonging to a group, but of being part of something of a higher order. It generates the sense of being part of a *spiritual* community based on faith, not secular culture. It is the sense, in the Christian case, of being part of the common discipleship of Jesus Christ. To indicate the distinctiveness of this type of community, Turner gave it a new name, that of *communitas*.

Turner has analyzed *communitas* in reference to liminality. To the extent that, in a rite of passage, individuals are in a threshold situation (liminality) in the "betwixt and between"[121] state, between the old status and the new one, they create among themselves a new type of community, a *communitas*, no longer based on status, power, race, or ethnicity, but on their common bond as humans in transition. This is a utopian type of society that breaks away from social classes, with their inequalities of status and wealth. This antistructural type of society can only be temporary, yet it lurks underneath all social structures as a dream, a utopia, and an ultimate goal.[122] Christians similarly are in a state of liminality when they come to church with the attitude of being betwixt and between two worlds, the temporal and the eternal. "If anyone is in Christ, he is a new creation; the old has gone, the new has come!" (2 Corinthians 5:17). Christians are in the liminal state when they follow this advice: "Put off your old self, which is being corrupted by its deceitful desires, and put on the new self, created to be like God in true righteousness and holiness" (Ephesians 4:22–24). For Turner, liminality and *communitas* are coextensive; *communitas* grows with liminality. As people put on the new self, they create a new community based not on "structure" (status and power), but "antistructure" (universality and equality of all in God).

In most churches, the sense of *communitas* is a fleeting one, lasting only a few minutes if it is present at all. However, if liminality is repeatedly reinforced through feedback intensification, it may grow to become a nearly permanent state. I have indicated above how at Sunday services at Bayville, various phases of entrainment lead to ever higher levels of emotionality. At each of these apogees, people get a sense of spiritual community when glancing casually at their neighbors. The Sunday morning *communitas*, however, will fade away if not reactivated throughout the week. I have also shown that at the various prayer meetings, an instant sense of spiritual community often occurs when people share their needs, along with those of family members and friends, and tell stories about their lived faith.

Rather than repeating my analysis of liminality and feedback intensification in the various ministries, I want to give a more quantitative account of the involvement of church members under the assumption that the more involved they are, the more likely their community is to be spiritual rather than mainly social.

According to the pastor of missions, "We are a ministry-based church, so that our sense of community comes from the various ministries. In my ministry of missions, I meet with my team leaders, the coordinators for each team, at least five times a month. Then they meet with their groups once a month. And then those little groups also meet for prayer, telephone calls, and contact with each other." There is a clear awareness, here, that Sunday services bringing together hundreds of members are not sufficient in creating a strong sense of community. There are 70 to 90 ministries. If each of these, let us say 80 in total, has 10 members, then about 800 people are involved—a third of the congregation. But if the 80 ministries have 20 members each, that would be two-thirds of the congregation. The latter is probably more correct, as the choir counts 100 members, prayer partners 400, the hospitality ministry 80 ushers, and so on.

Financial contributions are another form of personal involvement. How many people tithe? According to a pastor, about 80 percent of the members "are good tithers." This is extremely high in comparison to a national average of 42.7 percent for evangelical church attenders (N=8,190), and 14.5 percent for Catholic Church attenders (N=6,525).[123]

Religious knowledge is another indicator of religious involvement. How many people can name the first five books of the New Testament? "I'd say 75 percent. I don't think I'm exaggerating," was the answer of a pastor. Such a high number results from the practice of daily Bible reading and also from the attendance at Bible study classes. Reading the Bible from cover to cover is not uncommon; some of the senior members have read it ten or twenty times or more.

As for classes, there are about fifteen to choose from, each of an hour and half, lasting thirteen weeks. There are two cycles of classes of thirteen weeks per year. If each class has 20 students, that makes 600 per year. We cannot add 1,600 people in ministries to the 600 in classes, because some people participate in several ministries and also take classes. Yet the impression of *communitas* is evident as one chats with core members, even in the absence of compelling statistics.

The following data should corroborate this impression. The couples' class is usually attended by 50 to 60 people. This is not a formal class, since students begin class with bagels and coffee, sitting around tables in the cafeteria. The class on prayer draws a crowd of the same size, and so does the worship choir and orchestra class. Two membership classes had a combined student body of 110–120 in 2007, according to the pastor in charge. Special events are equally well attended. The Christmas and Easter plays draw several thousand people, some of whom come back year after year. The men and women's breakfast draws about 400 people several times a year. The church is nearly full at the spiritual concerts several times a year on a Friday night, with maybe 600 people. The special yearly week of prayer has three special prayer services during the week, and as many workshops on prayer, all well attended. There is a "full house" during the yearly missions convention, when about 30 missionaries come back from the fields to give testimonies about their work. About 100 men attend the men's retreat each year, and as many women. Special weekend retreats (e.g., "Ancient Paths") are often sold out, having a limit of 50 participants. Each of these is usually intense: the Ancient Paths retreat lasts four hours on both Thursday and Friday, and ten hours on Saturday. With such intense rhythmic entrainment, a strong sense of *communitas* is to be expected.

5. *Emotionalism.* One often hears that evangelical churches are too emotional. To answer that criticism, I will look at emotions, first in a

sociological perspective, next within the context of spirituality, and finally in the light of social movements.

Sociologically speaking, it is a truism that emotions are socially conditioned. People in the south are more expressive than those in the north, lower classes more than upper classes, the uneducated more than the well educated, the fans of rock music more than the lovers of Bach and Mozart, and, more generally, those brought up in the celebrity culture that emphasizes expressiveness, technological prowess, and loud music more than those educated in the humanities, reflexivity, inwardness, and silence. Since the expression of emotions is socially conditioned, any criticism of emotionalism is likely to be ethnocentric. Yet the criticism remains; it is valid in reference to superficial emotionalism defined below. Undeniably, the strong expression of emotions of Bayville does not suit everyone. It is, however, more attuned to the generation of rock-music lovers than to that of classical-music aficionados.

From a social-psychological perspective, we learn that emotions are the powerhouse of our psyches. Memory, intelligence, and willpower are heightened by strong emotions. We all remember where we were, and with whom, on the day of 9/11 (or, for the ancients, the day of Kennedy's assassination). A difficult topic is made easy by an enthusiastic teacher, a painful decision smoother by friendly encouragement, and the sorrow of death softened by compassion. Laughter can be used as therapy. Gentle dolphins can soothe, under supervision, the emotional problems of children. The other side of the coin is that negative emotions can lead to destruction, murder, and war. If we had no emotions, we would have little drive to get out of bed in the morning.

Emotions are also central in spirituality, because religious memory, intelligence, and willpower are heightened by emotions. Of special interest is the gift of tears. Although not listed among spiritual gifts by Paul (in 2 Corinthians 12), this gift has been known since antiquity. The early desert fathers had the highest regard for the gift of tears. Among Eastern Christians, this gift was highly praised for centuries. It was called "the second baptism" because the water of tears was thought to wash away current sins, as baptism washed away past sins.[124] In the Middle Ages, tears came to be seen as symbols and means of union with God. Emotions came to be part of devotional life.[125] There are the tears of contrition for sins, but also the tears of spiritual joy. The gift of tears is to be sought after, like all spiritual gifts, not for personal benefit but for the edification of the body of Christ (1 Corinthians 14:12). Spiritual tears flow without strain or effort, with only gentle sobbing; they are consolation for the soul, a refreshing well within the heart, peace deep within.

At times of conversion, however, tears may be loud and full of sorrow. In the Catholic tradition, the gift of tears has been more common than the gift of tongues. It can be found in the lives of many saints. At the Bayside church, tears are common for a few, intermittent for a few more, and occasional for many. Tears put us in contact with the depth of our souls, whether at a wedding or a funeral, whether we are alone or in a crowd, as at the passing of Princess Diana, Mother Teresa, or Pope John Paul II. [126] Tears are common at all important times of life. Similarly in spirituality, tears are often associated with important moments in people's growth and development.

The effect of emotions is noticeable at the end of a concert, play, movie, lecture, or church service: do people leave at once, or do they hang on, as if spellbound? What do they talk about as soon as they walk out through the doors? At Bayside, after Sunday worship or a prayer meeting, people often remain in their seats for a while and exit only slowly, engaging in small conversation. As they exit through the doors, the conversation goes on, usually about spiritual matters. The religious emotions linger on, maybe for one or several hours. If people come back to another service or prayer group or engage in prolonged daily prayer, their spiritual emotions will remain high most of the time.

Emotions produce emotional energy. Emotions and emotional energy can be channeled outward, as in speaking and singing, or inward, in reflection and meditation. Extroverted personalities are more likely to follow the first, and introverted people the second. The outward expression of emotions is more likely to use hyperbole and may lead to *superficial* emotionalism—that is, exaggerated emotions in reference to the substance at hand. The inward expression of emotions may use litotes and ultimately may lead to silence. Apart from the two undesirable extremes, superficial emotionalism and empty silence, emotions lead to action and, if properly channeled, to a social movement.

Missions and Evangelism

In the narthex, or vestibule, of Bayville's sanctuary is a map of the world, four by eight feet wide, with pictures of about 60 missionaries and the indication of their place of work in the world. Also in the narthex, looking toward the outside, is an inscription saying, "You are now entering your mission field" (see picture). Missionary work begins here, in the Bayville neighborhood, and extends to the whole world. Once a month, the Sunday service is dedicated to the missions. That day the pastor of missions gives the sermon, which is often followed by greetings from a returning missionary or the sending away of a missionary. In January 2008, a couple was sent to the Ishilhayn or Souss Berbers, estimated to be three to five million strong, living in the mountains of Morocco. The Berbers are Sunni Muslims, and no church has ever been established there. The couple left with about 100 prayer partners committed to pray for their work daily. Missionaries who go to the "unreached peoples" (where no church has yet been established) attract the greatest number of prayer partners. In February 2008, about forty high school and college students left for Georgia for a week of missionary work and help with the Hurricane Katrina disaster. The assignment of such groups is to entertain children and adults in schools, churches, nursing homes, hospitals, or prisons. They would perform short sketches on biblical themes, sing spiritual songs, recite poetry, and play music in a small band. Some have mastered the art of puppetry; puppet shows are popular among children and adults alike, as they can convey biblical messages easily and pleasantly.

Every year there are two missions conventions: one in the spring and one in the fall (see the whole program on page 73). Church members are usually invited to host the missionaries in their homes. Each convention lasts about four or five days. On the first evening of the April 2008 convention, a Saturday, 28 missionary teams spoke about their work at a sold-out banquet of more than 400 people. These husband-wife teams represented 50 to 60 missionaries at the convention. Nearly all of them are nonordained, which means that they are free from any clerical supervision. On Sunday,

2008 MISSIONS CONVENTION

Missions Convention Activities for Children

Sunday, April 13
"Be A Missionary" at Kidz for Christ (Gym), 8:30 a.m. & 12:15 p.m. Missions Candidate School For Kids (ages 5 to grade 4)
"The Trip Around The World" (Auditorium), 6:00 p.m., Join us on our imaginary airplane to 4 different countries (ages 4 to grade 4). Don't forget your passport!

Wednesday, April 16
"The Missions Experience" (Gym), 7:30 p.m., Join us as we play games that kids play around the globe (ages 5 to grade 6)

there was a guest speaker at the main service, after which missionaries spoke for an hour in six Sunday classes On Monday evening, a missions film was shown in the sanctuary. On Tuesday there were four missions workshops. On the last day, activities were scheduled from 10:00 a.m. to 9:00 p.m.: prayer meetings with missionaries in the morning, missionary-to-missionary interaction at lunch, and a guest speaker in the evening. During that week, missionaries and their prayer partners organized display tables in the narthex, with volunteers giving explanations and handing out pamphlets. The utmost importance of missions is suggested by the missions activities of children, which took up one-third of the printed program (see picture above); three different activities at the 2008 Missions Convention involved children and adolescents.

Evangelism is divided into three categories: career missionary work in the United States and abroad; short-term (two- to three-week) missionary ventures, either foreign or national; and local evangelization in the neighborhoods and adjacent towns. According to the pastor of missions, by the end of 2007, close to 80 missionaries were supported by the Bayville church. Of these, only 5 were sent out by the church itself; they were selected, trained, and are financed (including health insurance and retirement) by the church. All others were simply supported financially through a monthly stipend. Any missionary or evangelization organization can petition the missions board for financial support. The world map in the narthex indicates the missions that are supported throughout the world. Not shown are local efforts, such as the following: the Lightinghouse Mission, which helps the needy seven days a week, materially and spiritually; Teen Challenge, which helps addicted teenagers recover; Mission to the Americas, which works among American Muslims; Hope for the Future Ministries, a "church without walls" for the disenfranchised of society; Shaarei Hashamayim, a messianic Jewish synagogue; and Abba, a ministry for black men. Each of these organizations (and a few others) had a display table in the narthex during the missions convention. The participants in these missions all have prayer partners in the church. They come to ask for prayers, not money. Each missionary is supposed to have at least six prayer partners, and most of them do.

The second type of missionary work is that of short-term missions trips, like the student trip to Georgia mentioned above, sent out to evangelize, build a small church, or repair a church or school. This type of work may seem like Peace Corps work, but it is not. Here are some of the requirements:

1. Adults must use their vacation time or get a leave from work without pay.
2. All must pay their own expenses, whether to Georgia or South America (thus the seventh- and eighth-graders who plan to work for six days in a nearby metropolitan area in July 2008 must raise $150, and the ninth- to twelfth-graders planning a trip to Brazil must raise $1,500).
3. All must attend six missions classes.
4. All must attend three Thursday night prayer meetings.
5. All must complete two service projects locally to learn teamwork.

6. All must read two missionary biographies.
7. All must be interviewed and be accepted by the missions committee.
8. All must begin "journaling" from the day of the application.

Moreover, according to the missions pastor, "If they go to Africa to build a church or build outhouses or a school or paint, each participant also donates $100 for that work. So if there are 22 students going, that's $2,200." How many Peace Corps volunteers would accept all of these requirements? Here volunteers must be driven by evangelistic zeal, not the desire of adventure.

In 2007 there were five church-sponsored short-term missions and about fifteen individual trips. The church sponsored small group trips (three to fifteen participants) to Belize, to Guyana, to Cameroon, to Tanzania, and to Brazil. Not included is the group of about twenty students helping after Hurricane Katrina, because that trip was sponsored by the Christian school of the church, not the missions board. Individual trips are open to everyone: any prayer partner may visit his or her missionaries for help, support, or comfort. About fifteen such trips occurred that year. For instance, according to the pastor of missions, "On a missions day, I said, 'You need to think about spending your vacation encouraging a missionary, like going there and working and blessing them.' Then a man and his wife and his daughter who were sitting there just decided to go to an orphanage in Mexico." Other trips were initiated by individuals in various ministries.

Local evangelization is alive and well. "If you don't evangelize, you fossilize," could be the church's motto. Most people need some training for sharing faith in public. There is, for instance, an introduction on a Saturday from 9:00 a.m. to 3:00 p.m., which hopefully will lead the participants to take the thirteen-week course on evangelization. "For ten weeks of these thirteen," said the director of evangelization, "we'll go out in teams of three. We'll go to malls or to 7-Eleven, or we'll visit people that visit the church." Paying a visit to people who expressed an interest in the church is the easiest form of evangelization. The team does about fifteen such visits per month and double that number in the summer. Each team of three has two trainees who have little to do or say. Their most important job is prayer; moreover, each trainee must have two prayer partners. "Prayer is foundational to all that we do, because when we pray, we're seeking God's will—God's direction in what we're doing. So before we meet on Wednesday to go out to share our faith, we have already prayed with two prayer partners."

A volunteer may begin as a prayer partner and then become a captain of prayer partners or an evangelist; later, that same volunteer might go on a short-term mission. One may also become involved in more than one ministry, and at retirement, one may contemplate doing missionary work full time, I was told in a few interviews. "This church has a real missions mission," said a pastor. When I expressed the opinion that evangelization was the greatest factor of growth of the Bayville church, the pastor of missions replied, "You have caught a very important truth. There's an old statement that says, 'The light that shines farthest, shines brightest close by.'"

Conclusion: From *Communitas* to Social Movement

Liminality, feedback intensification, and *communitas* are dynamic processes leading to ever greater emotional energy. At Bayville, most people come to church in a state of liminality, with the expectation that something important will happen. Most services and meetings are intense, frequent, and enduring. I expected the Saturday introduction to evangelization to last a couple of hours, at most; it lasted six, without a lunch break (pizza was brought in). The Thursday and Friday "Ancient Paths" seminar was scheduled to end at 10:00 p.m., but participants were urged to stay longer; I decided not to, but actually I did for half an hour. Yet time passes quickly: psychological time becomes shorter than chronological time, as I discovered while checking my watch for observation purposes.

Emotionality becomes high: at the end of services and meetings, people linger on, as if not wanting to leave. On February 24, 2008, the North Korean audience gave a five-minute standing ovation to the New York Philharmonic at the end of its concert, as if not wanting to leave. The same happens here, in a more subdued fashion.

Emotionality creates a community of high intensity, while theology creates a community of low intensity, if any. Faith usually unites; creeds often divide (e.g., Catholics from Protestants, and Western Christians from Eastern Christians). Emotional energy can be directed outward, into singing, praying aloud, prayer walking, evangelizing in homes or public places—this would be the tendency of extroverted personalities. It may also be directed inward, into silence, reflection, planning, and strategizing—a tendency cultivated by education and introversion. The first will lead to evangelism, the desire to share one's faith; the second to evangelization, or structured missionary work. Both are present at Bayville.

The intimate connection between *communitas*, evangelism, and evangelization is clearly visible in the following excerpt from an interview:

> In prayer we can actually travel in the spirit to the fields where our missionaries are, stand with them shoulder to shoulder, and really share in their struggles and their victories. So there is no distance. It enables brothers and sisters here to actually be part of their work. Our missionaries count on us very much: they feel our love and support from afar. They can communicate with us whatever is happening. They will be encouraged that there will be people responding in prayer to them.
> ["That's the communion of saints?" I asked.] That's right. There are no boundaries. Scripture says that we're one body, but each member is doing its part. We're not all the head. We're not all the hands. We're all different parts of one body working together.

Communitas is the sense of one spiritual body working together. A church can be seen as a family in which all are treated as relatives, as brothers and sisters. It can also be seen as a team of people working together on a common task. It can also be seen as an army, legions marching forward. The official motto of Bayville is "We are a family, a team, an army." The military image of the church as army did not impress me favorably at first, yet it seems accurate in reference to Bayville, where *communitas* leads to mass participation and resource mobilization. For every missionary, there are to be six prayer partners, and some have up to a hundred. What an army!

One last word about voice, to return to the beginning of this chapter: Bayville is not an army of anonymous legionnaires. As stated in the interview quoted above, "We're one body, but each member is doing its part. We're not all the head. We're not all the hands." Each member has found his or her own function and voice: "In Christ, [we are] a new creation; the old has gone, the new has come!" (2 Corinthians 5:17). Paradoxically, to the extent that each individual has found his or her own voice, everyone can hear the voice of others in his own language.

CHAPTER 5

~

THE COMMUNITY OF COMMUNITIES: ST. MARY

There are striking differences between the Bayville Community Church and St. Mary, Star of Hope (henceforth St. Mary's), which is a Catholic parish. Unless we identify the differences, a comparison between the two may prove misleading. Bayville is an independent denomination of about 2,700 people that started as a house church and can be considered today as an extended house church. It is not a "sect" in the sociological sense: it did not break away from a mother church over theological or pastoral differences. It is a "small church," or "*ecclesiola*," a term coined by Joachim Wach (1898–1955).[127] St. Mary's, on the other hand, is part of an organization that has local branches and embassies in most countries of the world; in other words, it is part of a "church" in the sociological sense. As an introduction to the study of St. Mary's, I will first present a sociology of church and *ecclesiola* and an overview of the development of post-Vatican II small Christian communities. It is only after this theoretical introduction that we will turn to the parish life at St. Mary's.

1. Sociology of Church and *Ecclesiola*

There is a great deal of sociological reflection on the differences between "churches" and "sects" (when "church" and "sect" are printed in quotation marks, they are used in the sociological sense), but little on the differences between "churches" and *ecclesiolas*. Although "church" has many dimensions, I will restrict myself to one: a "church" fosters *institutional* religion, while an *ecclesiola* favors *individual* religiosity. Joachim Wach, who coined the term *ecclesiola*, gives as examples the German pietistic brotherhoods and the Catholic religious orders,[128] both of which emphasize conversion and personal piety. These two characteristics, institutional and personal religiosity, are not mutually exclusive: pre-Vatican II Catholicism strongly encouraged intense personal devotions within the institutional framework of the universal church.

Historically, Christianity started as a personal religion in house churches that became progressively institutionalized. As a reaction against institutionalization, reform movements appeared as early as the fourth century, in the form of eremitism in Egypt, and later as monachism throughout the West. The first chain of stable independent monasteries (*ecclesiolas*) was that of the Benedictine order in the sixth century. A practical definition of an *ecclesiola* is found in the opening paragraph of St. Benedict's rule: it consists of "those who live in a monastery waging their [spiritual] war under a rule and an abbot."[129] *Ecclesiolas* are independent elite religious communities.

From the sixth century on, the *ecclesiolas* of monasteries and religious orders consisted of *stable economically independent religious communities seeking spiritual growth in the light of a tradition (or rule) under the guidance of a leader (or abbot) who is free from external control*. The two main characteristics of this definition, economic and ecclesiastical independence and spiritual growth within a tradition, apply to all "small churches within a church" (the common definition of *ecclesiolas*)—that is, to all religious orders, congregations, third orders, fraternities, and confraternities of past and present. As *ecclesiolas* materially flourish over time, gaining wealth and power, they tend to decline. The numerous reformation movements before the Protestant Reformation started as *ecclesiolas*. However, Protestantism itself developed not as a chain of *ecclesiolas*, but as an ocean of "sects"—that is, breakaway churches seceding specifically from the Catholic Church. Reform within Protestantism also developed in the form of breakaway "sects." In evangelical Protestantism of today, however, reform often comes in the creation of nondenominational, independent *ecclesiolas* with the two main characteristics mentioned above: emphasis on personal religiosity and independence from outside control.

When Christianity became the religion of the Roman Empire under Constantine (more precisely, under Theodosius I, in 392), it changed its course forever. As long as it had been mainly a web of house churches, it had only had to consider the domestic affairs of the household; as a state religion, it now had to consider matters of the state. Primitive Christianity enjoyed great theological diversity, even conflicting differences, between local churches. While decentralized *ecclesiolas* may tolerate conflictive diversity, a centralized Empire could not. In 325, Constantine convened the Council of Nicaea to create a unified creed to be enforced in a unified Empire with a unified state religion. Henceforth affairs of the state (or of the civil society, its culture, and its institutions) became a major concern of the Catholic Church. Henceforth, Catholicism would define official creeds and rituals to be imposed on all its members. Let us look at the differences between "church" and *ecclesiola* in reference to these two points: the affairs of the state or civil society, and the uniformity of beliefs and practices. I will look at these differences not in the abstract, but in reference to the differences between Bayville and St. Mary's.

At Bayville, there is concern for neither the affairs of the state and the civil society, nor for the uniformity of beliefs and practices. What is this church's position on capitalism? Socialism? Social justice? Globalization? There is none. The implication, common throughout American evangelicalism, is that individual conversion to Jesus Christ will solve all social problems. How? The prevailing anti-intellectualism may even prevent such a question. And what are the uniform beliefs and practices of the Bayville community? A sociologist would be needed to survey them, and a theologian to systematize them. Their beliefs and theology follow their practices (*lex orandi, lex credendi*), not the other way around. There is no resident theologian at Bayville, and there is no office for the doctrine of the faith.

At St. Mary's we find some of the major characteristics of a "church" with, first of all, the prominence of an institutionalized priesthood set apart by celibacy; second, a concern for all members, not just for elite members, as in *ecclesiolas*; third, involvement in cultural and social affairs of the town and the nation; and fourth, a concern for the orthodoxy of beliefs and practices. The consequence of these four factors is often the creation of cultural Christians. Let me explain briefly these five points.

In the world church of Catholicism, the priesthood is institutionalized in a great variety of ways—as deacons, priests, bishops, the Curia, and the papacy—and each rank has its assigned power, status, and role. The balance of these forces has always been unstable. Nineteenth-century Europe was wrecked by the opposing forces of clericalism and anticlericalism. Since Vatican II and the creation of episcopal conferences, bishops have increased their presence on the local and national scenes, while the Roman Curia has for a long time enjoyed supremacy over local bishops, and the papacy always exercised supreme power over all. Add to this the conflictive agendas of conservatives and liberals. In a local parish like St. Mary's, the various forces of liberalism versus conservatism, clericalism versus anticlericalism, episcopalism, curialism, and papalism are likely to be at work, even if in subdued form. Moreover, because of the strongly hierarchical nature of Catholic Church, appointments of bishops and pastors (St. Mary's is expecting a new pastor in 2009) are always likely to be "political"—that is, in response to the "politics" at work at the local level.

When Christianity became a mass religion, the crowds were given requirements appropriate to their low level, like "Don't extort money, don't accuse people falsely, be content with your pay" (Luke 3:14). In Catholic terms, the basic requirements are baptism, confirmation, marriage, Sunday Mass attendance, and confession once a year. A "church" must have low requirements if it wants to be attractive to all, but these institutional requirements may be so low as to become trivial. Theologically, a "church" teaches salvation through good works (implicitly, of course; never explicitly)—that is, salvation through obedience and sacramental compliance (ritualism). When this is the case on a wide scale, the very notions of sacrament, salvation, and faith become opaque in the common consciousness. Any parish, including St. Mary's, has to struggle with keeping standards low enough for the masses without becoming trivial.

Catholicism has always been involved in the social, cultural, and political affairs of the secular society. Roman Catholicism developed its own art, architecture, and discourse from within its cultural environment. Great are the achievements of Christian artists and intellectuals over the centuries. Yet cultural involvement is always a double-edged sword, as illustrated by the artistic achievements of the Re-

> **What Does It Mean to Be Catholic?**
> "Regarding one of my homilies, I was ordered by the chancery to read the *Catholic Catechism* on a certain aspect of faith. Is that what it means to be Catholic, to adhere to everything that is said in the *Roman Catechism*?"
> —A parish pastor

naissance popes. Catholicism in Poland became a source of national pride at the time of Solidarity, the trade union that changed the world in the 1980s, only to become an embarrassment one generation later, when archives revealed some of the Catholic hierarchy's involvement as informants to the Communist regime. Cultural involvement in the United States led to the creation of numerous Catholic schools, hospitals, universities, and social services, but today we may ask, "How religious are these so-called Catholic institutions?" This is a question St. Mary's parish cannot ignore, since it operates a Catholic school as well as numerous social services.

Theologians seek to understand faith in the context of the secular culture. Theology can be proactive as well as reactive; it can become normative as well as legitimizing; it can define what people *should* believe, as well as justify rationally what they actually believe. During the first millennium, to a great extent the *lex credendi* (what people should believe) followed what they practiced (the *lex orandi*), as in the dogmatic definitions of the first great church councils, but in an increasingly hierarchical church, this tendency has been reversed. Over the last century, the papacy has increasingly assumed the role of Grand Theologian of the church. Both the Catholic sexual morality and the so-called social doctrine of the Church are to a great extent papal creations; they are mainly utopian and are practically ignored by the faithful, which jeopardizes the church's moral authority. To put it another way, official Catholic beliefs (*lex credendi*) often do not inspire the spiritual lives of Catholics (their *lex orandi*). At the local level, official teaching often looks like an albatross, a bird with wings too big to walk with; it flies high in the air but is awkward on the ground of everyday life. At the parish level, abstract or rigid definitions of faith, morals, and rubrics, and discourses about world peace or "faithful discipleship" (the bishops' recommendations for the 2008 presidential election) are often of little help for people's everyday *lex orandi*.

Finally, the standardization of religious practices in mass religion and the institutionalization of these standards in a cultural environment produce *cultural Christians*, which will lead to spiritual decline. A cultural Christian is one who does what is expected of him or her, one whose identity is fused with his or her role expectations. Children in Christian homes first become cultural Christians by following their parents' example; hopefully they will become adult Christians through personal growth later in life. Pre-Vatican II produced its well-known vintage of cultural Christians, those who could say "I have done my duties" (to God), "my life is in order,"

> **Ritualism ...**
> ... is salvation by works rather than grace
> ... is low-intensity interaction with God
> ... is priestly monologue in front of the assembly
> ... is assembly without *communitas*, without liminality
> ... is the choir singing instead of the people
> ... is salvation by conformity to the letter of the law: "What do I have to do to enter the Kingdom of God?" "Observe the teachings of the church, and you'll have it made."

"I have done all my sacraments," or in Latin American parlance, "I'm Catholic but not fanatical" (I do not practice, like everybody else). Cultural Christians exist at all levels and in all denominations, including among evangelical Protestants, liberal as well as conservative Catholics, and priests as well as bishops. I have defined spirituality in Chapter 2 as self-transcendence, as moving from a low level of need satisfaction in Maslow's pyramid to a higher level of actualization. Cultural religion is the opposite of self-actualization: it is the refusal to grow on the conviction that one has achieved all that is to be achieved because one is a "regular" church attender, or a "regular" priest, or a "regular" bishop. Then spiritual growth has stopped, and a comfortable mediocrity is likely to set in. Most parishes struggle with regular attenders who have accomplished all the church requirements and see no further need for personal growth.

Let me now briefly summarize the advantages and disadvantages of "churches" and *ecclesiolas.*

1. "Churches" offer salvation to all, while *ecclesiolas* cater to religious elites. The former need to have standards low enough to appeal to the masses, while the latter may reject those who do not accept their rules. The religion of the former is likely to be highly institutionalized in rote prayers, formal rituals, and submission to authority figures, while the religiosity of the latter aims at conversion through personal prayer and devotions, often as islands of piety.

2. "Churches" are involved in their environment, the popular and elite cultures, the visual arts, music, literature, the humanities, politics, social justice, and so forth. As a consequence, they appeal to cultural elites and often attract high-caliber intellectuals. But being involved in politics and holding substantial wealth, they often appear as corrupt. *Ecclesiolas*, on the other hand, may retreat in spiritual cenacles that, to outsiders, may appears as ghettos. Anti-intellectualism is prevalent at Bayville, where all teachings are centered exclusively on the Bible, with little knowledge of theology, exegesis, and spirituality beyond what was common at the apostolic age, and scant acknowledgment of the contributions of the social sciences to family life and social life in general. *Ecclesiolas* tend to retreat from the world and, as a consequence, often have little influence on worldly affairs.

3. "Churches" aim at the common good from the perspective of the institution, *ecclesiolas* from the perspective of the individuals they serve. Appointments in "churches" always have a "political" dimension; they are made by those at the top, in response to the expectations of religious, social, and political local leaders. Appointments tend to be conservative, favoring a kind of happy mediocrity that will avoid abysmal failure as well as institutionally disturbing success, and as a consequence, "churches" are likely to prevail for centuries. *Ecclesiolas* have a life cycle of their own; they may shine like a new star and spread like fire, but later fade away and die out. Their appointed leaders can be daring, in success as well as in failure. No outside control exists to prevent *ecclesiolas* from growing exponentially; no outside agency saves them from failure and extinction. According to Wittberg, most religious orders and congregations have a life span of about

two or three centuries.[130] They arise out of nowhere and later fade away and die.

What is the future of "churches" in the light of the above? Writing before WWI, Troeltsch argued that the future belongs to neither "churches" nor "sects" but to a third category, mystical communities,[131] or *ecclesiolas*. There is little doubt that *ecclesiolas* have mushroomed since then, especially in evangelical Protestantism. Is Catholicism doomed as a "church?" As suggested above, one of the major achievements of Catholicism is that it has integrated *ecclesiolas* (religious orders and congregations) into its own structure and, as a result, has often prospered.[132] Does this apply to Catholic parishes?

2. Post-Vatican II Development of Catholic *Ecclesiolas*

The concept of *ecclesiola* created by J. Wach has received little attention in the sociology of religion, so why resurrect it? Mainly because it has been given a new boost in post-Vatican II theology in three interrelated areas: the family as a "domestic church," baptism as a process in RCIA, and the church as a community of communities.

Vatican II resurrected the old image already found in Tertullian that the family is a small church where people pray together and support one another. According to the Dogmatic Constitution on the Church, "the family is, so to speak, the domestic Church. In it parents should, by their word and example, be the first preachers of the faith to their children."[133] The domestic family is defined here as an intact nuclear family with

---

Pope John Paul II on Parish Renewal

"One way of renewing parishes might be to consider the parish as a *community of communities*. It seems timely therefore to form ecclesial communities and groups of a size that allow for true human relationships. In such a human context it will be easier to gather to hear the word of God, to reflect on the range of human problems in light of this word and gradually make responsible decisions inspired by the all embracing love of Christ."
—Quoted in "The Church," *America*, January 22, 1999

---

children still at home. How many such families are there? The divorce rate among Catholics is about the same as among non-Catholics. In a 2007 survey, only 7 percent of Catholics considered divorce not acceptable in any case. According to this same survey, only 15 percent of divorced Catholics sought an annulment. Considering that only 53 percent of adult Catholics are married, only 65 percent of the married Catholics have been married in the Catholic Church,[134] and probably only half of them have children at home, the notion of domestic church seems to apply only to a small minority of families.

In a sociological perspective, the family as a legal institution *of social roles* is increasingly obsolete at the theoretical level. Well before the emphasis on relationships propagated by the cultural revolution of the 1970s, Ernst Burgess had documented the historical change in his 1945 book *The Family, from Institution to Companionship*. Past marriages were based on social roles (e.g., of breadwinners and homemakers) and institutionalized in the legal contracts of marriage, with no possibility of divorce except through the admission of guilt. Today's marriages are based mainly on relationships, with few established social roles and the possibility of divorce by mutual consent. In Burgess's words, today's family is based on "companionship," "interpersonal relations," and "mutual affection."[135] On the theological side, reflection has brought forth the realization that active participation in the Christian family is based not on biology and the marriage contract, but on the universal priesthood of Christ; it is based on baptism rather than (or as much as) the sacrament of matrimony.[136]

Before Vatican II (and even today), baptism was a five- to ten-minute ritual performed on a passive infant in an empty church at the request of parents—a request that was seldom denied. As long as Catholics lived in enclaves reminiscent of Christendom, such a practice could perdure. Totally different is the conception of baptism in the Rite of Christian Initiation for Adults (RCIA) introduced in 1972.[137] In short, it is not a ten-minute ritual but a one-year *process*; it is not to be performed on single individuals in an empty church but on the catechumens as a community, before the whole parish assembly; finally, it is not automatically granted, but requires the progressive integration of the "candidates" into the church, around the bishop at the beginning and at the end of the journey. Details will be described below.

In the 1970s, the Medellin conference and liberation theology brought forth a new social consciousness, which led to the mushrooming of *comunidades de base* (base communities). In the United States, the 1970s was the time of the flower generation and their utopian communes. It was also the time of the charismatic renewal sweeping across the American churches. In contrast to the Catholic liturgy, based on rubrics and rote prayers, charismatic worship was spontaneous and expressive, often accompanied by praying and singing in tongues. Scripture readings and faith sharing became standard features, which often made Catholic and Protestant prayer groups indistinguishable. Moreover, the Holy Spirit being considered the main mover in the praying assembly, the role of the clergy in charismatic prayer groups became marginal, their contribution based on their spiritual gifts, not their clerical status. Being Christ-centered rather than church-centered, the charismatic movement led to increased Scripture reading, more active prayer life, and a greater sense of community. As the charismatic movement faded away, a new wave of small communities emerged in parishes in various parts of the United States, more particularly under the influence of RENEW, created in Newark in 1976. These small communities, often first initiated by parish priests, quickly become lay managed and lay animated. They are centered on Scripture, faith sharing, and community interaction. Small Christian communities are now found in most US dioceses.

Let me now summarize the contributions of postconciliar theologies for the understanding of *ecclesiolas*. Since Vatican II, the church is increasingly seen as a community of communities. Although such a philosophy does not hold true at the global level (the Catholic Church remains a hierarchical organization), parishes can truly be clusters of vibrant communities. These small communities are increasingly Christ- and Scripture-centered, with faith sharing a major means of mutual support. Thus the family can be a small Christian community (or "domestic church") when the family is defined by companionship and affection, as in the civil society, not by biology and the proper "canonical form" of the wedding ceremony. The first Christians were in domestic churches (*domus* in Latin refers to the household, not just the nuclear family), and their domestic churches involved their extended families and the families of their servants and slaves. Today domestic churches (the term is seldom used) can include not only the extended family but neighbors and friends as well. Conversion in and through the death and resurrection of Jesus Christ is central to both RCIA and Christian life; hence, RCIA as a conversion process undertaken in a small community has become a model for parish renewal. Finally, small communities come in a variety of types, as seen within and across our national borders. In democratic parishes seen as communities of communities, a great variety of smaller communities is likely to emerge, reflecting the variety of special gifts and personal characteristics of the members.

So far we have seen that the Catholic Church is both a "church," or top-down clerical organization, and a cluster of *ecclesiolas*, or bottom-up lay or religious renewal initiatives. Let us now see how this combination works at St. Mary's.

St. Mary's Community of Communities

St. Mary is said to have been founded as a response to the perceived threat of a growing evangelical church, which I will call the Jonesville church (not related to the Bayville church). The Jonesville church evolved out of a successful youth ministry that emphasized music, drama, and biblical teaching. By the early 1980s, it had its own church building with thousands of worshippers. Since then, the church attendance has doubled.[138] The Sunday services cater to new members, especially the unchurched, while the Wednesday meetings provide in-depth formation to committed members. The theology of the Jonesville church is not very different from that of Bayville, although they are unrelated denominationally.

> **Legend or History?**
> "Jonesville started because a group of disenfranchised Catholics decided to knock on doors to find out if there were other dissatisfied people. They built a faith community out of people who weren't getting what they needed to get out of Catholic Christianity or out of Christianity in general. Places like Jonesville have grown exponentially over the past ten years."
> —Interview

The majority of the attendees in both Jonesville and Bayville seem to be former Catholics; guesses or rumors for Jonesville vary from 60 to 80 percent. This situation prompted the local bishop to do something. Around 1982 he approached Father Tom (no real names are used) about starting a new parish that would be evangelical in the Catholic tradition, innovative in its liturgy and music, and centered on the laity in the spirit of Vatican II. This new church was supposed to offer an alternative to Catholics attracted to evangelicalism and also to those dissatisfied with traditional ritualism. It was not going to be a geographical parish, and there was no indication of its exact location, except in the vicinity of Jonesville. There was no money, no staff, no parish site, but there was warm episcopal support. The reaction was swift. From neighboring parishes, people flocked to Father Tom's home Masses. In October 1984, he was officially appointed to the new parish—still to be located—and two months later, the first Mass was celebrated in the cafeteria of a local public high school. Out of the blue, six months later, came the offer to purchase sixteen acres of farmland a few miles away from Jonesville (an offer negotiated on a napkin in a restaurant between a farmer and a representative of the parish-to-be). Later, over a thousand families pledged more than $5 million. The new church was completed in 1988 and paid off in three years.

Three factors explain such enthusiastic support.

1) *Intentional parish.*

"The new parish," as it was first called euphemistically, was supposed to be nonterritorial, intentional, and theologically inclusive (open to those usually excluded). This was a canonical innovation. According to an old-timer, "When we met Father Tom, he invited us to come to his church. We were going to another parish, but he said that parish boundaries didn't really matter anymore, and we should feel free to come to his. We came, and we liked it." Many Catholics are doing that, but they are not supposed to. If they do, they may get into trouble. According to another interviewee, "When my husband and I went to get married, a lot of churches wouldn't marry us, because we were not members of any parish. We had a really hard time." This couple then saw a bulletin article that said, "We are a church with no boundaries"; of course they joined it. What were people looking for at "the new parish," and what did they find? "I'd been in Catholic churches all over the world, and there really is a sameness about them," one member said. "This one was a little different. What's different, frankly, is the quality. Great music and good sermons and just a beautiful facility: a lot of that was a little unusual. Most parishes are more sedate. There was almost a feeling of an evangelical televangelist type of thing."

In the Catholic Church, to be "different" is a double-edged sword, because the parishes affected by the "quality drain" that takes away some of their best members are likely to complain. Catholicism is a sociological "church"; it is a hierarchical organization of territorial parishes where the notion of subsidiarity (a Catholic form of decentralization) is often more a concept than a reality. Intentional parishes can succeed only with strong episcopal support; without it, they may falter and wane. The "new parish" was to be an intentional parish with episcopal support.

2) *Creative lay participation.*

Quality participation, great music, and good sermons require creativity, found more often in *ecclesiolas* than in "churches." Vatican II created a theology appropriate for small communities. According to one member, "Vatican II expressed a concept which shocked and scared the Tridentine fundamentalists to their foundations: the priesthood of the laity, the return to the earliest traditions of the Church in which the local churches selected their priests and their bishops and in which women were spiritual leaders." This view goes beyond the official interpretation of Vatican II; if shared by the laity, however, it is likely to generate much creativity.

> **"Wow! They've Got Great Music."**
> "I'm 71. My liturgy experience has been mostly conservative, mainstream. My first experience with St. Mary's was 'Wow! They've got great music.' I picked up their bulletin, and it was twenty pages, easily at least fifteen pages more than what I was ever used to."
> —Interview

At the "new parish," a liturgy committee presided over liturgical creations. They often selected the readings of the Sunday Mass, trying to find texts more in harmony with the Gospel of a given Sunday than the assigned readings from Paul's letters.

At times they changed all the readings. They used dramatizations and visualization (e.g., illuminations and visual effects in the church, a Passion play during the holy week in lieu of the passion readings, or the office of *tenebrae* delivered in a dramatized way). They would decorate the church according to the theme of the day, and select or create their own music. In all of this, the laity essentially controlled the liturgy. They had the support of Father Tom, who gave them great latitude to be creative. (As time passed, however, official support discouraged such initiatives.)

One ministry that flourished under Father Tom was the ministry to the separated, divorced, and widowed, offered from an ecumenical perspective. It was to assist people from any denomination through their emotional crisis; it did not concentrate on Catholic doctrine and annulment seeking. One of its goals was to reach non-Catholics in an ecumenical spirit, as was actually the practice at Jonesville's Sunday services. At that time, it was the largest ministry of the church, with the encouragement of Father Tom. (Later, however, this ministry was geared to greater orthodoxy).

3) *Small Christian communities.*

Father Tom became aware of the importance of small communities in Latin America and felt they were the way of the future. He created a committee to investigate. This committee received material from a variety of sources, from both Catholic and non-Catholic churches. Some of its members went to experience faith communities and observe leadership in different Catholic churches, while others attended the seminar of a prominent propagator of small communities of the time. The final proposal was an original creation that borrowed ideas from existing communities, but also included innovations. When the first sign-up was announced, about seven hundred people in a parish of maybe two thousand families registered for what henceforth will be called small Christian communities (SCCs).

The process of creating small faith communities was typical of "the new parish," which, by then had become St. Mary's. It was not a top-down creation of the pastor, but a team work. Father Tom had initiated the project, but he later allowed the team, the communities, and ministry leaders to develop according to their talents. He empowered the people; he did not impose his views or reformulate made decisions in his own terms. According to an old-timer, "People were inspired by Father Tom and were induced to become a part of something more dynamic than the traditional parish and traditional Catholicism. He gave his parishioners the opportunity to do just about everything the laity should do as priesthood of the people." Given the opportunity, a great variety of small faith communities emerged over the years, thus making the parish a true community of communities.

When Father Tom retired, he was replaced by Father Frank, who built on the foundations laid by his predecessor. I visited St. Mary's in 2007 and 2008. It is today's church that I now want to describe.

At the Bayville Church Assembly, one is immediately struck by the emphasis on prayer and foreign mission. There is no such emphasis at St. Mary's. When I asked staff members about the main focus of the church (its ministries and spirituality, in other words), I was told that there was no central focus; for some it could be social justice; for others the liturgy and its readings; for others the Eucharist; for others the faith communities. Observation confirms this lack of a visible central focus. Yet in all the ministries, I found a unified, implicit theology—more specifically, a theology of the laity based on baptism and conversion. This implicit theology is found most clearly in the RCIA.

My analysis of St. Mary's will be divided into two parts, the sacraments on one hand and the Small Christian Communities on the other. I will show that at St. Mary's, all sacraments tend to follow the format of initiation/transformation of RCIA. Next I will analyze the various *ecclesiolas* and their spirituality.

A. Baptismal sacramentality: The sacraments as rites of transformation

At St. Mary's, all sacraments tend to be rites of initiation and transformation, rather than rites of passage. It was not so in the Catholic Church of the past. In *Les rites de passage*[139] published in 1909, Arnold van Gennep described what he saw, namely sacraments as rites of passage. The very moment when Catholic sacraments were supposed to take effect (the moment that marks the "passage") could be identified precisely. For example, one is baptized upon the words "I baptize you ...'; one is married upon "I declare you husband and wife"; and Christ is "really" present at *"Hoc est corpus meum ..."* ("This is my body ..."). Today the *ex opere operato* sacramentality inherited from the Council of Trent is on the wane. By following the evolution from rites of passage to rites of initiation, social scientists have come to see rituals as interaction—as interaction ritual *chains*, as described in the previous chapter. What is special about St. Mary's is that both the sacraments and the *ecclesiolas* are inspired by a baptismal spirituality of transformation.

The seven sacraments upheld by the Council of Trent do not form a unified system in which all sacraments are equally important. Luther and the Anglicans emphasized baptism and the Eucharist as major sacraments, a view that is often shared by Catholics today. Trent emphasized priestly ordination and the Eucharist, thus giving birth to a priestly spirituality of the Eucharist as sacrifice. The sacraments came to be objectified in space and time, under the control of the clergy. Baptism washed away the stain of Original Sin; matrimony made intercourse acceptable to Church and God; the extreme unction saved the souls from eternal damnation. Progressively, the trend became "the more sacraments, the better"—that is, frequent communion (daily); frequent confession (weekly); two Sunday Masses for the pious (a Low Mass and a High Mass); and according to the old *ordo*, three low Masses in a row by priests on Christmas Eve. Even today pious brochures may invite the faithful to "purchase" one or two "novenas" of Masses, as if nine Masses were better than eight, and two novenas better than one. In the Tridentine sacramentality, the priest is central, and the assembly absent or passive.

The tendency today is to see Christ as the primary sacrament, and baptism into his death and resurrection as the center of sacramental life. From this perspective, the Eucharist becomes a celebration rather than a sacrifice, with an emphasis on thanksgiving (the actual meaning of *eucharistein*) rather than on "the real presence" in the bread and wine; it is celebrated by the whole assembly, with the priest as presider rather than celebrant. This spirituality is to inspire *all* sacraments and *all* ministries. Let us now look at the sacramental practice at St. Mary's.

1. The Rite of Christian Initiation of Adults

Only about a dozen non-Catholics become members of St. Mary's church through RCIA every year (plus a few Catholics who receive confirmation), which represents an insignificant increase for a parish of 3,800 registered families (about 12,000 people). The symbolic nature of RCIA is highly significant, however, for the whole parish. The fonts for baptism by immersion at the Easter vigil are located at the geometric center of the sanctuary, which is shaped like an amphitheater; hence, visually, the baptismal fonts are as central as the altar itself. The presence of catechumens is felt throughout most of the year, from about September to May: every Sunday after the homily, they are ritually and publicly dismissed. During Lent, they go through three public "scrutinies," asking God, for themselves and the whole community, to "heal all that is weak, defective or sinful in their hearts."[140] At the Easter vigil, they come as penitents, barefoot in brown sackcloth, and don white tunics after the baptism. The Easter vigil lasts over three hours. Even after that, their training is not over; they will continue their intense transformation for another forty days until Pentecost. Clearly the whole parish is affected by the RCIA process, which is both an initiation and a transformation.

RCIA consists of four periods and three rites. The first period is one of inquiry, a time of free discussion to find out whether the inquirer is willing and ready to embark upon this serious journey. At the rite of acceptance, scheduled here in September, the candidates will have to answer several questions, standing with their sponsor in the aisle of the church at the beginning of a Sunday Mass: "Why do you want to be baptized [in a society where everyone can attend any church, no questions asked]?" "Why join this parish [rather than another one, where the requirements are easier]?" They are then presented with a copy of the Bible not by the priest, but by a member of the community, to emphasize their incorporation into the parish family of believers.

Having been accepted into the Order of Catechumens, the candidates begin their training in earnest. From September to May, there are weekly meetings of about two hours, beginning with the reading of the Gospel and moving to the presentation of a topic for about forty-five minutes (sacraments, doctrine, history of the church, communion of saints, and so forth), followed by sharing and discussion. At the Sunday Mass, they hear the Gospel again. After the homily, they are "sent off to break open the Word of God." They convene in a separate room, read again the Gospel of the day (for the third time that week!), and discuss it for the entire duration of the church service. Hence, RCIA is Christ- and Scripture-centered, rather than Church-centered. It is experiential and dialogical, rather than dogmatic and cerebral.

The rites of sending and election take place at the beginning of Lent. In front of the community, the sponsors testify publicly about the transformation they have seen in the candidates and their readiness to move to the next level. The community then *sends* them to the cathedral (a bus is waiting outside) where the bishop will accept them, individually and personally, as being among the *elect* who have been chosen to prepare for baptism and who also have freely chosen to do so. The Lent period is a time of purification and enlightenment. The third, fourth, and fifth Sundays of Lent are times of "scrutiny," or self-examination. In their weekly meetings, the elect will reflect on their failings. At the Masses of three Sundays, they will kneel in the aisle with parishioners laying hands on them while an anonymous list of their failings is read publicly. The scrutinies are exercises of penance and reconciliation involving not only the elect but the whole congregation. At all times, the process is community- rather than priest-centered. The rituals involve elaborate dramatization in choreography, words, and sounds, leading to high emotionality. These are rites of transformation, not rites of passage.

The culminating point is the baptism itself during the Easter vigil. The church is dark and cold (with snow in 2007). In front of the church, a fire is blessed for giving light to the Easter candle, which at St. Mary's, is big enough to be carried by three men. The triple immersion of baptism is dramatic. The priest in full liturgical garments enters barefoot into the pool. The church is dark except for the light of the Easter candle. The elect proceed barefoot in their brown sackcloth. They are immersed three times. confirmation follows. Then they are given a candle lit at the Easter candle and a white tunic, symbolizing their new lives. Communion in the body and blood of Christ is seen as the culmination of the baptism into his death and resurrection. The three-hour ceremony leaves an indelible memory. Six more weeks of mystagogy remain until Pentecost.

2. Confirmation

The unity of baptism-confirmation-Eucharist found in the patristic era has been broken, first in Reformation theology, and increasingly in Catholic theology and practice. Today in the United States, confirmation comes *after* First Communion, as the culmination of Christian catechesis, while theologically it should come before, not after.[141] While canon law leaves great latitude for its administration, the American bishops could only agree that confirmation should be administered between ages 7 and 18. Each diocese or parish is also free to organize its preparation. At St. Mary's, confirmation preparation is very much inspired by the baptismal sacramentality of RCIA, as a ritual of transformation. Scripture, community, and dramatization are essential, as in RCIA.

The confirmation preparation is part of a program that may cover four to six years. During junior high, students from St. Mary's participate in small group catechesis meetings weekly for about two hours. Confirmation preparation similarly covers two years of weekly catechesis, usually during the first two years of high school. When students graduate from the junior high program and move into high-school catechesis, their catechists often move along with them, so that students may stay together with their adult facilitators for at least four years. Some students stay together in small groups from grade 2, at First Communion, to grade 10. The two years of junior high formation can be compared to the period of the catechumenate in RCIA (from September to Lent), and the two years of high school to the period of purification (during Lent). The last two years of high school correspond to mystagogy (from Easter to Pentecost). After confirmation, students are encouraged to become peer ministers to lead the weekly discussion of an incoming confirmation group, together with an adult. In terms of numbers, 90 percent of those entering confirmation preparation have already undertaken two years of junior-high catechesis, and about 40 to 50 percent of those confirmed volunteer to become peer ministers during their last two years of high school. Clearly confirmation is a transformation process rather than a rite of passage.

The various groups meet for the 4:00 p.m. Sunday teen Mass. Although only about 120 are confirmed each year, this Mass is attended by about 500 to 800 people—namely the students of various groups, some of their parents, their adult facilitators (sometimes a husband-wife team), the peer ministers, and friends. Each week a different group of students is in charge of the Sunday liturgy, which involves making arrangements for the music, the singing, the readings, ushering, greeting visitors, and refreshments after Mass. The catechesis itself—from 5:15 to 7:00 p.m.—consists of a short lecture followed by discussion in groups of ten to twelve, co-led by peer ministers and an adult. Spending three hours at church every Sunday for up to six years represents a very high standard of intensity, allowing for intense interaction and transformation.

There is an important social justice component that is not always found in RCIA. Two evenings each year are dedicated to learning and discussing the social doctrine of the church. Students are expected to get involved— junior high kids locally, and high school students in the metropolitan area. Some will visit a halfway house for ex-convicts, preparing and serving meals for them. Other will visit a homeless center to help the homeless medically and educationally, as well as with food. Other service projects include (or have included) Habitat for Humanity, PADS (service to the homeless), downtown social activities, Assist-a-Family, and so on. They may also join a teen social service group that has chosen social services as its main ministry. All of this is done under the guidance of ministering adults, in light of the message of the Gospel and Catholic social teaching.

As in RCIA, various dramatizations highlight events and teachings. Dramatization is an important form of feedback intensification leading to high intensity of emotions and shared symbols. There is the rite of enrollment, which makes the confirmands officially part of the confirmation program. There is the rite of selection of a Christian name: students select a saint who will be both their patron saint and their role model, and it is under that name that they will be confirmed. As in RCIA, students select a sponsor who will accompany them through confirmation. This sponsorship, first dramatized socially by a dinner with all the sponsors, highlights the role of adults as spiritual parents. There is "the pizza with Father Frank," which highlights the role of the priest in a catechesis totally managed by laypeople (except, of course, for the celebration of the Sunday Mass). Finally, there are yearly retreats: mini-retreat 101, mini-retreat 201, and mini-retreat 301, which take place one evening at various times during the year, and two retreats at the end of the first and second year of confirmation preparation. A two-day peer ministry retreat is available to those who have volunteered to serve. There is an overnight social awareness retreat for all high-school students to help them "walk in the shoes of the homeless and hungry ... as they investigate social issues that face impoverished individuals and families." Finally there is a four-day Kairos retreat that consists of testimonies in small group discussions by students who have participated in a Kairos retreat in a previous year. In spite of these high standards and the high cost of $350, about a hundred students participate each year in this four-day retreat. Other forms of dramatization are the performance of the Living Stations of the Cross by junior-high students during the Lent season at neighborhood Masses; the Passion play during holy week, and Gospel dramatizations at the Sunday peer Mass. It is likely that these Gospel dramatizations, created by students and performed in front of peers in lieu of the priestly homily, will lead to intense identification with the Gospel symbols. Generally speaking, dramatizations are rituals of interaction of high intensity, especially if they are performed by peers. Confirmation itself is an important dramatization ritual in the life of an adolescent, and so is the Eucharistic celebration for the whole community.

RCIA is a process, not a program; as such, it has a beginning but no end. To only perform a ritual (e.g., that of baptism) would empty it of its meaning as a rite of initiation and transformation. The same can be said about confirmation at St. Mary's. If all students there had been confirmed at baptism, the four- or six-year process of transformation taking place at St. Mary's could go on unchanged, because as a process of transformation it is the continuation of baptism. Hence, we may say that the confirmation process there is inspired by a baptismal spirituality of death and resurrection. This is also the spirituality of the Eucharistic celebrations.

3. Eucharistic Concelebrations

Church documents can be read sociologically as well as theologically. Let us look at the Constitution on the Sacred Liturgy sociologically. "The liturgy is an outstanding means by which the faithful can *express in their lives ... the mystery of Christ.*"[142] Such a recommendation for the faithful to express through the liturgy their lived participation in the mystery of Christ assumes that they can have an input into the liturgy, and that the latter is not totally in clerical hands. "Mother Church earnestly desires that all the faithful be led to that full, conscious, and active participation in the liturgy."[143] Who is "Mother Church"? Obviously it is Mother Hierarchy. "The Church earnestly desires that Christ's faithful ... should not be there as strangers or silent spectators."[144] Here "Church" stands for hierarchy, as if Mother Hierarchy were *the* Church. It has been official Catholic teaching for centuries that "the Pope, bishops, and priests, are called the Teaching Church, or simply *the* Church [emphasis added]."[145] Hence, it is understandable that most priests and theologians (even the most "liberal" ones) say "church" when they mean "hierarchy" (as in, "the church teaches that ..."). Most importantly, this Constitution implicitly recognizes that the faithful *are* usually "strangers or silent spectators" precisely because the clergy *is* "the Church," with the implicit or explicit exclusion of the laity from active participation in the liturgy.

The "desire" of the church hierarchy, however, is the opposite. "At the table of the Lord, they should give thanks to God by offering the Immaculate Victim, not only through the hands of the priest, but also with him, they should learn to offer themselves too."[146] But if "Mother Church earnestly desires that all the faithful be led to that full, conscious, and active participation in the liturgy," what is actually the case in the liturgy of the Mass? Most often during the liturgy, "the Church" refers to the hierarchy or teaching Church (the *lex credendi*) and only seldom to the Church as universal body of believers (the *lex orandi*).

All liturgical celebrations can be said to be concelebrations *in the broad sense* not only in the sense of involving several priests. This is clearly indicated in the Roman canon of the Mass. Who is the Church? According to the *lex orandi* of the Mass, it is, first of all, the communion of saints. The Preface invokes the angels and all the saints to praise God as holy. The threefold holiness of God of the *sanctus* refers to Isaiah; hence, the patriarchs, prophets, and holy men and women of Israel are included among "all the saints" referred to in the Preface (Abel, Abraham, and Melchisedech are mentioned later). The *communicantes* mentions a long list of saints, such as "Mary, the ever-virgin mother of Jesus Christ our Lord and God. We honor Joseph, her husband, the apostles and martyrs Peter and Paul, Andrew," and many more mentioned in parentheses. In the *nobis quoque peccatoribus*, the church prays to "share in the fellowship of your apostles and martyrs, with John the Baptist, Stephen, Mathias, Barnabas," and again many more are mentioned in parentheses. Finally, in the *supplices rogamus*, we invoke again the angels: "We pray that your angel may take this sacrifice to your altar in heaven." Clearly the church appears here primarily as the communion of saints.

The people of God are mentioned in the Eucharistic Prayer in the most unexpected way. The pope and bishops are mentioned first, not as concelebrants but as sinners who need our prayers. The faithful are mentioned next, but they got somewhat lost in the 1970 English translation. Let us look at the Latin text,[147] with the official English translation underneath (number one) and my *literal* rendering next (number two). In bold are the Latin words that are left out in the English version and my literal translation of these missing words.

Memento, Domine	**famulorum famularumque** tuarum
1. Remember, Lord,	(missing 1) (missing 2)
2 Remember, Lord,	**your servants, men and women,**

et omnium circumstantium, pro quibus tibi offerimus:

1. (missing 3) we offer

2. **and all those around us for whom** we offer

vel qui tibi offerunt   hoc sacrificium laudis,

1 (missing 4) this sacrifice of praise

2. **or who themselves offer**   this sacrifice of praise,

pro se suisque omnibus: pro redemtione animarum suarum,

1. (missing 5) (missing 6) (missing 7)

2. **for themselves and all of theirs: for the redemption of their souls.**

tibique **reddunt** vota **sua** aeterno.

1. (missing 8)

2. **they offer their** prayers

There are no missing words in the official French translation[148] and only one missing word in Spanish, as can be seen:

Souvenez-vous, Seigneur de vos **serviteurs et servantes et de tous** ceux **ici réunis.** Nous t'offrons pour eux, **ou ils t'offrent** ce sacrifice de louange, **pour eux-mêmes et tous les leurs** pour leur propre rédemption.

Acuédate, Señor, de tus hijos (missing 2, about women) **y de todos los aquí reunidos** te ofrecemos, **por ellos y todos los suyos, y ellos te ofrecen**, este sacrificio de alabanza.

What the English translation "Remember, Lord, your people" leaves out is, first of all, the specificity of this people as men and women, priests and faithful. The Latin, French, and Spanish use gender-specific words for male and female servants and sons, not the neutral word "people" used in the English translation (the Latin does not use *populus*, or "people"); the effect of this choice is, intentionally or not, to make women invisible, as does the Spanish, which mentions sons (*hijos*) but not daughters. Next the translation "We offer this sacrifice ..." takes out the faithful "who *themselves offer* this sacrifice ... for *themselves* ... for *their* souls; *they offer their* prayers." In the Latin text, the faithful are active participants (concelebrants) with the priest. In English, the faithful—"who themselves offer this sacrifice of praise for themselves and theirs, for the redemption of their souls, they prayer their prayers" —are made invisible[149].

There is one more example in the Eucharistic Prayer I where in the English translation (fourth column; my translation is in the last column) makes the people of God invisible[150].

Unde et memores, Domine, nos **servi** tui, **sed et plebs tua sancta,** eiusdem Christi, Filii Tui, Domini nostri, tam beatae passionis, necnon et ab inferis resurrectionis ...	C'est pourquoi nous aussi, tes serviteurs **et ton peuple saint avec nous,** faisant mémoire de la Passion bienheureuse de ton Fils, Jésus Christ ...	Por eso, Padre, nosotros, tus siervos, **y todo su pueblo santo,** al celebrar este momorial de la muerte gloriosa de Jusucristo, tu Hijo...	Father, we celebrate ... *We, your people and your ministers,* ... (missing) (we) recall his passion, his resurrection from the dead ...	Lord, **we your servants, and also your holy common people** celebrate the memory of Christ ...

Here, the Latin mentions first the priests as "your *servants*," and next *(and also)* "your *holy common people*" as separate participants in the Eucharistic celebration. Both the French and Spanish translations faithfully follow the Latin: "we your servants (serviteurs, siervos) and *also* your *holy common people* (ton peuple *saint avec nous*; y *todo* su pueblo *santo*)." The English translation does not mention the faithful as *holy*. Moreover, the translation of "servi" as "ministers" rather than "servants" is confusing: are not all the faithful "ministers" by virtue of their baptism? Priests are both servants of the Lord and, in a post-Vatican II perspective, servants of the people of God; then why call them ministers when the Latin says *servi* and not *ministri*? The celebrant may be speaking for all when he says "We your *people* and your ministers ..." but the Latin does not use *populus* (people) but *plebs* (from which *plebeian* is derived), or common people; in the Latin, the priests as servants and the "*common people*" are two separate entities. By not recognizing the presence of the *holy common people* (sed et plebs tua *santa*) the English translation makes the assembly invisible, as if the priest were saying Mass alone, privately.

Again in this example, the presence of the faithful—"your servants, men and women ... who themselves offer this sacrifice of praise, for themselves and all theirs: for the redemption of their souls ..."—is Made invisible. Happily these mistranslations will be corrected in the New Roman Missal of 2011. There are times the faithful are made invisible not only in words, but also in reality. Thus at the papal Mass at the World Youth Day in Sydney in 2008, there were 400 bishops and 5,000 priests around the altar (plus scores of male acolytes) but no females, not even altar girls. Moreover, the crowd of 400,000 people was made invisible by having all the singing either done in Latin or performed by a professional-quality choir and orchestra, with no invitation to the crowd at any time to join in the singing. It was like a TV show in front of cameras. The same happened at the Opening Mass by Cardinal Pell a few days before and the Commissioning Mass one week earlier. How can we explain the implicit theological assumptions at work here? A theological review should help answer this question.

The Constitution on the Sacred Liturgy (no. 7) recognizes the manifold presences of Christ not only in the sacramental species, but also in the celebrating priest and the assembly. Most sacramental churches recognize the triple presence of God in Jesus of Nazareth, his church, and the Eucharist. The relationship between the three, however, has changed over time, with additional differences emerging between Catholics and Protestants. The first Christians gathered on Sunday to celebrate Jesus's resurrection. They did not gather on Fridays to mourn his death. They did not come to pray for the atonement of their sins or flagellate themselves for God's mercy. They came to "celebrate" God's power of resurrection. In brief, they saw themselves as one people in the glorious body of the resurrected Jesus of Nazareth. They took communion in that glorious body and brought the consecrated bread to the sick members of the congregation. This vision changed, according to de Lubac,[151] Chauvet,[152] and Martos,[153] during the Middle Ages (or as a consequence of the Council of Trent) when the Eucharistic celebration became privatized as an act of devotion, clericalized mainly (or even exclusively) as a clerical celebration, and objectified, in time at the consecration and in space when the host is carried processionally through town, or worshipped in the Blessed Sacrament. During the Reformation, many Protestants rejected the presence of Christ in the sacraments, emphasizing instead his presence in history, Scripture, and the Church. In reaction, Catholics came to emphasize even more their privatized, clericalized, and objectified understanding of the sacraments.

The *Novo Ordo* of 1969 and the *Roman Missal* of 2000 returned to the ancient unified vision of Christ as present in history, Church, and sacraments. According to the *General Instruction of the Roman Missal* (2000), what is now called the Eucharistic Prayer rather than the canon is seen now essentially as a prayer of thanksgiving. What is new is "the recovery here of the ancient understanding of the Eucharistic Prayer as the great thanksgiving,"[154] rather than supplication and expiation. The canon was traditionally divided into three parts: the preface, the consecration, and the Communion. The Novo Ordo obviously does not change this traditional division, but somewhat gives it new meaning. It states, "The chief elements making up the Eucharistic Prayer may be distinguished in this way: Thanksgiving (especially in the Preface) ... *Acclamation ... Epiclesis ... Institution narrative and consecration ... Anamnesis ... Offering ... Intercessions ... Final doxology* [italics in the text]," and communion.[155] The use of Greek words (*epiclesis* and *anamnesis*) clearly suggest a return to early Christian practice. Again, what is changed is not the content but some of the meaning. The significance of this change became prominent when in 2001 the Congregation of the Doctrine of the Faith recognized the validity of a Eucharistic prayer (the Anaphora Addai and Mari still used in small East Syrian churches, the Syro-Malabar Catholic Church, and the Chaldean Catholic Church) although it does not include the words of the consecration (now called "words of institution"). If Christ was, is, and will be, he is present in and out of time, in and out of space, and should not be objectified in ritualism and localism.

Let me now summarize these two visions of the Mass, old and new.

In the Tridentine tradition, the Mass is seen first as a sacrifice where Christ is "really present" in the bread and wine. Second it is essentially a priestly function, as only one altar boy needs to be present. Third, as the Mass is said in Latin (or today when the choir sings as though giving a performance), the faithful have little part in it. Fourth, it is mainly an individual devotion, celebrated by priests every day and encouraged for the laity. Fifth, the most important moment of the Mass is the consecration—

more specifically the Elevation of the Host, as seen in the picture to the left.[156] Sixth, its spirituality is one of sacrifice and reparation, particularly in the adoration of the Blessed Sacrament and nocturnal adoration, in silence and private meditation. Seventh, the sacraments are seen as absolutely necessary, with a quasiautomatic effect *ex opere operato*. Eighth, implicitly the fundamental sacrament is priestly ordination, since it makes possible all other sacraments, especially the Eucharist. In short, the clergy *are* the church, because priests, by their teaching, personal example, and the administration of the sacraments, are the necessary channels of salvation. Finally, for the faithful, the church is mainly the place where they receive the sacraments, usually passively.

This is the model of the High Mass celebrated at Santa Maria Maggiore, described at the beginning of chapter 3. There was a processional entrance of about twenty priests, all in garments showing their clerical rank, presided over by Cardinal Law. The high moment was the consecration and Elevation of the Host, with lots of incense and bells ringing. All the prayers and songs were in Latin. There was little faithful participation. The Mass was followed by the exposition of the Blessed Sacrament and nocturnal adoration. This High Mass took place in Rome on December 31, 2007.

The following characteristics refer to a post-Vatican II vision. First, the Mass is more commonly called the Eucharist or the Eucharistic celebration.

Second, it is Trinitarian as the cosmic celebration of the Lamb (as in Revelation 5:6–14). Third, it is always a concelebration involving the communion of the saints, the living and the dead. Fourth, it is a public celebration of the spiritual body of Christ in the Christian community, not a private devotion. Fifth, it is deeply rooted in and connected to the early Christian practices. Sixth, its sacramentality sees God in all things (not just the seven sacraments) and Christ in all the baptized, especially all the poor of the world. Seventh, it values enthusiastic singing and contemporary music as much as or more than silence. Eighth, it is ecumenical in intent. Ninth, the fundamental sacrament is baptism as the initiation into Christ's transforming power. Tenth, "The ministerial priesthood is at the service of the common priesthood" (CCC no. 1547). And finally, for all the faithful, priests and laypeople, the church is a place of ministry to both the Christian community and the outside world, which implies an active involvement of all, not just the somewhat passive reception of sacraments.

These two visions of the Eucharist tend to be mutually exclusive but may easily coexist. Most people—laypeople, clergy, and bishops—find themselves with one foot in one and one foot in the other. Because these two visions imply different ecclesiologies and soteriologies, they are fundamental in one's perception of the Church, its teaching, and its liturgy, and hence are likely to color how a priest or bishop understands the Mass, the meaning of its canon, and the roles of priesthood and laity.

What do we find at St. Mary's?

The Choir and Church Singing

The more actors participate in the feedback intensification of a church service, the more likely will people be involved in the service's religious symbols and mysteries. In a traditional Catholic Sunday Mass, there are usually three actors: the priest, who does most of the praying; the choir (on the balcony or a side chapel), often invisible to those facing the altar; and the organ, which plays loudest when people are expected to sing. At St. Mary's, there are five major actors: the choir in front of the church, for all to see; the band that supports the choir; the director of worship and music; the assembly, which joins in the singing most of the time; and finally, the celebrant. Here the priest does not monopolize worship leadership. At this parish, there are three "codirectors of word and worship": a female pastoral associate who is also codirector of pastoral ministry; the director of music, with a Master's of Divinity and a diploma in sacred music; a pastoral associate; and the pastor, the only priest in this parish. At St. Mary's, there is no organ to cover the silence of the assembly; therefore, there better be lively music! Let us consider the role of the choir and its director, also called the "director of worship and music." What is outstanding is that the ministries of word and worship are not considered the exclusive monopoly of the ordained.

"I am responsible for everything that happens in the worship space when we gather for prayer and worship," said the director of worship and music. His responsibilities range from making creative flower arrangements around the altar, to dramatizations of liturgical texts, to paraliturgical readings, to artistic performances, to the spiritual animation of the choir and the whole church. Since the pastor and his codirector of worship have been working together for about ten years, great mutual trust has developed between them. According to the director of worship and music, "There is a wonderful level of freedom that is provided by [the pastor's] understanding that there is a shared priesthood of the faithful." Over the years, the pastor's vision of the parish has increasingly become a reality. "His vision is that we are a community of communities and that the ministry is done by the laity; the role of the staff is to animate the work of the faithful." Hence, "there is a wonderful level of freedom and collaboration." The collaboration is such that the pastor and the director of music meet only about once a month.

The Catholic liturgy can be compared to a chain of restaurants that has 150 dishes on its menu (a three-year cycle), but only offers one specific dish per week. Such a situation

> **I Loved the Music**
> "My background is Protestant and evangelical. When I became a Catholic, I missed the modern music. I went to St. Mary's, which is half an hour away from where I live, and I loved the music. It's modern. It's upbeat. It's like the music I hear on the radio, because I listen to Christian music. It's music I can sing along with."
> —Interview

would lead many chefs to desperation, since it seems to exclude culinary creativity. The McDonald's chain has franchises all over the world, but local restaurants are not allowed to offer their own versions of hamburgers and french fries; hence, McDonald's cooks are usually unskilled and low-paid laborers. The Catholic liturgy consists of mandatory readings over a three-year period with no (or little) choice. Will the Catholic parishes go the way of the McDonald's chain and make their liturgies endlessly similar and often quite dull? Not so at St. Mary's. If there is no choice about the readings, one must be extra creative about how to handle them. "What we need is to prepare, prepare ourselves," said the music director. "I talk a lot about liturgical *preparation*, instead of liturgy planning, because the liturgy is already planned for us. What we need to do is *prepare!*" While an average parish may follow the liturgical prescriptions mechanically, at St. Mary's each liturgy is personalized: "Almost all of our liturgies are personalized so much that almost all become creations."

For this codirector of word and worship, preparation begins at home, in the choir. There are two- to three-hour rehearsals once a week throughout the year, twice during the weeks before Christmas and Easter, and nearly daily during the last days before the holy days. "What I do with them is not just teaching them music; it's very pastoral, and it's very ministerial. We try to begin and end with prayer, and then, we're very clear that what we're doing is not performance, that it's ministry." There is also a small choir Christian community (SCC) that meets before the rehearsals and short retreats every year.

Who will join the choir? According to a prominent member of the choir, "There are people who cannot read music, but no one is excluded, and it is my job in the parish to invite people to join the choir. 'Just come, and see if it is right for you!' I would say." Some people join because they like to sing and perform, without much of a sense of ministry, but this is a "church"! At Bayville, one must go through a one-hour interview and be accepted into the choir (some candidates are not). By definition, a "sect" is an elite group with high standards. Bayville describes itself as an "army" of well-trained soldiers integrated into teams with "captains" as leaders (e.g., in teams of prayer partners). St. Mary's parish is a "church" that sets standards low enough for the masses to join; hence, its pastoral strategy is quite different from that of a "sect." A "church" takes people where they are and endeavors to move them up. Thus, at St. Mary's, the prayer meetings before the choir rehearsals are optional, without pressure to attend. About ten to fifteen people attend regularly. Low number? Not really, when one considers that many choir members already participate in one of the many small Christian communities of the parish; moreover, many women (and men) with family and/or professional responsibilities are already stretched to their limits by the three-hour rehearsal once a week. By definition, a "church" is a place where the believers can grow, but they may also stagnate if there is no leadership. But leadership—as opposed to canonical authority—is something relatively new in the Catholic Church.

The Catholic liturgy gives the celebrant a quasimonopoly in prayer leadership: it is the priest who invites the faithful to prayer (e.g., when he says "*Oremus*," or let us pray); the assembly's role is to respond (e.g., with a song). This division of labor, however, does not exclude creativity. It is the job of the director of worship and music to "personalize" the liturgy. And so it appears to many faithful, as stated by a member of the choir, "I bring people here at least half a dozen times a year, if not more, and they come back. Here you are not looking at your watch, no matter how long it is, and the Masses go for an hour and fifteen minutes and sometimes longer. In my other church, the Mass was forty-five minutes, and you couldn't wait until it was over." This cantor is personally involved in his music ministry: "Before I sing, I always look up at the cross [in the middle of the sanctuary] and ask God to give me the strength and the ability to deliver his message to the congregation." The cross in the middle of the sanctuary is indeed an inspiring work of art. "When I brought my mother here," one member said, "tears were rolling off her eyes when she saw the cross. I just couldn't believe how overwhelmed she was." At its best, a Catholic liturgy is complex, but this complexity allows for creativity. It consists of mandatory readings; dramatizations in words, music, and works of art; and feedback intensification, with many actors involved, leading to the internalization of shared values and a deeper participation in the religious mysteries. At St. Mary's, the "holy common people" are not made invisible; on the contrary, they participate as separate participants, together with the priest, in the Eucharistic celebration.

The Homilies

In the wake of the Catholic renewal in biblical studies, Vatican II mandated that the Sunday readings be explained in homilies,[157] not sermons. "Origen was the first to distinguish between *logos* (*sermo*, sermon) and *homilia* (*tractatus*, homily). Since Origen's time homily has meant, and still means, a commentary, without formal introduction, division, or conclusion, on some part of Sacred Scripture, the aim being to explain the literal, and evolve the spiritual, meaning of the Sacred Text."[158] Only the priest can give the homily. Moreover, according to an instruction to implement the Vatican II reform, a homily is to be a lecture, not a lecture-discussion or other forms of modern teaching, because "the faithful are to refrain from comments, dialogue, and similar activities" in response to the priest's explanations.[159] The homily is to comment mainly on the liturgical readings. This excludes most current or burning issues about which the faithful would expect information, clarifications, and direction, but which are not mentioned in the readings. A homily is not the place to develop at length topics like private confession versus general absolution, prayer, sacrificial giving, tithing, money management, grief, redemptive suffering, divorce, or lay and priestly vocations, not to mention the burning issues of church accountability, celibacy and premarital sexuality, and the need of gender equality in the church; indeed, no Sunday reading leads itself to such comments. Nor is it the place to explain St. Paul's understanding of faith in his letter to the Romans, the common priesthood of the faithful in contemporary theology, or the historical background of Jeremiah or Isaiah. A homily is to give a literal or spiritual interpretation of the readings of the day. The problem is that most of Jesus's sayings are self-explanatory; they were so even to the illiterate masses of his day. Rare are geniuses like Origen or Augustine, who can comment insightfully. The consequences of the replacement of the sermon by the homily are unmeasurable. By excluding the burning issues of the day as topics for Sunday homilies, the Catholic Church has somewhat given up, *in its Sunday teachings*, the traditional role of a "church" to be involved in the social, cultural and political affairs of the secular society (see above pages 105). And by limiting the commentary to the readings of a given Sunday, Catholicism has defined the scope of its Sunday teaching even more narrowly than most evangelical churches. Is it surprising, then, that many or most Catholics are dissatisfied with their Sunday preaching?

In such a context—and independently of it—the homilies of Father Frank are praised very highly. In most parishes, the format of the Sunday homilies is an explanation of the Gospel followed by applications to everyday life. Father Frank does not follow this format. Actually he tends to reverse it, beginning with everyday life and then illuminating it with Gospel quotations. He may begin with the headlines of the week's newspapers, or an important book, or a personal experience like taking his dog to the park at night, or an image, like Mountain Time. As a result, he captures people's attention from the beginning, and the homily becomes a kind of mystery story, with everyone wondering where it's going. Let me give examples.

> "The first time I went to St. Mary's, I made an immediate connection with Father Frank's homily. It seemed like he was talking to me. What he was talking about was the church and religious legalism, the stuff that I was really struggling with. I figured, if this guy's willing to take a stand and talk about this stuff, that's a hell of a lot more than any other parish pastor has in other churches that I had been to."
> —Interview

I care for two dogs: Bingo, a five-year-old Schnauzer whom I inherited from my mother; and K. C., whom I share with my office workers ... K. C. is very easy to take care of. Bingo, on the other hand, demands long walks. Recently, I took Bingo to a park. It was early evening, but it was so dark and filled with bushes and trees where other creatures could hide. All of a sudden, from the cold darkness, there came another creature. It was either a coyote or a fox, I couldn't tell which, but he stood his ground and stared at us. I yelled at him, or her, and picked Bingo up and carried him away. The coyote/fox did not pursue us. I will never enter a park in the darkness again.[160]

Where do we go from here? "Darkness. Darkness is a primary symbol for fear, anxiety, apprehension, depression, hopelessness. Both the first reading from Isaiah and then the gospel speak of people dwelling in darkness ..." We are in the middle of the winter; outside it is cold and dark. It is also the beginning of Lent. At the time of Isaiah, there was the darkness of Assyrian invasion, but also the prophet's message that "God will bring light again." At the time of Jesus, there was the darkness of Roman occupation, but also the promise that "darkness will never prevail." Today among us, there are many forms of darkness; some are chemically induced, while others are social, or psychological, or spiritual. "Is there darkness in your life? Jesus wants to help us with any darkness we might be lost in ... Let us walk toward Jesus. Let us walk toward light." The imagery here is comforting rather than frightening; we first relate to a small dog's fear of darkness at night in the park and then witness its experience of being carried away by its owner. It is the imagery of the lost sheep and the good shepherd.

Headlines make easy beginnings. "The cover story of ... was about a resurgence of people going to confession ... on the Internet. There is something like twenty-four websites where people can now post their sins. This custom has increased 139 percent in the last year. One cluster of sites reports a hundred thousand confessions in a month. An individual site reports two thousand confessions a month; another, two hundred a day." One feels like flipping through the newspaper, wanting to know more. "Many people are quite sincere in confessing. They have been carrying the guilt of sin around with them, and they feel a need for catharsis, a need to release that material to other people in a spirit of honesty." This introduction naturally leads to good teaching about conversion according to the Sunday readings. "The first step in repentance is naming our sin. ... Sin is hurtfulness. ... Sin is idolatry. ... Sin is being irresponsible with the gift of life that God has blessed us with. ... If we are truly to repent this Advent, we need to name our sin." The conclusion comes in the form of an owned statement, "I believe that the Sacrament of Reconciliation is a great resource, a great tool that we have in Catholic tradition." At St. Mary's, reconciliation is celebrated in formal liturgies with readings and songs, and also in large communal services before Christmas and Easter. Through this homily, reconciliation has been made easy, like the two thousand confessions a month, or the two hundred a day, on the web.

The homily may begin with a personal testimony. "Whenever I experience pain or struggle in my life, I try to think of someone else who is having pain and struggle, and I try to offer my pain and struggle as a living prayer for that other person. When I do this, it helps me to see my struggle in perspective. Usually mine is nothing in comparison to the difficulties of that other person. Then I very much feel one with God and one with that other person. When we pray this redemptive suffering, we experience a oneness in consciousness with God and other people." Such an example makes the teaching of the day all the more acceptable; it makes redemptive suffering bearable. "When the cross emerges in our lives, we are not to walk away from it. We are to walk toward it. We are to embrace it. We are to carry it. We are to allow ourselves to be nailed to the cross. We are to feel and experience all that the pain of the cross brings into our lives, and then, we are to engage in trust and surrender."

Going shopping is an experience that most people can relate to. Father Frank looks at it reflectively. "John Kavanaugh's book, *Following Christ in a Consumer Society* … had an impact on me when it was first released in 1981. … John Kavanaugh's basic recommendation … is to develop a *spirituality of resistance* toward the culture around us. This spirituality of resistance involves a revaluing of interiority, solitude, and prayer." How does shopping look in such a perspective? "As I walked through a couple of stores, Christmas decorations were up. The store environments were screaming at customers, 'Buy! Buy! Buy!' It is curious that the day that marks the birth of Jesus has become a day, indeed a season, that emphasizes commodity-form living to an extreme." This leads naturally to the Gospel reading: "In the Gospel today, we are reminded that living the Gospel is a countercultural phenomenon that very well may cost us some struggle and pain. We may find ourselves at variance in terms of values with people who are very close to us." Here the reference to shopping is made a negative experience: too often shopping is what it should *not* be, namely a commodity form of living, a surrender to the voices of conformity, a nonresistance to the culture around us.

Testimonies are always touching, especially if they come from ordinary folks. On the occasion of Christmas, Father Frank asked people to write about the real-life manger that they would like to invite Jesus to be born into. Here are some answers:

—Jesus, come and be born in my marriage, and help me to be more patient with my sick wife.

—Jesus, please come and be born in my loneliness.

—Jesus, help me to be a better father to my children.

—Jesus, please help me to be less indulgent when it comes to food and drink.

—Jesus, help me to be more patient and less judgmental of other people.

—Jesus, come into my heart; help me to wake up to how I am too self-focused. Help me to turn some of this focus toward others.

—Jesus, help me to experience you daily and feel your presence.

—Jesus, come into my life and help me to be more prayerful and more attentive to the needs of others.

Children, too, were invited to participate:

—Jesus, come into my room and stop the fighting with my brother.

—Jesus, come into my relationship with my brothers and sisters and help me to allow them to play with my toys.

It is not just children who fight; it is not just children who do not share their toys. To give people, including children, a voice about their weaknesses is to give them the strength to overcome them. The homily, then, becomes empowering, teaching from below.

One last example about Mountain Time: "For too many of us, life is characterized by hurry, tension, high expectations, and polyphasic thinking and doing, or multitasking." People need Mountain Time! "Sometimes when I hear people describe their vacations, I walk away and wonder quietly, 'How was all that activity recreation for them?'" They really needed Mountain Time. Like Jesus, we can walk on water—that

Sunday's reading—"if we make adequate Mountain Time to be filled with grace and Spirit, to become one with God. So … let's make sure that each day we carve out time and space for Mountain Time, and on the mountain, with the Lord, let us be quiet, let us listen, and let us pray." Indeed, we have learned from the Gospels that "Jesus went to a mountain to be alone and to pray." After this homily, it will be easier to remember the meaning and importance of Mountain Time.

In summary, many characteristics of Father Frank's homilies account for his success. There is, first of all, a populist tone that levels with the audience: Frank is not speaking *to* the assembly but *from* the middle of it (the church building is circular, like an amphitheater). He is also a scholar and an intellectual (he holds a PhD in the social sciences) who gives references to important books and concepts. Not least important, his wisdom is Scripture-based; he does not quote the Greek text, but often refers to the contemporary state of historical and exegetical studies. His basic outlook is not church-centeredness and clerical subservience—far from it. He often makes biting comments about the institutional church (e.g., on Christ-King's Sunday, "The leaders of the Church have embraced a monarchical model of governance. We hear cardinals spoken of as the *princes of the Church.* They wear garb that speaks of royalty. There is a stark contrast between the symbols of such leadership and the throne from which Jesus led and leads his Kingdom: the cross." There is here an evangelical, countercultural tone that comes from making the death and resurrection of Christ *of the Gospels*—which is somewhat different from the Tridentine church-centered emphasis on sacrifice—the center of Christian spiritual life. And this spirituality is a baptismal spirituality, to be considered in the second part of this chapter.

The Sunday Liturgies

There are two Sunday Masses in the morning and a teen Mass in the afternoon, along with two Saturday services. Small children have their own age-appropriate liturgy, but not a Mass. Attendance fluctuates from a low of 2,500 in July to a high of 3,200 in December and May.

Several indicators show the active participation of the faithful in the liturgy. Clapping is a spontaneous expression of approval that has become relatively common at Catholic Masses. At St. Mary's, clapping occurs not only at exceptional performances, as elsewhere, but also at many other times, such as at the end of the homily, or even during the homily, when a statement strikes a chord in the audience. Newcomers at Masses are usually recognized individually and are welcomed with applause. At the end of the eleven o'clock Mass, the faithful wait until the end of the final hymn to break into applause in appreciation of the choir's work. More generally, while it is common for the faithful in many Catholic parishes to start exiting soon after the *Ite missa est*, at St. Mary's, most people stay until the end of the singing, like at the end of a good concert, and clap in appreciation. They will then exit slowly into the narthex for refreshments, and linger on chatting with friends or remain in silence. Another indicator of high participation is the recitation of "Our Father," which is quite emotional here. For the "Our Father," all the faithful hold hands, as is increasingly common practice in Catholic churches. But at St. Mary's, the faithful form a chain throughout the circular church, with the Eucharistic ministers standing on both sides of the celebrant, all raising hands in one chain through all the pews and across the nave, around the altar and starting from the priest to the Eucharistic ministers to all the faithful. This is a very emotional moment. The hands remain raised throughout the *Libera nos*, the priest's prayer after the "Our Father," until the celebrant invites all to offer each other a sign of peace, at which time the handshakes of peace are warm and profuse. The St. Mary's parishioners seem to have come to identify this ritual as their trademark, as the emotional and spiritual symbol of their collective identity and involvement. Another indicator of participation is the teen Mass, for and by teenagers. The readings, the singing, the music, the offertory, and the refreshments are performed by teenagers, to the great satisfaction of their parents, who attend in great numbers. One final example of vibrant participation is the custom of raising hands to pray over others—again, an increasingly common practice, but done with more fervor here. During Lent the whole assembly prays over the RCIA candidates; the candidates in turn pray over their sponsors, kneeling in front of them at the ephpheta ceremony. At First Communion, the communicants pray over their parents, kneeling before them, and those parents will in turn will pray over their kneeling children, laying their hands on them. At the funeral Masses, the close relatives surround the casket of their loved one to pray, extending their hands, while the assembly prays over both the departed and the grieving family.

In terms of interactive or feedback intensification leading to increased participation in shared symbols and values, the Eucharistic celebrations can be seen as true concelebrations involving not only "we your servants" (the priest) and "your holy common people," as stated in the Eucharistic Prayer I, but actually a great variety of participants. The service of the altar involves the traditional altar servers; the lectors of the liturgical texts; the readers of invocations at the Prayer of the Faithful; the homilist, who occasionally may be a layperson; the presenters of the gifts at the Offertory; and about a dozen Eucharistic ministers. The music ministry consists of a worship and music director, a pianist, a small band, a choir, and a dozen cantors who sing the responsories at the different Masses. Two big screens above the altar allow for easy participation in the singing. At the end of the celebration, one finds tables with beverages and snacks. Everything is geared to active participation.

At Masses, praying seems particularly fervent during the collective prayers recited together: the Confiteor, the Kyrie, the Gloria, the Credo, and the Our Father. In festive times, these are sung rather than recited. More generally, the singing consists of well-known hymns, as well as modern and contemporary songs. Some of the singing at St. Mary's is the same as at Bayville described in the previous chapter; Bayville may use songs by Catholic artists (e.g., "Your Grace Is Enough") and St. Mary's some evangelical ones (e.g., "Amazing Grace"). There is, however, a great difference in participation between the two churches. At Bayville the singing is at all times loud enough for everyone to hear one's neighbors in any direction; this singing is never overpowered by the choir or the orchestra. Not so at St. Mary's. At all times, one can see people singing along—or rather, humming along—but never loudly enough to be able to hear one's neighbors (except maybe in the front pews). The same can be said about the rote prayers recited together: they are said in a soft but barely audible voice. What explains these differences?

A major characteristic of Catholic worship is that the "Competent ecclesiastical authority alone has the right ... to promote public worship" (canon 301). All Catholic public worship is and must be directed from above. Over the centuries, it has always been the clergy that has defined the appropriate sacramental rites and the acceptable forms of public prayers, of pilgrimages, and of the veneration of the saints. At many churches today, the faithful are told when to stand, when to kneel, when to bow, when to sing, when to pray, and when to be silent. There are also unwritten rules. Two such rules that differentiate the Catholic religious subculture from the American culture at large are silence and majestic performance. Silence is a major rule in monastic institutions, which often practice the "great silence" (no talking whatsoever) between late evening and morning hours. Silence is also expected in any Catholic church before and after the services; the loud music of contemporary pop artists is seen as inappropriate in a Catholic setting. Catholic worship is expected to reflect the majesty of the Creator; hence, no cathedral can be too lavish, no altar ornaments too expensive, no processional pageantry too slow, and no liturgical prayer or reading too ornate if they are deemed to honor God in public services. This unwritten rule was often stated at the beginning of the traditional catechisms: man is created "to honor God" through church worship. To a certain extent, it states that man was made for the Sabbath, and not the Sabbath for men and women.

> **Recommendations for St. Mary's**
>
> "St. Mary's is one of the few Catholic Churches where you can take somebody who is not a Catholic but might be wanting to explore it, because it's very hard for me as a Catholic to be able to recommend other churches."
> —Interview
>
> "At St. Mary's the small Christian communities form a bond between the parishioners and the church that I've never seen before in any Catholic church."
> —Interview

Protestant Reformation churches have often taken stands opposite to Catholic practices. Monasteries were abolished, and so was the rule of silence. The visual decoration of churches through images and statues was rejected with iconoclastic fervor, but singing and music were encouraged. Today many Protestant churches still favor the iconoclastic rejection of images in favor of profuse sound productions with an extensive choir, a major orchestra, and a sound system that may rival that of music halls. There, the faithful may experience God through sound and music (and in Pentecostal churches, through glossolalia and prophecy), but seldom through silent prayer. In mainline churches, the divine is experienced more visually—in extreme cases, through personal visions and apparitions. Silence and mediation are valued, and so is the study of tradition, for which Reformers expressed contempt. Evangelicals often study the Bible as a meteorite that appeared two thousand years ago, to be interpreted literally, not through historical criticism. Before WWII, many Protestants were attracted to the silence of Catholic monasteries and the monasteries' beautiful Gregorian music. Today the younger generation finds silence empty, if not boring, and the contemporary pop music of many evangelical churches attractive. The Roman Catholic liturgy is a subculture that seems foreign to those not born or raised into it, as would be, to most Catholics, the Byzantine liturgy of the Greek-Catholic churches. Most of the enthusiastic supporters of the music at St. Mary's that I have interviewed are cradle Catholics who have been involved in the Catholic subculture since childhood. Nationwide, 9 out of 10 Catholics are cradle Catholics. Today, American Catholicism attracts few converts, a topic that deserves further discussion in the conclusion.

Let me now summarize our findings about the baptismal sacramentality found at St. Mary's.

In this section, I have shown that the Catholic sacramental theory and practice are slowly evolving from rites of passage to rites of transformation. Most Catholics still think in terms of (having been taught so, up to this day) *attending* Mass, *receiving their* sacraments, going to confession *once a year*, and so on. Even at St. Mary's, the change is slow. At the Sunday Mass at the end of Advent in 2007, all were reminded that "Christmas is a *day of obligation*." The notion of obligation persists. Thus Carol, a regular Sunday Mass attender who had not been confirmed in childhood, told RCIA, "I am looking to *finish my sacraments*," and at the rite of acceptance, in front of the church: "They asked me why I was there; I said I wanted to *finish my sacraments* [emphasis added]." A sacramentality of obligation and automatic rituals is probably one of the leading causes of Catholic decline. The Catholic Church lost maybe half of its regular attenders over the last two generations, dropping to only about 30 percent today in the United States, 15 percent in Australia, 7–8 percent in many European countries, 3–4 percent in the Netherlands, and 1–2 percent in Scandinavia. Unless the notion of religious obligation is replaced in the minds of Catholics by a positive desire for participation, the decline may continue—a paradox contrary to traditional wisdom based on obligation and law enforcement.

While the faithful have internalized the Tridentine notion of sacramental obligation, it is the clergy who created it and continue to foster it—but not so at St. Mary's. The lengthy process of preparation and transformation through RCIA is accepted in most Catholic parishes today, but few, like St. Mary's, make it the model of their sacramentality. The current practice of confirmation is highly questionable when con-*firm*-ation (the action of af*firm*ing one's faith) is followed by the abandonment of religious practice; yet its current practice is also open to innovation (e.g., in the form of a two- to four-year preparation). At St. Mary's, after two years of weekly teen Masses and instructions; a public rite of selection; a personal sponsor, a peer team minister, and an adult team facilitator; two years of involvement in social services and works of charity; and several mini-retreats and a longer Kairos retreat, it is not likely that those thus "made firm" (confirmed) will drop out. In religion, as in sports, training makes one stronger, and leadership is crucial. At St. Mary's, the sacramentality is one not of ritual passages performed by the ordained, but one of participation and transformation in the name of the common priesthood of the faithful. This is most visible at the Sunday Eucharistic celebration, which has traditionally been seen, as in the Tridentine Mass, as the monopoly of the clergy. If feedback intensification is the most important aspect of the ritual interaction, the Tridentine Mass, with its silent or passive assembly, is not conducive to much intensification—and this type of Mass is still prevalent in many parishes. At St. Mary's, Sunday Masses are both celebrations and concelebrations. The unwritten rules of silence and majesty of the Catholic subculture remain, but within these limitations, the Sunday concelebrations are joyous, enthusiastic, prayerful, and deeply appreciated by the parishioners. They can, indeed, be seen as a model for Catholic renewal.

B. *Ecclesiolas* and Baptismal Spirituality

St. Mary's parish can best be described as a community of communities. Thus married couples form various small communities, but among the married couples, those with children can form their own communities, and among those with children are various smaller communities organized according to the age and the activities of the children. Among the married with children are also communities to serve special educational needs (e.g., those of children with Down syndrome, autism, and even cerebral palsy). A more detailed description of the various communities will be given throughout this section.

1. Governance

The functioning of the St. Mary's parish is illustrated by its governing body. All ministries (about 140, but there is no official list) are divided into seven areas, each supervised by a director, which are worship, youth, family life, adult formation and outreach, justice and peace, pastoral care, and maintenance. These seven areas consist of many ministries, and each ministry may consist of several teams. Representatives from all the ministries meet once a month at the Leadership Committee. Moreover, a representative from each of the seven areas, together with their directors and the parish staff (about fifteen to eighteen people altogether) also meet once a month as the Pastoral Council, which is the governing body of the parish.

All meetings are public, and all are invited. The monthly meetings of the Leadership Committee attract between eighty and a hundred people.

As an example of the great variety of ministries in each of the seven areas, here are the ministries within worship: art and environment; audiovisual ministries; children's liturgy of the word; Eucharistic ministries; hospitality; liturgy preparation; living arts; Mass coordinators; music ministry; prayer and devotion; proclaimers; sacristan; sign-language interpretation; special events; table and light ministers; ushers; and wedding rehearsals. The leaders of each of these eighteen ministries (which may consist of several independent teams of volunteers) attend the monthly meeting of the Leadership Committee, the purpose of which is mainly pastoral and educational. Leadership in this parish goes two ways: from the top down as well as from the bottom up. The question at the leadership meeting is, in its most general form: "What information will benefit, let us say, the proclaimers, the ushers, and the nursing-home visitors, and what will the representatives of these ministries take back to the members of their ministries?" Topics discussed at the Leadership Committee often involve current issues reported by the pastor, general topics like prayer, the liturgy, catechesis opportunities, formation issues, new ministries, liturgical events, or specific needs of the parish at a given time. Often, an outside speaker provides a theme for discussion. The meetings of the Leadership Committee last about two hours. The first half is a presentation and the second half a general discussion in breakout groups by areas. All reconvene at the end to share conclusions. These meetings allow for two-way information: from the bottom up to the directors and pastor, and from the top down to the ministry volunteers.

All meetings—of staff, directors, leaders, and volunteers in ministries— begin with "faith first." After an introductory prayer by the group leader, the upcoming Sunday's readings are proclaimed, followed by comments, reactions, and a closing prayer. The meeting may likewise end with a prayer (often the recitation of Our Father) while all hold or raise hands. A Mass is celebrated once or twice a year at the Leadership Community meeting during Lent or Advent. These meetings are neither just business meetings nor mainly devotional gatherings. They reaffirm the community in its diversity and its religious identity.

The Pastoral Council is the decision-making body of the parish, although officially it is only advisory to the pastor. The tension between the advisory and decision-making roles is resolved in the consensus model of governance at work here. Consensus is not reached through agreement at the lowest common denominator but rather through mutual listening, as stated by a council member: "Each person coming here must be willing to listen to the other and perhaps be influenced by the other." Moreover, the issues are not presented in the form of motions to be accepted or rejected, but as joint projects, like "I am thinking of doing this or that. I need your input about it." Proposals may also come from representatives of the various ministries (e.g., proposals for new or expanded ministries, or requests for financial support). Interestingly, the Pastoral Council also includes four parishioners "at large" who represent no particular group, but may give input from the perspective of the average parishioner. Although decisions are reached collegially by consensus, decisions are finalized in the form of motions and votes recorded in the minutes.

The success of any decision made by an advisory pastoral council or even a pastor depends on the collaboration of the volunteers who will carry out this decision. Father Frank may air his proposals not only at the Pastoral Council but also at the Leadership Committee meeting in an effort to get feedback from the grassroots, saying, "I'd like your support on this, and I'd like you to bring it back to your communities, and I seek their support for it." In a certain sense, the parish is co-owned by the parishioners and the pastor. It is a co-ownership of responsibilities, not of rights. The sense of ownership comes from the invitation to all parishioners to participate in ministries as well as governance. As a result, decisions come from the basic sense of citizenship in the parish, from the emotional and functional involvement of the parishioners in the parish's present and future. This sense of ownership is fostered institutionally by having the meetings of the Leadership Committee and the Pastoral Council take place the same day, back to back, so that the discussions in one can automatically be taken up in the other. The Pastoral Council is at the service of the various ministries, not the other way around.

As a basic principle, according to a member of the Pastoral Council, "the extent to which a pastor is willing to be advised determines how successful the Pastoral Council will be." The relationship between the pastor and the Pastoral Council cannot be unilateral, in the form of advice given by one to the other; it must be mutual, in the form of seeking advice as well as giving advice. Father Frank, I was told, is always willing to be advised. Thus consensus in both decision making and ministry leadership involves not only mutual listening, but also the willingness to be influenced by others; it involves and requires *communitas* according to a baptismal spirituality.

2. Community formation

Following Ferdinand Toennies, social scientists distinguish between face-to-face communities (like families) and impersonal societies (like businesses). In common parlance, however, we usually call our town a community, although we may not know most people. A more restrictive concept is that of a moral community, of people sharing common values and interests, like a church or a parent-teacher association. Within the moral community of a parish, there may be implicit small moral communities sharing common values like married couples, parents with children, or parents with children of a given age group. Hence, in any church, there may be many implicit small moral communities that can become formal Christian communities.

We have seen that a "church" tends to be involved in the social and cultural affairs of its society, while a "sect" tends to withdraw from secular activities, fostering mainly devotional groups. Thus, in a church-type parish, there may be a great variety of religious societies, while in a sectarian parish, we may find only devotional societies centered on, for example, the rosary, adoration of the Blessed Sacrament, the miraculous medal, novenas, or the devotion to a particular saint. At St. Mary's, there are small Christian communities for teenagers as well as for singles over fifty, for the married as well as for the divorced, or for people interested in baking and sewing, as well as those interested in digital technology. As we have seen, all ministries are divided into seven areas. Here are the ministries in service, peace, and justice: assist-a-family, clothing, food pantry, habitat, Hispanic ministry, homelessness, individual needs, care for creation, peace and justice, respect for life, social justice network, St. Joseph's home (for the elderly), St. Michael (a sister parish), and wings (for women in need). The other six areas include as many or even more ministries, each with a few or many teams of volunteers. These ministries are clearly those of a church-type parish.

All groups are called communities, which may be confusing for outsiders. Of special interest—and a major characteristic of St. Mary's church—are the small Christian communities, or SCCs, as they are commonly called here. There are about eighty such SCCs involving about a thousand people, but these are only one of the many ministries listed as "Outreach Communities." Among the latter we find bookstore; Internet; radio and TV; youth audio; annulment support; baptismal preparation of parents; Bible-study groups; Center for Inner Peace and Hope; Wednesday community; foundations; greeters and ushers; inactive Catholics; mini-retreats; multicultural ministry; neighborhood ministry; parish missions; Pathways (for singles); Footsteps (RCIA); Rising from Divorce; sewing ministry; Simbang Gabi (Filipino ministry); SPREAD; welcoming; and young adult ministry. All of these are included in the area of adult evangelization and catechesis, which contains many more ministries.

There are many ways to become involved in ministry. Although members feel a general push to become involved, they also feel encouragement to find what suits them best. In a "church" that caters to all, not just the elite, there have to be low-level entries. Carol did not attend a Catholic school, and she dropped out of church in college. After her daughter was born, "The realization that she needed some kind of religious education brought me back." At first, she just accompanied her mother at the monthly pancake breakfast and occasionally helped her serve coffee and cookies at the hospitality committee. At one point, the Knights of Columbus advertised the creation of the "Ladies Auxiliary" in the parish bulletin. This was her turning point: "When I grew up, my young career was in the restaurant business. I told the Knights that I would join if they let me flip pancakes at the pancake breakfast. So I became the pancake queen. That was the start of it. It just snowballed from there." At the time of the interview, Carol was the vice president of the Ladies Auxiliary, a long way from being the self-proclaimed pancake queen.

There are many humble ways to become involved, because there are many needs. Every Sunday night, about three hundred volunteers divide into teams to help shelter the homeless in the parish gym once a week. No special knowledge is needed to set up the hundred or so beds and serve the food to the homeless. There are fifteen hospitality teams to bake cookies and serve them with coffee after Mass. Baking fans are welcome, and their involvement may, as Carol put it, snowball from there.

Education is another entry into ministry. Many Wednesdays throughout the year feature public lectures by well-known authors in a series known as "Community on Wednesday." The speakers are sometimes nationally known personalities (like Andrew Greeley and Paul Lakeland) that even wealthy Catholic colleges cannot easily attract. The topics are usually related to the role of the laity, post-Vatican II theology, or social justice. As no registration is required, one may select the lectures of one's choice.

Bible studies are also a common entry into the Catholic subculture. There are popular courses like "For Women, By Women, About Women," offered both in the morning and the evening; general introductory courses about the Bible; and the study of the great passages of the Bible, as well as in-depth Bible studies (e.g., of the beatitudes, the historical Jesus, or a single book of the Bible). About 350 people are registered for these courses. Weekend workshops center on the discovery of one's talents and the matching of these talents with the needs of the parish. Finally, a two-year cycle of adult Catholic education courses is open to all, as well as an academic program of courses given locally that lead to a master's degree in ministry. Not least, there are courses and learning opportunity in spirituality—for example, parish retreats, monthly spirituality meetings, and professional spiritual guidance (known as companioning).

Implicit moral communities offer another entrance into ministry. For a moral community to become a Christian community, a transformation is necessary; thus parents with children attending religious education must come to see one another as co-workers in Christ rather than just Christian parents with kids in CCD. In the religious education program, called Gathered at Table, parents meet for an hour of instruction during the first week of the month while the children attend classes of five to ten students. The following week, the parents meet again during the children's classes, this time for informal interaction among themselves. The third week, the parents join the children in common activities involving both the parents and the children (e.g., making a manger for Christmas or a poster and pictures for the wall at other times). There will be some teaching (Gospel stories about the manger or the posters), praying, singing, and working together as a family. Everybody learns and teaches, and the whole family grows in faith together. Two or three families may interact and work together, so that when the parents meet informally again two weeks later, they may have a lot to tell one another. This process may go on for years, from first to sixth grade. As time passes, both the family units and the parents as a group develop into *communitas*, spiritual communities rather than interest groups. Another option for parents is home teaching, or Home Faith. Six enrichment sessions during the year help both parents and children learn cooperation in their respective roles of teacher and listener at grade level. The parents do the home teaching the rest of the year. They are also encouraged to join the family activities of Gathered at Table on the third Sunday of every month. This option intensifies the parent-child interaction while opening up the family unit to group activities once a month. It is likely that these parents will develop a strong bond with both their children and fellow Christian parents.

Engaged couples are dyads that may only have dreams in common, being self-centered to the point of obliviousness of others. At St. Mary's, marriage preparation begins and ends as a group activity (and, hopefully, as a Christian community activity). The first session is an orientation ending with a blessing, followed by a dinner together. About halfway through the program, the couples are invited to the steps of the altar in front of the Sunday assembly to publicly state, in the presence of family, friends, and guests, that yes, they are going to prepare seriously for the upcoming marriage to make it last forever. Toward the end of the program, there is a reconciliation service just for them. After a few readings and music, the couples go into separate spaces, where they say to each other that they are sorry for whatever they are sorry about. Throughout the program are many opportunities for disagreement, conflict, and unkind words. Couples usually know each other's weaknesses as well as their own. They have known for months that they will be coming to this reconciliation, and for weeks, they have prepared for it, so it is not a frightening experience. They talk to each other, forgive each other, and perform some ritual of cleansing and forgiveness. They may wash each other's hands, or, during Lent, they may use ashes and wipe the ashes off each other. This emotional encounter is followed by a little celebration, like wine and cheese. This communal experience, although not exactly a community activity, will not be easily forgotten. Over five or six weeks of marriage prep, three or four couples meet in the home of their sponsors to discuss the basic issues of marriage, talking among themselves and between couples, listening as much to themselves as they do to their sponsors. After all, the sponsors are mainly facilitators. The art of listening is more difficult to learn than the art of speaking. The engaged couples must learn to listen to one another, to their sponsors, and to the wider church, thus creating a community of memory that is as real as a physical community. When it is all over, the evaluations suggest that the program has indeed created a community of memory that will last for years. We all remember people in special circumstances that we will never forget, and that memory creates for us a spiritual community of minds. Happy are those who thus remember their marriage preparation!

Funerals are another opportunity to create communities of memory. Death brings families together as temporary moral communities, but these may become lasting communities of memory. At St. Mary's, the female pastoral associate in charge of bereavement meets with the grieving family to offer moral support and arrange for the funeral liturgy, inviting them to select the readings, songs, and music. Volunteers in the bereavement ministry will provide food and take care of the setup before and after the funeral. The prayer service at the funeral parlor may be taken care of by other volunteers. After the funeral Mass, the celebrant will accompany the family to the cemetery, but if he cannot, someone from the parish will. The day of the funeral, parishioners prepare salads or desserts to be taken for the funeral luncheon. While death and grief often create disruption in the everyday routine, the help of trained volunteers can smooth the process and make everyone feel comfortable under these trying circumstances. Funerals only last hours, but they often leave indelible memories, especially the memory of togetherness and comfort, and the memory of a *communitas* in which social ranks are erased in favor of a spiritual community of equals.

3. Christian communities as ecclesiolas.

St. Mary's is a community of communities, but it is not held together by a conservative-versus-liberal ideology. Its ideological diversity is shown symbolically in the topography of the church compound: on the right side there is a chapel with Eucharistic adoration, and on the left an office for social justice; the left and right are not ideological either, since from the opposite direction, the left becomes the right and the right the left. There is a rosary society that meets weekly, a charismatic group praying in tongues as in any Pentecostal church, and a centering prayer group, all of which are small. The creation of new ministries is entrusted to the imagination of the parishioners. Thus one member of the Ladies Auxiliary started a burial service for infants abandoned in morgues, sometimes for years; this service was quickly adopted by her group. Several parishioners took courses at a specialized institute to become certified spiritual directors; they now operate in the parish as "spiritual companions." One of them started a new program called Spiritual Journey that was successful from its inception. On one or two evenings per month, people meet to pray and read Scripture together, then talk about their spiritual journeys for half an hour in groups of two, a very uncommon practice that was warmly received. The various ministries of care depend on the creativity and generosity of the members, as their ministry is "one of supportive listening, presence, prayer, and sacrament ... when the path [of those ministered to] is difficult or even obstructed." On the more mundane side, there is the wedding rehearsal ministry and the coffee and cookies after Mass.

What holds these ministries together? It is not ideology, but rather a ministerial structure of concentric circles. A good example is that of family ministries. There is a men's ministry; women's Bible-study groups; the Knights of Columbus for men and the Ladies Auxiliary for women; marriage preparation with sponsoring couples; various ministries for the married—namely, the Honeymooners, the Couples' Night Out, marriage workshops, Evening of Romance, Marriage Encounters, and Retrouvailles retreats; the moms' groups; religious education in Gathered at Table and Home Faith; the Spirit Camp (a summer Bible camp for about 350 children); two to four years of teen ministry in high school, teen Masses, and various teen retreats; and finally, a ministry for singles in their twenties and thirties, a ministry for college students, and a group for singles over fifty. What holds these groups together is first of all the focus of their particular group (e.g., singlehood or the children's religious education), but also many other ministries to which the members may belong. Thus the thousand members of the Small Christian Communities may also be involved in Gathered at Table or Home Faith with their children; in social justice or ministry to the poor, the sick, or the bereaved; or more simply, in baking or wedding rehearsals. When parishioners get involved, they progressively join more than one ministry. We have seen above that all the parish ministries are organized into ever-wider concentric circles: the ministries are divided into seven areas; a representative from each ministry participates in the Leadership Committee; a representative from each area is nominated to the Pastoral Council; all parishioners are invited to all meetings; any individual can make a proposal at the Pastoral Council; and Father Frank is available at all levels.

St. Mary's great achievement is these small Christian communities (SCCs), which exist in a variety of formats. Some groups only meet for Advent or Lent, often used as a trial involvement by newcomers. Others will discuss a book, often one of national significance like Jimmy Carter's *Our Endangered Values: America's Moral Crisis*, or *Jesus of Nazareth* by Pope Benedict XVI. These discussion groups, too, may only be temporary. Two or three times a year (e.g., at the beginning of Lent or Advent) is a recruiting drive by Father Frank after his homily. Everyone is invited to fill out a card indicating their preferences: whether it is preferable to meet in the morning or evening or only on specific days of the week; whether it is desirable to meet in a group for singles, or couples, or single moms, or parents, or young adults, or men or women, or widows or widowers; which five to ten book discussion groups might be appealing; and which prayer groups are preferred. Based on these data, new members are added to existing SCCs—some of which have been existence for over a decade (one up to twenty years!)—or new SCCs are created.

The SCCs are modeled after the group of the twelve apostles around Jesus. Likewise, they meet in small groups of three or four couples around a facilitator. According to a member whose group has been active for thirteen years, "It's almost like going back in time to the way the church started, people meeting in homes, and those gatherings became the basic cells of the church." The four major dimensions are prayer, Scripture, faith sharing, and social justice, but each group will tailor these goals to its own needs. The beginning of the one-and-a-half- to two-hour session may be taken up by small talk about family, work, the parish, or religious events of the previous week, followed (or preceded) by a short prayer. Then come the Bible readings of the forthcoming Sunday, each one by a different member, followed by comments and reactions. Most SCCs are lectionary based, offering reflections on the readings of the forthcoming Sunday. There is a video of commentaries on the Gospel readings recorded by Father Frank. This DVD is available to all groups and is widely appreciated for the information provided, including the suggested parameters for the discussion.

Faith sharing happens naturally, in the form of one's reaction to the readings, or "What's going on in *your* life?" According to a member, "Sharing is quite important, because it gives me an insight into another person's views. Also, it brings me closer to people within that community. I don't think it's a natural occurrence in other parishes. As a matter of fact, I don't remember anything like that elsewhere." Indeed, many Catholics are closet Catholics: they do not easily let others know about their private spiritual lives. Some communities may become narcissistic, centered too much on therapeutics. Involvement in social justice will prevent this self-centeredness. There are always discussion questions on Father Frank's video about social involvement in the parish or the wider world. In some groups, there may be a time for prayer petitions for family members, friends, and acquaintances. The evening ends with a short prayer. Refreshments may be provided at the beginning or the end. Satisfaction with the evening will determine whether people will come back; nearly all of them do, sometimes for years.

To be successful, *ecclesiolas* must be integrated into the life of the parish or church in which they develop. At St. Mary's, the SCCs and the other Christian groups are undoubtedly well integrated into the fabric of the parish. But are they independent enough to be able to withstand adverse local circumstances? What will happen if the new pastor to be nominated in 2009 will be indifferent or even hostile to the existing *ecclesiolas*? The ministries that do not depend on the parish financially or administratively are likely to survive—more particularly the Knights of Columbus, the Christian Family Movement, and the SCCs.

The Knights of Columbus are likely to survive because they are a national organization with local chapters. Members have their own national goals and religious practices of monthly meetings, Marian devotion, and retreats. They have their own fund drives (e.g., to support the mentally disabled) nationally and locally. Each council is headed by a Grand Knight, who defines the priorities for the year. The Knights at St. Mary's have recruited 170 members since their inception ten years ago. Their goal here is mainly to support the parish materially, socially, and spiritually. One of their most visible activities here is "the café," a big breakfast the last Sunday of every month to foster parish communication and unity, which feeds about 500 parishioners. According to the chancellor of the local Knights, "We try to put people together at tables; if they come in as a large group and want to have breakfast together, that's fine. If a family comes in alone, we try to put them at a table with another family, so that they can start to meet other people and build community. So building community has been one of the big missions of the Knights of Columbus." They also sponsor the parish picnic and the food service at the special RCIA meetings. Besides their monthly meetings, they have their own SCCs, and many are involved in the various ministries of the parish. In short, they give to the parish much more than they receive from it. They are a good example of an independent *ecclesiola* actively involved in its environment.

The Christian Family Movement (CFM) was most popular in the 1960s and '70s. It is more a movement or network than an organization, relying more on local initiative than on national directives and structures. One characteristic is that members invite and involve children, not just parents, at their meetings. Joan did not come from a very religious family, and she did not attend a Catholic school. When she started attending an SCC at St. Mary's, she did not like that children were not invited. Indeed, it is hard to imagine what children can do in a couples' meeting discussing adult issues. So she initiated a CFM group of her own. The meetings were first held in the homes, but this practice quickly became impractical. As the group grew—up to 40 families now with many more children—everything had to be reinvented. Now they first meet briefly in church and next split into small groups. They tend to have three major priorities. First, community building: each time they split into groups, they gather with different families in order to keep in touch with all of them; they have an annual picnic, an annual camping trip, a monthly ladies' night out, a men's night out, and a couples' night out, on a rotating basis. Second, social outreach: they plan activities they can do with their kids, and each month brings something different, such as yard work and gardening for a local pregnancy center, or visiting nursing homes, or packaging boxes for soldiers and Marines. Third, the religious education of their children: many would do Home Faith, teaching their own children, but as the group became larger and the number of children increased, they started their own classes, consisting of a short lecture followed by small group instruction according to age. CFM is a community of its own, a community of parents together with their children, and a community of children taking classes together. CFM even has its own liturgies. "We also do our own First Communion every year. They involve the whole family. Siblings of the first communicant are the readers, they're the gift bearers, they're the ushers, they're the greeters—they're everything. There's a lot of family involvement in celebrating this child's special day. There's a beautiful little ritual that we always do: the parents of the First Communion kids kneel down in front of their First Communion child, and the First Communion child blesses the parents. It's really incredible. It's one of the nicest Masses I've ever seen."

CFM is a good example of a dependent/independent *ecclesiola*, making no demands on the parish but making many contributions; Joan is actually now in charge of all family ministries at St. Mary's.

The SCCs are well organized. The SCC office keeps track of all groups and members. There is a Steering Committee of six core members who plan and direct the movement. These core members keep in touch with the facilitators of the SCCs, offering help and advice, DVDs and brochures, and information about coming events. It is also the task of the Steering Committee to organize three major events: a spring dinner free of charge for all, an outdoors Mass followed by a potluck dinner in the summer to foster a sense of community, and an SCC institute for reflection and resourcement. This institute may also offer workshops about the four dimensions of SCC meetings: faith sharing ("God sightings"), Scripture interpretation ("breaking open the Word"), social justice, and evangelization. Although the Steering Committee meets with Father Frank once a month, most of the work is done by its core members without him. According to the parish SCC leader, "The one thing you really need a pastor for is to do the recruiting from the altar. He has to give a very strong pitch so that people join SCCs. When laypeople have done that, it's been hard to increase the membership." Indeed, many parishes that started small Christian communities with the help of RENEW have seen their numbers dwindle for lack of support from the parish priest. "Another way we recruit is encouraging members to evangelize a new person into their group. I would even recommend that much stronger," said this leader.

In summary, "SCC will survive, and will survive strongly because there are so many committed people, and it's so enriching for the members." For the time being, the strongest asset of the SCC is the commitment and enthusiasm of the members: it's so enriching! The SCCs are local creations that are self-sustaining, not needing affiliation with a national organization. For the time being, they depend on the pastor for recruitment and thus do not need grassroots evangelization on their own. What will the future bring? Will they continue to grow? Or, after a high-level plateau, will they begin an inevitable decline?

Conclusion: Renewal and Decline

Few parishes in the United States are as vibrant in their celebrations, as dynamic in their ministries, as Gospel-centered in their spirituality, and as democratic in their governance as St. Mary's, which can be seen as a model for many. Yet St. Mary's is not growing. It is even declining.

From 2002 to 2008, the Sunday collections have remained stable, but adjusting for inflation, they decreased by 15 percent while the number of registered families increased. St. Mary's is located in a wealthy suburb of about 2,300 households, according to the 2000 census. The average household size was 2.91, and the average family size was 3.12. That year, the median income per family was $155,000, and today it is likely to be about $200,000. At St. Mary's, the 2008 average Sunday contribution was $14.50 per person per week (an average weekly collection of $42,500 for an average weekly Mass attendance of 2,940 parishioners), or $2,260 per year for a family of three. This yearly contribution represents about 1 percent of an average family's income. This does not compare favorably with the Bayville community church, where the majority of the members tithe. Now according to the National Parish Inventory conducted by CARA in 2001, Catholic households donated an average of $438 to their parish in the Sunday collection, or $167.80 per individual per year (about $3.00 per Sunday)—which represents 1.04 percent of the median household income for American households in the entire United States. Hence, the financial contributions at St. Mary's are no better than the national average for Catholics.[161]

Sunday church attendance hovers around 24 percent. In such a vibrant parish, one would expect a higher attendance. The parish keeps very accurate records of its registered families and Sunday attendance each week; hence, the low attendance cannot be imputed to inaccurate information. One cannot impute, either, the quality of the services, which are among the best. It seems, rather, that the missing 75 percent are not interested in the kind of Sunday service offered here or elsewhere. This raises the question of the ministry to the unchurched, which in the Catholic Church seems inadequate or nonexistent.

Attendance is also declining. Since 2002 the church has lost about 500 regular Sunday attenders, while the number of registered families has increased from about 3,000 in 1995 to 3,800 in 2008. It is true that most Catholic parishes are experiencing attendance decline, but also St. Mary's? This was an unexpected finding that only came at the end of this research.

Another indicator of decline is the low number of confirmations, which are about 20–25 percent lower than the number of First Communions. Parents may select to have their children confirmed in another parish, presumably because the requirements are lower, or drop out altogether. In either case, there seems to be a flight from excellence, a flight from high demands. It is doubtful that higher demands will attract them. Are there Christians out there who are satisfied with minimum standards?

The most common factor of church growth is the addition of new members through evangelization. St. Mary's attracts about a dozen converts per year through RCIA, which is insignificant. This leads us to wonder about the emphasis on evangelization in the various ministries. One of the seven areas is evangelization outreach; it includes the following ministries: annulment support, baptism hospitality, baptism prep, Bible study, bookstore, Christian Family Movement (CFM), Wednesday community, creative sewing, Foundations, Landings (for returning Catholics), multicultural ministry, neighborhood ministry, Pathways (for older singles), RCIA/Footsteps, Rising from Divorce, small Christian communities, welcoming, TV and radio, and the most recent addition, greeter ministry. These may be seen as outreach ministries in the broadest sense, but they are not evangelization as the term is/was commonly used. There is little or no interest in foreign missions, although a missionary may occasionally celebrate the Sunday Mass and ask for a second collection. The Financial Report of 2008 mentions $3,500 given at a missions appeal, as opposed to $56,000 at the bishop's appeal; missions are clearly not a priority.

Two ministries are specifically designed for evangelization: one to cater to returning Catholics and the other to evangelize in the parish neighborhoods. According to the person in charge of Landings, "Our job is to welcome back returning Catholics, to make them feel at home again, and to provide an environment over the course of several months, where they feel they can get reconnected. We know they're out there. I've seen statistics that say that for every person sitting at Mass in a Catholic Church, there may be as many as ten who were born Catholic who are not sitting there. The big challenge that we have is finding them." The problem is that they are not coming; for the time being, Landings is a ministry that has a leader and no followers, and it has been so for several years.

The neighborhood ministry is a special creation of St. Mary's. The parish is divided geographically into twenty miniparishes headed by coordinators, and each is divided again into ten to twenty neighborhoods, each with its own representative. The representatives and coordinators update vital statistics about all parishioners each year, after which they draw an updated map of the parish; thus they are working with accurate statistics. The evangelization effort is twofold: informative and evangelical. It is the job of representatives to keep their neighborhoods (especially the newcomers) informed about upcoming events at the parish. They are also encouraged to organize neighborhood Masses and Station of the Cross followed by a fish-fry dinner. "Last year we were very successful, with probably 1,500 to 1,700 people total," according to the parish coordinator.

How does it work? Here is the testimony of a coordinator of a miniparish of about 250 families, who is also the local representative of a neighborhood of fifteen families living within three blocks of his house. "I've walked to all of those houses, and I've talked to each of them and got acquainted. I just wanted to touch base. No particular purpose. Usually you want to have some reason. When we started out—and we haven't been doing it so much lately—we would deliver something, like an Advent packet, or a little calendar, or some literature. One year we had one prayer for each day of Advent, most of them written by members of the parish. It was a difficult thing to put together, which is probably why they didn't do it again. … The neighborhood concept, I'm one of the earliest ones to buy into it, but it really has never taken off very much. It's very difficult. We're still active, and we still do things, but it hasn't taken off to the point where I thought it might." Among other issues, the problem seems to lie in the strategy: to hand out a calendar or a book of prayers is not enough to convert or evangelize anybody. Too much was expected from the geographical mapping of the parish without enough evangelical salesmanship.

Here is a more general assessment. "The SCCs support each other and provide for their own spiritual growth. I have yet to see more than a handful that reach out to the rest of the parish or their local community. They tend to be islands in the sea. There has been a reduction in outreach, in mission. Their mission is self-centered, as it is in all the parishes in the Catholic system. ... Things are now the traditional way of before Vatican II." This assessment is overly pessimistic, but to what extent is it correct about evangelization in the Catholic Church today?

The big push for evangelization came with John Paul II's "new evangelization." Here is a summary from the numerous writings and speeches of the late pontiff on the topic: "In its writings about evangelization, the Church means most fundamentally the proclamation of the basic Christian message: salvation through Jesus Christ," because, according to John Paul II, "evangelization cannot be new in its content since its very theme is always the one gospel given in Jesus Christ." What is new is not the content but the emphasis; again quoting the pope, "Evangelization can be new in its ardor, methods and expression."[162] Throughout the world, all dioceses now have an office of new evangelization. A look at their web pages reveals that the content of the new evangelization is essentially adult education, sacramental instruction, and spiritual retreats. So it is at St. Mary's. I have given above a list of the ministries associated with evangelization outreach; they range from annulment support to greeter ministry. The new evangelization is basically a re-evangelization plan for inactive Catholics—that is, an invitation to return to the sacraments for those who have abandoned them. Moreover, the baptismal spirituality of Christian transformation, rather than rite of passage (so highly praised in this chapter), only applies to adult baptisms that are very few and far between; for the vast majority of Catholics, maybe 99 percent, infant baptism remains the rule, and with it the Tridentine theology of washing away original sin to avoid eternal damnation. In many parishes, the official rhetoric is one of Christian initiation, but the practice often remains one of automatic rituals. Does this constitute a return to pre-Vatican II? Yes, at least in part.

Is the rhetoric of the new evangelization attractive to the inactive Catholics (60–70 percent of Catholics) who do not attend church on a weekly basis? Apparently not. For the generations past, guilt and the fear of hell were enough to drive inactive Catholics back into the fold. Instead of this negative push characteristic of the past, we now have the positive pull of the mass media and celebrity culture to consumerism, at times to the point of addiction. This considered, any new evangelization would have to begin with a sociological analysis of what holds people back in order to devise pastoral ways to help them at their own level. We may now realize that, with all its vibrancy, St. Mary's is a model for parish life, but not for church growth. Its vibrant liturgy and the dynamism of its ministries generate lots of emotional and spiritual energy, but this energy is directed *ad intra*, not *ad extra*, as it is in the rest of the church. Hence, we have next to look outside the church for renewal models.

CHAPTER 6

~

PLANNED RENEWAL

I n this chapter, I want to discuss the various programs created to bring renewal and spiritual growth to parishes and churches. I will consider first the programs supported by the United States Conference of Catholic Bishops and next the various Protestant and Catholic proposals.

How effective are these programs? Rather than just look at their success rates, which may be difficult to interpret, I will analyze them in light of the factors of decline outlined in chapters 2 and 3, the three factors of spiritual decline that apply to all American churches, and the three factors that pertain specifically to Catholicism. A brief review may be useful.

1. Evaluation Criteria for Renewal Programs

1. The nontransmission of values and the disaffection of the young are pressing issues. In 1955 about 75 percent of Catholics of ages 8 to 25 attended church regularly, at the same rate as the other age groups of the Catholic population, but only 35 percent did so thirty years later, at about the same rate as their Protestant counterparts (as shown in the graph 1 of chapter 1, page 15). Today their attendance rate is about 15 percent—that is, half of thirty years ago. Analyzing data from the 1960s, Wuthnow showed in 1976 that the decline was statistically explained by involvement in the counterculture.[163] The flower culture has faded away, but not the

youth subculture into which the young have retreated. The technology of mass culture (DVDs, digital music players, cell phones, social media, and so on) has increasingly made that subculture more pervasive and alienated from religion. Any renewal program should address this pressing issue.

2. Another factor of decline affecting most American churches is confusion about the very nature of religion, which centers not on self-gratification and individualism, but spiritual growth and individuality. The political ideology of equality and equal rights—the very heart of democracy as we understand it—is not the essence of religion, although authoritarian religions may gain from greater equality and equal rights. More generally speaking, religion should not be an ideology, whether liberal or conservative. Since Vatican II (which happened at the time of the counterculture), Catholics have invested much of their energies into either a liberal program of institutional reform that did not materialize or into a reactionary return to the past. This ideological battle often found (or finds) the hierarchy on one side and the laity on the other, or worse, finds Rome in opposition with the rest of the Western church. Any reform must be spiritual, rather than ideological, and heal the gap between conservatives and liberals and between the teaching church and the listening church.

3. At the heart of the decline is the relationship between the churches and the world, which sociologists analyze in terms of "church" versus "sect"; churches tend to compromise with the world, and sects to retreat from it. The Christian ideal is to be in the world but not of the world. The opposition between church and sect may at times be simplistic, as there is an obvious overlap between the two. Yet the prevalence and insidious effect of consumerism cannot be ignored. As an addiction rather than wise consumption, consumerism has created two world problems of inordinate proportion: a health problem associated with being overweight, which affects two-thirds of Americans; and today's financial and economic crisis, which results in unemployment and financial hardship. What propels consumption is advertising, a form of information that should allow customers to make wise choices. But when people submit themselves, on

average, to 4 hours of television a day for 365 days (or 2 months per year at 8 hours a day and 5 days per week), the root of consumerism is mass media addiction—that is, a lifestyle that has lost control over its environment. What happened to Christian asceticism? Even that word has become obsolete, if not unknown. Any reform must teach in one way or another that Christians are in the world but not of the world.

Spiritual growth can be discussed in light of Maslow's pyramid of needs, because it exemplifies the dynamics of self-transcendence: lower-level needs must be satisfied before a higher level can be achieved. Much insight into self-development has been gained since 1943, when Maslow proposed his theory of human motivation, yet the overall structure remains valid, particularly because of its simplicity. I will present it in the light of subsequent developments, especially Alderfer's simplification (which reduces it to three levels), Erikson's theory of human development,[164] and Fowler's stages of faith.[165]

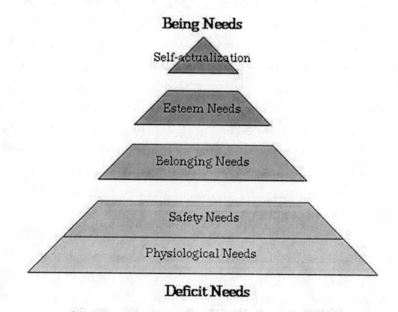

http://age-of-the-sage.org/psychology/maslow_pyramid.html

At the lower level are the physical and psychological survival needs. In 2007, 12.5 percent of Americans (37.3 million people) and 18 percent of children under 18 lived in poverty, including 8.2 percent of non-Hispanic whites and 24.5 percent of blacks.[166] Poverty has increased, not decreased, since the year 2000, and so did hunger. In 2007, 36.2 million people lived in food insecurity. Churches and individuals contribute considerable amounts of time and money to alleviate poverty, and the food pantries are stretched to their limits. Financial poverty is often a multidimensional symptom associated with the lack of skills, poor health, lack of education, depression, and so on. The question, then, is whether the poor only need food and shelter, or also need support for spiritual growth. The question is whether charity is enough—is spiritual help also needed? (Catholic charities usually only offer material support; evangelical charities often include spiritual help.)

This question is more pressing when it comes to security needs. Indeed, mental health requires the security of steady food, shelter, income, and physical health, especially in insecure situations. Addiction creates its own form of insecurity. At the end of 2007, the USA household debt as a percentage of annual disposable personal income was 142 percent versus 101 percent in 1999. The household debt grew from $705 billion in 1974 to $14.5 trillion at the end of 2008. There are real reasons to feel insecure today, even with a steady job and good health. About 60 percent of high-school teens report that drugs are used or sold at their schools, making the teens themselves three times more likely to use them.[167] Today, half of all college students reportedly binge drink and/or use illegal drugs. Nearly one in four meets the medical criteria for substance abuse or dependency. Most rates are up since 1993.[168] Again, is charity enough? We will further examine the answer to this question shortly.

The middle level of the pyramid refers to the emotional needs of belonging to a group in which one finds acceptance and love. The physiological and security needs of the child are usually met in the family, but at adolescence, one increasingly wants friends and close relationships in school, and later at work, and, for some, in church. Here the problem is not that one cannot find them; it is rather that the new environment may be so gratifying that it becomes a prison or ghetto. Infatuated lovers and peer groups are well-known examples of small ghettos. Growth comes to an end, and complacency sets in; self-transcendence is edged out by a gratifying routine. To submit to the requirements of one's group in order to be accepted corresponds to stage three in Fowler's scheme of faith development. Most parishioners operate at this level, according to Fowler: they submit and obey; they fulfill all the requirements of their church and say "I have made all my sacraments." They can be called cultural Christians, found in all churches, found among practicing as well as nonpracticing believers. There are cultural priests, cultural bishops, cultural atheists, cultural students, and cultural professors: they conform to what is expected of them. Church renewal should encourage both docility toward and independence from authority figures. This is a nearly impossible balance, and it is usually tilted toward submission.

Finally, at the highest level of the pyramid is self-actualization based on values transcending rationality—values like self-giving, inner peace, harmony, truth, beauty, and so on. This level corresponds to stages 5 and 6 in Fowler. This is the level at which church reform and personal growth should aim, while most people are stuck at lower levels. Any proposal must endeavor to *move people up* to a higher level, recognizing the various stages of human development.

There are factors of decline specific to the Catholic Church. In chapter 3, I have outlined three main obstacles to Catholic faith *for outsiders.* Insiders may disagree; these factors may be foreign to them. Outsiders perceive the church as a power structure, the sacraments as unnecessary, and Catholic morality as confusing. Let me review these points briefly.

4. Catholicism as a *church* is an enterprise of communal salvation, not a *sect* or *ecclesiola* where individuals pursue their own religious quest. As an enterprise, it is like any business: it will use all reasonable means available—including power and wealth—to achieve its end, which is salvation. Neoscholasticism defined the church as a "perfect society" —that is, a society that has (or must have) all means toward its end, which in the nineteenth and early twentieth centuries included papal sovereignty over the Papal States. Such a view is difficult to accept for those not raised in this mainly clerical Catholic subculture. The theory of the church as perfect

society has been abandoned, but not rejected, by Vatican II, but its spirit lingers on. Moreover, as an enterprise of communal salvation, the Church (which here means the hierarchy) feels responsible for the masses; hence, it will endeavor to impose objectively correct behavior, even at times against people's will. Until Vatican II, the Catholic Church considered itself as the objective realization of the kingdom of God, and its doctrine the absolute truth of God, valid for all times and all cultures. This subculture perdures somewhat. For example, in the United States, the hierarchy works for the abolition of abortion and even wishes for the abolition of divorce, if it is possible. Since the abortion and divorce rates of Catholics are not very different from those of non-Catholics, it may seem to outsiders that the church (i.e., its hierarchy) is trying to impose by law a behavior that its members do not follow by choice. The antiabortion campaign remained at the top of the bishops' agenda in the 2008 election year. It is divisive to the extent that it encourages a dualistic vision of the church and society: pro-life versus pro-choice, religious conservatism versus secular liberalism, Catholic truth versus non-Catholic error, obedience to the church versus Protestant individualism, and emphasis on church rather than Jesus Christ—or, more succinctly, "us" versus "them." If this is how the church tends to be viewed by the outsiders—as it has been my thesis—what changes must renewal programs instigate in order to heal these dualisms?

5. One can look at morality as either a theory or a practice. As a theory, morality belongs to philosophy and moral theology; as a practice, it belongs to the people who practice it. From a sociological perspective, all societies have some form of morality. At the most fundamental level, what differentiates humans from animals is morality, rather than just intelligence—conscience rather than IQ. There are instances of killing, infanticide, and other forms of violence in the animal kingdom, among animals with and without much intelligence. Among humans, a value judgment is always associated with these behaviors. Every society has its own moral code defining what is acceptable behavior and what is not. While philosophy reflects on difficult moral issues at the theoretical level, concrete societies inculcate appropriate behavior in everyday life through

socialization. Every society is a moral society; every society has a moral culture defining proper eating and drinking behavior, appropriate dress, acceptable sexual behavior, professionalism, and so on. Thus those born into the pre-Vatican II Catholic moral culture knew what to eat on Fridays, on weekdays, on Sundays, on ordinary days, during Advent, and during Lent. They knew how to spend the Sunday morning and how to enjoy leisure on Sunday afternoon. They knew what behavior was appropriate in both work and leisure, and both were seen as means of sanctification. They were told about modesty in dress and self-control in all forms

> **Does Church Attendance Create a Catholic Moral Culture?**
> "My mom has always been very active in the church, giving time and talent. She was a gifted musician, [a] professional singer and composer, and the church made great use of her talents. What did she gain from all that? She was a good person, but so is my dad, who seldom went to church. They put me in a Catholic school. After a career teaching in public schools, I don't see much of a difference between Catholic and public schools. What did I gain from all this? I don't know, but I have little use of going to church. In fact, I don't, and seldom have."
> —Interview

of consumption. They were told to pray every day, morning and evening, and most did. In short, there *was* a Catholic moral culture, the way that today there is an Amish moral culture, a Baptist or an evangelical moral culture, or a Latino moral culture. But there seems to be no more non-Latino Catholic moral culture in the United States; very little differentiates non-Latino Catholics from non-Catholics in what they do, eat, drink, or consume; how they date, marry, and divorce; and how they die. In religious societies, the moral culture is imbedded in their spirituality and rituals, because a person's moral culture springs from his or her religiosity, not from the moral philosophy or moral theology of the elite.

Indeed there is a philosophical and theological Catholic moral culture (e.g., in books and Catholic universities), but the latter does not belong to the everyday life of ordinary people. The two strong points of Catholic moral theology, social justice and the official sexual morality, are not much related to people's everyday moral practices the way the pre-Vatican II moral culture was related to the spirituality and devotional life of the time.

We have come to the same conclusion as in chapter 3: one major factor of Catholic decline is the split between the teaching church and the listening church, but also between the listening practicing Catholics and the unchurched, who now constitute the majority. The unchurched often do not understand (or often disagree with) official Catholic moral teaching, and when they look at the everyday moral life of Catholics, they find it no different from that of non-Catholics. They see Catholic morality as a vacuum—but again, this is the outsiders' view. What can church renewal do to change this perception and the underlying reality?

6. In reference to sacraments, we can begin with a theological and sociological perspective that derives from the above: sacramentality belongs to the believers the same way morality belongs to the people of a given society. In the early church, each region had its own liturgical creations, with those of Jerusalem being different from those of Rome; today, those of the East differ from those of the West. Throughout the centuries, new religious orders and congregations brought forth new forms of spirituality and new ways of relating to God—that is, new forms of sacramentality. Today, Latin America still has its own form of popular piety, one that has often been viewed with suspicion by church authorities. In the pre-Vatican II church, the creativity of popular piety enriched the official liturgy through festive town processions, local pilgrimages, Christmas carols, and home altars. But today we have the same split about the sacraments as about morality—that is, an official morality and sacramentality from above, with little or no input from below. The romanization of the liturgy has made the faithful the object of liturgical reforms rather than its subject, leading to the withering away of popular piety.

As there is no human society without moral practices, there is hardly any religious culture without some form of sacramentality—that is, an implicit or explicit theory about and practice of relating to God through signs, nature, ritual, or sacred writs. Granted there is a negative (apophatic) way of relating to God, as in Buddhism, Islam, and iconoclastic forms of Christianity, but these are extremes. Most Christian churches seek the invisible through the visible (the kataphatic way).

An exclusive (as opposed to inclusive) definition of sacraments lists seven, but this number is theoretical rather than practical. Baptism and confirmation are usually conferred to children upon the request of the parents; marriage is usually celebrated only once, maybe twice, in a lifetime; ordination excludes women; the anointing of the sick is not for people in good health and will not happen before old age if one is not sick; the practice of reconciliation or penance is low, by all account. This leaves the Eucharistic celebration. To fully participate in and spiritually benefit from the Eucharistic celebration requires a level of spirituality that seems lacking in many Catholics, which explains why unchurched have little need for it. Many unchurched can be seen as pre-catechumens, and no form of sacramentality is available to them at their level.

An inclusive definition of sacraments (in the broadest sense) might begin with Jesus as the sacrament of God, and the church (i.e., the church as communion of saints and sinners, not just the hierarchy) as the sacrament of Jesus Christ. Next one could add Scripture, practically the primary sacrament of most Protestants. An inclusive definition would include not only the seven sacraments, but also practices like the traditional devotions to Mary and the saints. Next one might add the sacrament of daily life in which believers see God's hand, more often through painful rather than joyful experiences. This inclusive definition sees sacraments as forms of divine self-revelation; it does not weaken the practice of the traditional sacraments. On the contrary, it strengthens them, the way pre-Vatican II devotions strengthened sacramental practice.

In summary, one root cause of Catholic decline (and the concomitant growth of evangelical Protestantism) seems to come from the split between the upper and lower levels of the church. Vatican II was supposed to heal this wound by proclaiming the common priesthood of all Christians through baptism, and the organic unity of the people of God to which all make valuable contributions. This split makes people see the church as a bureaucracy, as a power structure that hides rather than illuminates the face of God (and the sex scandal did not help). This split often opposes the philosophical and theological morality of the educated to the practices of the masses, especially in the areas laypeople know best: namely, sex, family, work, and leisure activities. This split also often opposes the type of sacramentality inherited from the Council of Trent to the *lex orandi* of the masses. The unchurched do not "practice," but they still pray; there is a disjunction between their private prayer and the rubricized prayer of the liturgy. The pre-Vatican II church was probably more unequal and more authoritarian than the church today, but it suffered no such split, because the private devotions of the masses were also part of the public prayer of the church, as in the collective recitation of the rosary and the traditional devotions to Mary and the saints. It is a vibrant spirituality from both below and above, rather than new magisterial directives from above, that is needed. Let us now see what reform proposals have to offer.

2. Go and Make Disciples

In 1992 the Catholic Conference of American bishops adopted *Go and Make Disciples: A National Plan and Strategy for Catholic Evangelization in the United States.*[169] This long document can be summarized by its evangelization goals and strategies. The document outlines three major goals: make all Catholics share their faith, invite all people to listen, and promote values that will transform the nation (no. 46–56). Each goal lists various objectives, along with various strategies to achieve these objectives. There are 13 objectives and 57 strategies for goal I; 12 objectives and 63 strategies for goal II; and 7 objectives and 33 strategies for goal III, or a total of 32 objectives and

**The First Evening
at a Local Parish Mission**

It began with a hymn, followed by a prayer from a handout, read alternatively by people in the left and the right pews. Next came the sermon for half an hour, and then another prayer read from the special printout and a final hymn.

The sermon was about trusting God. It was a moral exhortation illustrated by many life experiences and quite a few Scripture quotations. It was not significantly different from secular moralism. Scripture was mainly quoted to justify the moral teaching; it was not implied that one has to read the Scripture oneself. The implicit message about prayer was the same: at no time was the audience invited to personally turn to God. It was always: "Here is a prayer I am going to read for you—no need to pray by yourself, and I won't give you any time for it."

Total time: a little more than an hour. In what sense is this a mission?

153 strategies. Most of these strategies are not new. Here are the strategies for objective 1 of goal I: "retreats; parish renewals; RENEW; Cursillo; involvement in the Charismatic movement; youth encounter weekends; marriage encounter; and other programs of renewal and conversion" (no. 91). This document casts a net too vast to catch many fish.

On its website, the committee on evangelization and catechesis of the USCCB lists ten programs that can be grouped into three categories: 1) Alpha for Catholics and CaFE (Catholic Faith Exploration); 2) Disciples in Mission, Envision, Follow Me, Parish Mission, the Parish Renewal Project, and Paulist Parish Based Evangelization; finally 3) RENEW and World Prayernet. The first two programs, Alpha for Catholics and café, were created in England; they are either unavailable or rarely found in the United States. The second group consists of parish missions of various length and intensity. In the third group, RENEW promotes small Christian communities, while Prayernet fosters individual prayer. I will briefly comment on the second and third group.

Parish missions, first popularized in Europe in the seventeenth century, became part of the apostolate of many religious congregations, especially the Eudist Fathers (the congregation of Jesus and Mary founded in 1643). In the United States, parish missions became part of the revivalist movement of the 1850s, and usually lasted eight to ten days. The sermons on topics like the last judgment, hell, repentance, forgiveness, and life everlasting were often highly emotional and often had dramatic effects. Today missions are preached mainly by the Paulist Fathers through the Paulist National Catholic Evangelization Association (PNCEA). They last a weekend rather than a week—that is, two or three evenings besides the Sunday homily. The evening talks (on Monday, Tuesday, and occasionally on Wednesday) last about an hour. They may be attended by 10 to 20 percent of the Sunday worshippers. They fail to reach 80 percent of the regular attenders and 100 percent of the nonattenders; in other words, they do not reach those who have abandoned religious practice. There are only a handful of Paulist priests to preach these missions for the whole of the United States; hence, their effect is limited.

Disciples in Mission and Envision are two long-term evangelization programs made available by the Paulist Fathers through the PNCEA. These self-administered plans use teaching and reflection materials of various kinds that must be purchased. Thus the Disciples in Mission parish kit for Lent contains a guidebook for small groups, a family activity booklet, bulletin inserts, a homily guide, prayer cards, novena cards, posters, lapel pins, and so on. The fruitful use of this material rests totally with the parish staff, as these programs are self-administered. As in distance learning through the mail or the Internet, these programs hold great promise, but as in distance learning, they require unusual dedication to begin and complete the program. A parish kit is like a textbook: all the work remains to be done.

In summary, the parish renewal programs consist of either directed parish missions of three or four evenings or self-administered guidelines that the parishes themselves have to follow. The two prayer programs are also to be run by the parishes themselves: Prayernet is a "campaign undertaken ecumenically through parishes and congregations to their members," while in the Discover Life in Christ Campaign, "parishes will invite their members to dedicate a certain amount of time to daily prayer."[170]

What images of church and society are implied in the programs outlined above? Is the implicit influence of the outside world on believers recognized? The traditional opposition between the teaching church and the listening church is still at work here: it is missionaries who come to preach parish missions, and it is the parish priests who must invite parishioners to participate in self-administered renewal programs. Parish lay ministers have no special role in these missions, as if they did not exist. The conciliar notion of "people of God" is used less and less; it is usually replaced by "the faithful,"

> "Non-growing churches focus on reenlisting inactive members. Growing churches focus on reaching receptive people."
> *The Purpose-Driven Church*, 183

which is more practical, as it clearly indicates who is to teach and who is to listen. Devotions are still alluded to, although their importance has waned over the years; the notion of *pietas* will be explained below. The importance of the outside world is not recognized, except indirectly in reference to nonpracticing Catholics.

Nonpracticing parishioners are often called "inactive Catholics." Following Fichter, this term is used instead of "dormant Catholics" prevalent in the past, but the implication is the same: inactive Catholics may come back as easily as one wakes up from sleep and becomes active again. The answer to a frequently asked question (FAQ) about inactive Catholics explains, "Almost every Catholic who goes to Mass regularly knows one or more inactive Catholics. The difference between the two is that inactive Catholics do not practice their faith." It may be true that "some inactive Catholics are more spiritually minded than those who go to Mass every Sunday. They believe, but do not belong." This may be true for seasonal attenders but for not for those who never attend church and often have not attended for years. For the latter, it is misleading to state that "They do not go to Mass as often, and are not involved in serving in parish ministries such as reading at Mass, teaching in the parish religious education program, or volunteering in parish support of the homeless."[171] This vision of inactive Catholics fails to recognize that the world has changed in the last fifty years. In the past, the parish teaching church— which consisted of several priests, catechists (usually priests), and Catholic school teachers (mostly priests, sisters and brothers)—had an overbearing influence on the listening church; Sunday Mass was considered mandatory, and about 70 to 80 percent complied. Today, the overbearing influence on most believers is the secular culture. In a 2005 survey, 76 percent of Catholics agreed that one can be a good Catholic without going to church every Sunday. While as many as 95 percent of Catholics of low commitment to the church believed so (mainly those inactive), half of the highly committed (that is, regular church attenders) also agreed.[172] Today it is the secular culture that shapes the religious beliefs and practices of most Catholics. Hence, it is a delusion to believe that a "Welcome Home liturgy once or twice a year" in which practicing parishioners invite inactive Catholics to come to church will bring the latter back to the sacraments.[173] If the faith trajectory of European "inactive" Catholics is of any indication, second-generation nonpracticing Catholics often fail to have their children baptized and instructed in the Christian faith before relinquishing the Catholic identity altogether. "Welcome Home liturgies" will not do.

3. RENEW and Small Christian Communities

The 1980s saw the proliferation of small Christian communities not only at St. Mary's, but throughout the United States. Lee estimates the number of SCCs in existence to be at least 37,000 at the time of his research in 1997–1998, with a membership of over a million people[174]. The majority of these groups were parish related, which means that one in twenty church attenders was part of an SCC. Three national networks coordinated these groups, Buena Vista, the National Forum for Small Christian Communities, and the National Alliance for Parishes Restructuring into Communities, each with publications, national meetings, and support systems. These communities exhibited great variety, with charismatic groups, Eucharist-centered communities, Hispanic-Latino groups, and various forms of parish small communities.

Small Christian communities came into existence on a grand scale in the archdiocese of Newark. The first such community of twenty people began in the fall of 1976. With the encouragement of Archbishop Gerety, over forty thousand people were involved in small groups in the three years of 1978 to 1980, fostering spiritual growth and renewal. The success proved contagious. as other dioceses invited members of RENEW, the organization to promote small communities, to spread the movement in their dioceses. For the millennium, RENEW created a three-year RENEW 2000 program in preparation for the Great Jubilee. Over 50 dioceses in the United States and Canada were involved. Since its inception, RENEW has reached over 25 million Americans in 13,000 parishes and 130 dioceses in 22 other countries.[175] It is probably accurate to state with D'Antonio that RENEW is the single most important factor in the creation of small Christian communities in parishes, and the success of RENEW was due, in part if not mainly, to its episcopal support. USCCB singles out RENEW as one of its tools for renewal on its website.

Two lessons learned at St. Mary's seem to apply to most SCCs. Firstly, *ecclesiolas* must be both independent from the controlling forces of centralization and in symbiosis with church leadership. St. Mary's lay leaders learned from experience that SCCs cannot thrive and expand without the strong support of the pastor, a discovery that has been repeated in many parishes. What is needed is a recruiting campaign once or twice a year on his part, not just moral support. Secondly, the greater the variety of SCCs, the more likely people will join. St. Mary's has SCCs for the married and the singles, for those with children and those without, for members of the Christian Family Movement, the Knights of Columbus, and the choir. There is a charismatic group as well as a rosary group. Moreover, the number of SCCs doubled when less-structured groups were created, like book discussion groups or other short-time groups for Lent or Advent. The faithful are not all of one type: those timid in their faith may only like to join a temporary book discussion group, with the option of joining again at a later time.

In 2002 the archdiocese of Westminster of London, England, launched small Christian communities with the help of RENEW. The program started with a three-year weekly training program, meeting for six weeks twice a year, during Lent and in the fall. About 170 parishes responded favorably to the archbishop's call, and about 20,000 people were involved in their parish SCCs. When the three years' training came to an end, participation dropped, as if parish priests had fulfilled their commitment. To this day, about 10,000 parishioners still meet in small communities, because the archbishop had established an office to foster small communities through the publication of group reflection pamphlets and the training of leaders. This experience illustrates the importance of both diocesan and parish leadership.[176]

Just before the millennium, a local US bishop instituted RENEW as his official diocesan program for the Jubilee Year. By the end of the year, a total of 1,146 groups involving 11,578 parishioners were functioning. At that time, 7 parishes had over 30 groups; 16 parishes between 20 and 30 groups; and 26 parishes had 10 to 20 SCCs. A total of 62 parishes were involved, with an average of 18 SCCs per parish, each of about 10 members. This is a phenomenal result, showing what can be achieved through strong clerical support in just one year. However, when I inquired in 2008 about the SCCs, I was given evasive answers, as if it were something of the past. Some SCCs remain in existence, but their pastors may be unaware of them—or oblivious to them—as if they are of no ecclesial significance. In 2001 a new bishop was appointed to this diocese, with new priorities and a new management style; as a consequence, SCCs became a program of the past. Apparently priests did little to keep it alive, and when parish priests do not personally recruit new members, SCCs slowly fade into nonexistence. This case illustrates the absence of continued leadership at both the diocesan and the parish levels. Moreover, it illustrates the weakness of the USCCB plan of renewal in its support of only one organization—RENEW—instead of a general concept: that of the church as community of communities with the possibility of a great variety of groups (charismatic, Latino, Eucharistic, devotional, intellectual, and so on).

What is the significance of SCCs in the landscape of the American church? From the above, one get the impression that SCCs are desirable parish organizations among others, nothing more. Today parishes need and usually have volunteer catechists, a choir, Eucharistic ministers, outreach activities, maybe a rosary society, and—why not?—a few Christian communities. The only concepts to bind these together are the traditional notions of *devotio* and *pietas*. Our notion of devotion is rooted in the *devotio moderna*, which, since the fourteenth century, has emphasized personal dedication to spirituality and the sacraments, and the conception of *pietas*, which, for the Romans, was dedication to the gods and the family, especially the parents. In Christianity, piety is dedication to God and the parents, as required in the first and fourth commandments ("Keep holy the Sabbath" and "Honor your father and your mother"). Thus, a devout or pious Catholic is one who frequently receives the sacraments, volunteers in the church ministries, and is a member of a pious association (e.g., the rosary society or an SCC). The stereotypical view of a devout is one who prays, pays, and obeys. There is no overall concept of church as community, *communitas*, or *communio* to unite into one entity the teaching church, the practicing faithful, and the inactive Catholics described above. In this perspective, the "church" is basically the teaching church, as taught in the *Baltimore Catechism.*

The above analysis of the USCCB program of renewal leads to the conclusion that there is nothing strikingly new in that proposal. As stated at the beginning of the first chapter, most Catholics seem unaware of the seriousness of the Catholic decline, or accept it as if nothing could be done. The US bishops seem to follow that trend, as their agenda of re-evangelization offers nothing original. Their 150 strategies and their proposals of parish missions and private or public prayer may appear as no more than holy water on the fire of decline. More drastic proposals are needed. We now turn to various renewal programs available to parishes—namely, the Gallup surveys, the Congregational Life Survey, Warren's *Purpose-Driven Church,* and the research undertaken at the Willow Creek church.

4. The Gallup Surveys and Belongingness

Using their vast collection of survey data, Gallup researchers found that successful businesses were those with the greatest worker satisfaction. Their analysis led them to conclude that worker satisfaction was the cause, not the effect, of business success. This theory allowed the Gallup organization to create a lucrative enterprise of helping businesses increase worker satisfaction. Could these findings also apply to religion? If yes, it would allow for another lucrative business, especially since clients are expected to take the Gallup survey year after year, to show improvement.

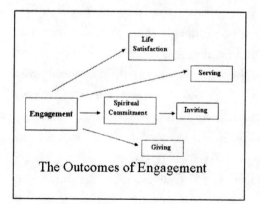

The Outcomes of Engagement

Gallup researchers claim to be able to explain the "failure of the past 35 years" of church decline and at the same time propose a simple course for renewal: "Spiritual commitment is usually a result of one big—and often overlooked—factor: congregational engagement. Focus on improving engagement, and increased commitment will follow."[177] Some parish priests agree: "My sense of a good Catholic or a good parishioner is someone who belongs. We can have people who attend church every day, but they don't belong. They're coming the consumer way. They're really not connected to the church." There is, indeed, a consumer tendency in the Catholic Church in which the faithful are encouraged to *receive* ("consume") sacraments somewhat passively; there is seldom much emphasis on community, especially in parishes of several thousand members. "For people who do not attend church on any regular basis, if I can get them involved in some project (we need to paint the pews, or we need to put windows in), very physical kind of stuff, we need to stuff mailings. Their belonging begins when they say, 'I matter.' And then they're going to start coming to church, because 'I feel like I belong here.'" From the Gallup perspective, involvement is good in itself; it does not matter what the involvement is about. Participation in Habitat for Humanity or the management of a garage sale for the church were examples of engagement given at the Gallup seminar described below, besides the examples of painting pews and putting up windows of the previous quotation. The basic assumption is that involvement precedes and leads to spiritual involvement, not the other way around, as illustrated in the Gallup proposal given above.[178]

There is some evidence to support this assumption. Participant observation in two CaFE (Catholic Faith Exploration) groups in London in 2008 (CaFE is a British renewal program also encouraged by the American bishops) found that the participants rated highest their sense of belonging in these groups. This is not too surprising, since they meet over coffee, wine, and cheese in small discussion groups. It was also found that they appreciated the social dimension (belonging) as much as the religious one (believing). The researchers were led to ask, "Does this drive to community best serve a maturing faith or is it rooted in a certain insecurity, or a search for a comfort zone?"[179] In other words, is this search for community rooted in the prevailing culture of belongingness? Is there any religious countercultural dimension at work here? These questions, however, are irrelevant from the Gallup perspective, which emphasizes engagement and belongingness uncritically.

The Gallup research made an "astounding" discovery: not all believers are of one kind. While in the US bishops' models of renewal, all believers are seen as "the faithful," with only a distinction between the practicing and the inactive Catholics, Gallup distinguishes between the engaged, the not-engaged, and the actively disengaged. Nationwide, in all churches, 29 percent of church members are classified as engaged, 54 percent as not-engaged, and 17 percent as actively disengaged. Among Catholic respondents, only 19 percent are classified as engaged, with higher percentages of the not-engaged and disengaged than among Protestants.

An obvious dynamic of renewal is evident in these findings: increase the number of engaged parishioners and decrease the number of the disengaged. How this can be achieved is usually the main topic of the Gallup seminars. In order to find out if there has been an improvement, one must take the Gallup survey again year after year.

This survey consists of twenty-five items, plus a few background questions. There are several technical flaws in this questionnaire. First, there are no negative or reversed questions, so that one is induced to answer mechanically "Yes, yes, yes," to all questions without much thinking; this goes against common practice in the social sciences. Second, there are six factual (nominal level) questions which are treated as intensity questions (ordinal level). For instance, "I have a best friend in my parish" should be answered positively or negatively, not on a five-point scale. Thus in a 2008 local parish survey, which I will use as an illustration, in response to having a best friend in the parish, 15 percent strongly disagreed (coded "1"), 12 percent answered "I disagree" (coded "2," double the previous weight), 15 percent answered "I don't know" (coded "3"), 24 percent agreed (coded "4"), and 34 percent "totally agreed" (coded "5"). To have six such factual questions out of a total of twenty-five questions coded as intensity questions rather than factual questions will inflate the scores, especially if one realizes that it is socially desirable to answer "2" rather than "1" and "5"(strongly agree) rather than "4" (agree) for the good reputation of the parish. Moreover, it is socially desirable to answer "I don't know" when confronted with an embarrassing question like having or not having a best friend in the parish—and 15 percent said so. How trustworthy are these answers, then? If the implicit message is, "If you don't like it, don't answer," is it surprising that only 543 answered the questionnaire (filled out at Mass) out of a total 1,800 Sunday attenders?

Social desirability is strongly at work here, as indicated by the highly positive answers to self-evaluation questions. Eighty percent "agree" or "strongly agree" with the statement "I have forgiven people who have hurt me deeply"; 84 percent agree with "I will take unpopular stands to defend my faith"; 90 percent said "My faith gives me inner peace"; 91 percent claim "I speak words of kindness to those in need of encouragement"; and 84 percent think of themselves as "spiritually committed." Knowing that the results of the survey will be published in the parish bulletin, one may be induced to answer positively, not only to feel good about oneself, but also to make the parish look good in its ratings, bringing up the number of engaged and down the number of disengaged.

It may take some courage to disagree; it is easier to skip the question or answer evasively (coded "3"). Thus only 4 percent disagreed or strongly disagreed with "As a member of my parish I know what is expected of me," while 15 percent answered "I don't know" and 3 percent skipped the question. Additionally, 6 percent disagreed with "My spiritual needs are met," while 14 percent answered evasively and another 5 percent did not answer; 8 percent disagreed with "My spiritual leaders care about me," while 12 percent selected option "3" and another 7 percent skipped the question. There is a strong bias in the Gallup perspective against those not conforming. Those actively disengaged are defined as "physically present but psychologically absent. They are unhappy with their congregation and insist on sharing that unhappiness with just about everyone."[180] This definition is repeated on several occasions. There is no empirical evidence in the survey that "they insist on sharing their unhappiness with just about everyone," rather the opposite: on the three items given above, three to four times more people answered evasively or skipped the question rather than answer negatively.

For about $8,000, a parish gets an analysis of its survey, a two-day seminar about the results (usually several parishes together), and one week of special training for parish leaders nationwide. In the two-day seminar, pastors will not learn how engagement is measured, since this is a business secret (if the secret were given out, Gallup would lose its customers); they can only learn how to improve their engagement scores. The basic principle is reaffirmed: "Focus on improving engagement, and increased commitment will follow." What is important is to make people *feel* engaged. Most questionnaire items are about feelings: "My needs are met"; "Spiritual leaders care about me"; they "encourage my spiritual development"; "My opinion counts"; "My participation is important"; "I have meaning and purpose in my life"; plus the other items already mentioned about inner peace, speaking words of kindness, and being a spiritual person. But these feelings are highly subjective. Indeed, these surveys are about perceptions, not reality; hence the FAQ (frequently asked question), "Why should congregational leaders pay attention to these results?" Answer: "Perceptions of a group's members influence the way they think and behave. In effect, their perceptions determine their level of engagement and their ultimate level of performance. Thus, these *perceptions are the group's reality* [emphasis added]."[181] It is true that for many people, especially as a consequence of advertising, perceptions are reality. Having learned this lesson from McLuhan, the campaign managers of President Nixon set out in 1967 to sell the presidency the way one sells cigarettes—that is, through controlled advertising and focus-group management.[182] But religion? Can one sell religion?

There is, indeed, a kind of religion that can be sold—namely the religion of belongingness, which has been prevalent, sociologists discovered, since Eisenhower's presidency. "The religiousness characteristic of America today is very often a religiousness without religion, a religiousness with almost any kind of content or none, a way of sociability or 'belonging,'" wrote Will Herberg in 1955. At the Gallup seminar of 2008, which I attended, religion, spirituality, and denominational characteristics were never mentioned. Religion seemed to be, now and then, in Herberg's terms, one of "adjustment, sociability and comfort, designed to give one a sense of 'belonging,' of being at home in the society and the universe."[183]

We have, however, learned something important from Gallup's research: all believers are not of one kind. Hence, different pastoral plans must be designed for the different audiences. A tripartite division of the faithful is also useful, because, as pointed out above, either the top group (the teaching church) influences the middle group, or the bottom group (the outside world) will predominate in the church. Gallup research is based on questionnaires from church attenders; there is no information about nonattenders, except indirectly. Thus in the parish survey presented above, only 7 percent of those less than 35 years old answered the questionnaire, but 59 percent of those aged 55 or older did. Hence, nothing could be learned about the young; yet according to the pastor, 80 to 90 percent of the young drop out of church attendance after confirmation. There is nothing in the Gallup strategy of religious belongingness that will change this trend. For young people, belongingness is very important, but belonging to a Christian church is not. This is a serious issue that cannot be ignored, as it is in the Gallup approach.

5. The US Congregational Life Surveys

In 2001 four countries (Australia, New Zealand, England, and the United States) launched a massive survey involving about .8 million faithful from many denominations (40 in the case of the United States). The questionnaire was filled out during a church service in April 2001; hence, it only gives information about church attenders. This research was financed by foundations; participation was free of charge for all churches involved. The findings and the data are public, which allows for further research. The items of the questionnaire, with only slight variations by country and denomination, can be divided according to either their rationale or their correlations. I will present the rationale of the questions first and the correlations later.

Nine broad core qualities supposedly define the life of any church. They can be divided into three dimensions: inward qualities (faith, worship, and community), outward qualities (service, faith sharing, and inclusion), and managerial qualities (vision, leadership, and innovation).[184] Although some of these qualities are also found in the Gallup questionnaire, the orientation is totally different. Instead of a single variable (engagement), there are three broad areas for improvement: the foundational dimension of faith, worship, and community; the outreach dimension of membership increase; and the administrative dimension dealing with change in an ever-changing world.

In the first dimension, faith is measured by asking not about beliefs, but about growth in faith, the frequency of prayer, and the importance of God in people's lives. There will be "nurturing worship" if preaching is found to be useful, churches' services inspirational and joyful rather than boring, and God's presence perceptible in the services. Finally, community is measured by the sense of belonging; the frequency of attendance in church and group activities; and the ease of making friends at the church. Some of the responses may surprise pastors, because in most churches, there is no feedback about preaching and church services, and no information about private prayer, the sense of growing in faith, or the sense of belonging. The findings may dictate new strategies for improvement.

Findings in the second dimension about outreach may also present surprises. Most churches have well-known outreach charities, but what about faith sharing and inclusiveness? There are questions about getting involved in evangelistic activities, sharing faith with others, inviting others to one's church, and discussing matters of faith at home. On these questions, the results may be embarrassingly low. Inclusion refers to welcoming visitors and following up on people who have been drifting away. Most churches welcome visitors but do not follow up on visitors and drifters. New pastoral strategies may be required.

Finally, on the dimension of leadership and change are questions about the pastor's vision of the church, his empowering leadership, and his encouragement of flexible innovations. Again pastors may be surprised to find that the faithful do not feel listened to or encouraged to use their gifts and talents, or see their church as open to change and innovation. The lack of leadership may also correlate with decreasing membership and the exodus of the young. Pastoral innovations may be necessary to curb the trend.

In studying correlations between variables, Woolever and Bruce found ten factors (called "strengths"), nine of which are similar to those presented above, plus one on participation (attendance in church and activities, financial contribution, and leadership role). These ten strengths are then correlated with one another.

Not surprisingly, the four strengths of spiritual growth, worship, participation, and sense of belonging are strongly interrelated. It is impossible to say which one is the cause and which one is the effect, contrary to Gallup's claim. A more obvious conclusion is that self-improvement will help others improve; thus a more meaningful worship will lead to spiritual growth, greater participation, and a stronger sense of belonging, and vice versa.

It may be difficult to increase spiritual growth, meaningful worship, and a sense of community; it may be easier to work at increasing participation (which is behavioral) through stewardship programs fostering the giving of time, talent, and treasure. This factor is important, because it correlates with membership growth. When members are strongly committed, they are more enthusiastic about their church and invite others. There is, however, a great difference between churches: Catholics rank lowest in participation, with only 44 percent answering positively on all participation questions, as opposed to 69 percent of conservative Protestants and 72 percent of black churches. Hence, it is not surprising that conservative Protestants are growing numerically, while Catholics are not.

I have briefly presented in the first chapter (pages 21-23) the findings of the 2001–2008 Congregational Life Survey based on 300,000 answers from over 2,000 congregations or parishes. These data allow us to compare Protestants and Catholics. Out of 10 basic variables or church strengths, Catholics rank lowest on 7: spirituality; church participation; sense of belonging; care of children and youth; faith sharing; empowering leadership; and looking for the future. Mainline Protestants, conservative Protestants, and black churches are lowest on one variable each.[185]

Any parish can fill out the US Congregational Life survey and receive a short analysis of the data for a small fee. There is, however, little push or pull in that direction. Why is this so? In the Roman society, *pietas* was mainly filial piety—that is, the dedication to the parents, especially the father. Filial piety requires giving honor to parents, the physical as well as the spiritual ones. In the Catholic Church, piety always involves giving honor to the church through words and deeds (e.g., by calling people by their right names: the pope as Your Holiness, a cardinal as Your Grace or Your Excellency, or a priest as Father). From such a perspective, a pastor is likely to be reluctant to have his parishioners tell him how poor his sermons and how uninspiring his services are or remind him that the church is losing members. How can those "above" ever be judged by those "below"? The notion of *pietas* is essentially conservative and hierarchical. The reluctance to have the church exposed to the judgment of the masses is part of this conservative and hierarchical mind-set. If the church, however, were to be one holy people of God—that is, a community of communities—the traditional notion of *pietas* toward the church as well as all the honorary titles of the clergy would be out of place. Then there would be no more "above" and "below." Then church members could listen to one another as brothers and sisters.

The analysts of the International Congregational Life Survey avoid offending the sensibilities of the churches by always emphasizing the positive, rather than the negative. There are ten "strengths" but no corresponding weaknesses; the strategy is to increase the strengths and ignore the weaknesses. Christian Schwarz came to the opposite conclusion: it is the weakest factor that impedes growth. Thus, if evangelization is the weakest, there will be no growth, and decline is predictable. Schwarz's research is based on 4.2 million replies to surveys conducted in 1,000 churches in 32 countries and on 6 continents. Any church or parish can take his Natural Church Development Survey. Schwarz singles out eight basic factors, which are, with the corresponding factors of the US Congregational Survey in parentheses, passionate spirituality (faith), inspiring worship (worship), small groups (community), loving relationships (community), gift-oriented ministry (service), evangelism (faith sharing and inclusion), empowering leadership (vision and leadership), and functional structures (leadership). The basic factors utilized in both surveys overlap greatly. However, the inclusion of negative factors allows for new discoveries. Thus in the leadership variable, it was found that "formal theological training has a negative correlation to both church growth and overall quality of churches,"[186] as theologically and canonically trained ministers are likely to preach theology and canon law rather than spirituality. In reference to functional structures, there is "an extremely negative relationship between traditionalism and both growth and quality within the church";[187] growth requires innovation, not ritualism and tradition (28). Finally, in reference to priorities, out of 170 variables, "small groups" was found to be the most important: "If we were to identify any *one* principle as the 'most important' ... without doubt it would be the multiplication of small groups."[188] There is little or no hierarchy in small groups; their purpose is not the increase of devotions but Scripture-centered discipleship. A church of small groups can only be a community of communities when there is no "above" and no "below." If the weakest factor impedes growth, that factor has to be attended to, even if the process is embarrassing to the authorities, because in a renewed church those in authority are servants of all.

6. The Purpose-Driven Church

Rick Warren's ministry at the Saddleback church in Southern California has been exceptionally successful among regular churchgoers as well as the unchurched. After having seen his success story analyzed in more than one hundred doctoral theses, he wrote his own account in *The Purpose-Driven Church* of 1995. The book sold over half a million copies, which suggests that it is of interest not just to pastors; it makes significant contributions to pastoral strategies for all denominations and churches.

In his early twenties, Warren decided to create a new church. After six months of prayer, he felt called to create a "missionary-sending" church in the United States rather than

> **"The ten most receptive groups of people that we've reached out to:**
> Second-time visitors to the church
> Close friends and relatives of new converts
> People going through a divorce
> Those who feel the need for a recovery program (alcohol, drugs, sexual, etc.)
> First-time parent
> The terminally ill and heir families
> Couples with major marriage problems
> Parents with problem children
> Recently unemployed or those with major financial problems
> New residents in the community"
> —*The Purpose-Driven Church*, 183

work personally abroad, a church characterized by its missionary "sending capacity" rather than its "seating capacity," a church designed "for turning members into ministers and missionaries."[189] More prayer and research made him discover that California was one of the most unchurched states of the Union, and Saddleback Valley in Southern California the fastest-growing county. "I heard God speak clearly to me: 'That's where I want you to plant a church'" (34).

Having no money and no local acquaintances, Warren started his first Bible-study group with seven people two weeks after his arrival. Feeling called to reach the unchurched rather than attract members from other churches, he spent twelve weeks going from door to door to talk with people. "I wanted to listen first to what *they* thought their most pressing needs were." Most unchurched people knew what they didn't want—namely, the traditional old stuff, and money collections. Just twelve weeks after his arrival, Warren sent out 15,000 invitations to attend a nontraditional service. At the first service, on Easter Sunday of 1980, 205 people showed up. "There weren't more than a dozen believers at that first service. Instead, it was filled with unchurched southern Californians." When he invited them to sing and pray, "people just looked around" with blank stares (44). Everything remained to be done. At that first church service, he proclaimed his vision, a dream of "sending out hundreds of career missionaries and church workers all around the world and empowering every member for a personal life mission in the world" (43). Was it naiveté, arrogance, or prophetic vision? The future would tell.

Warren quickly realized that different audiences required different pastoral strategies. This is something new: in the surveys presented above, the researchers did not deal with pastoral strategies, which were left to pastors; they alone had to decide to work on strengths or weaknesses, or both, or none. For Warren, strengths and weaknesses make sense only in conjunction with appropriate strategies. At the Saddleback church, he now addresses five different audiences. First are the unchurched and occasional attenders, with 31,000 names in the church data bank. Second are the 10,000 regular weekly attenders (all statistics are from his 1995 book). Next are the active church members who have taken a membership class, been baptized, and signed a membership covenant; they are 5,000 strong, and they will learn to grow in Christian fellowship. At the next level are those committed to discipleship, about 3,000; they committed themselves to daily prayer, tithing ten percent of their income, and being active in small groups, and their goal is to grow in spiritual maturity. Finally at the highest level is the core group, which has gone through the previous stages; these 1,500 members are committed to ministry in teaching, music, youth, outreach, and so on. The core group forms the heart of the church: "If I were to drop dead, Saddleback would continue to grow because of this base of 1,500 lay ministers" (134); they are all unpaid volunteers.

The global strategy is to move each group higher, one notch at a time. There is a general curriculum of moving up: "We bring people in, build them up, train them, and send them out. We bring them in as *members*, we build them up to *maturity*, we train them for *ministry*, and we send them out on *mission*" (108–09). There is a specific goal for each audience: for the unchurched, it is to learn about the Good News; for the Sunday regulars, to participate in worship; for the active members, to become involved in fellowship; for the committed, to grow in discipleship; and for the core members, to improve the evangelical skills of serving others. The Saddleback purpose statement has five clear goals: evangelization, worship, fellowship, discipleship, and service. The results on these goals are measurable, not just in numbers, but also in quality. Saddleback is a church with clear objectives at each level, and the results are measurable even without scientific surveys.

Having defined the goals, what are the strategies? Reaching out to the unchurched will be discussed in the next chapter. As to the regular Sunday attenders, there is no special requirement; all they have to do is participate in the worship with the hope that the music will relate to them and the sermon will speak to their hearts and minds.

Above the level of mere attendance, the requirements become more demanding. In order to be an active member, one must become a contributor, not just a consumer, thus getting a sense of ownership. Engagement gives a sense of belonging, Gallup found out, but not any type of involvement will do (e.g., painting the pews or fixing the church windows); the participation has to lead, in one way or another, to a greater commitment to God and his church. "If little is required to join, very little can be expected from members later on" (315). Most (including Catholic) churches are as welcoming as supermarkets; all that is expected is a financial offering, usually no more than a restaurant tip. "At Saddleback we have four requirements for membership: (1) a personal profession of faith of Christ as Lord and Savior, (2) baptism by immersion as a public symbol of one's faith, (3) completion of the membership class, and (4) a signed commitment to abide by Saddleback's membership covenant" (320). Becoming a full-fledged member is a rite of initiation, like RCIA, not just a rite of passage. The membership class is an initiation into the history, doctrine, and fellowship of the church. Baptism is a monthly and highly visible public celebration, with high-intensity religious emotions arising when each new member makes his public profession of faith, with feedback intensification from the community with applause, encouragement, photography, and congratulations. In the past, the pastor held a reception for new members in his home, thus presenting the church as a family rather than an organization. At other times, the church held a banquet for new members, paid for by previous new members, and thus the profession of faith became a table fellowship with other committed believers. The membership covenant summarizes the evangelical precepts in four points with numerous Bible quotations. In the last point, members are expected to support the church "by giving regularly," according to St. Paul's advice: "Each one of you, on the first day of each week, should set aside a specific sum of money in proportion to what you have earned, and use it for the offering" (322). There is no mention of tithing; that will come at a higher level of commitment. Too demanding? Not so for the 5,000 members (as of 1995). "If little is required, very little can be expected."

The everyday life of active members is a time of acclimatizing to Christian living before the steep climb to spiritual maturity, when all the requirements of knowledge, prayer, fellowship, and tithing will fall into place into a single vision. The climb begins with the 201 class, "Discovering Spiritual Maturity," to get people started. They will learn about four basic habits ("virtues" in traditional language): Bible reading, prayer, tithing, and fellowship. These habits can be started overnight, as suddenly as one gives up smoking or drinking cold turkey (except that this is much less painful). According to Warren, "people leave the class permanently changed" (349). It is not that they have made it to the top; rather, they have started the climbing in earnest by committing themselves to follow their signed covenant of growth. They will be supported all along. Most people are biblically illiterate, Warren found out (who would disagree?). Hence, the need for a nine-month introductory Bible course, "the largest program … written and taught by lay teachers" (315). The Bible is studied intellectually, but also prayerfully, as *lectio divina*. There is also a systematic theology course taught twice a week for twenty-seven weeks (nearly the equivalent of two university semesters). Finally, there are the Life Skills seminars, usually four to eight hours in a single day, on basic Christian skills (how to study the Bible, how to pray, how to handle temptations, how to make time for prayer and ministries, how to get along with others, and so on, described on page 359 of Warren's book). There are many other courses, seminars, lectures, and events, each and all of which will make the climbing easier. And then there is the participation in small groups.

These requirements may seem unreasonable. Yet about 3,000 people have accepted them at Saddleback church—more than double or triple the weekly attendance in most Catholic parishes. Those who would find them unreasonable probably have never tried them in one way or another. In that case, parishioners ready for such high standards may go (or have gone) elsewhere. As pointed out in chapter one, more Catholics are joining demanding churches than the other way around. Those whose personal high expectations remain unmet may simply drop out. Notice that the Saddleback expectations for mature Christians seem as demanding in their own way as those of religious orders in the Catholic church, for which there are fewer and fewer vocations today. Obviously something could be learned here.

The final goal is to turn members into ministers. What are the reasons to justify today's lay ministries? We may list the following. (1) Most churches need volunteers for their maintenance ministries so the clergy can take care of the spiritual ministries. Wrong! At Saddleback, maintenance is done by paid staff; the laity should not be used as cheap labor. (2) The laypeople have their own vocation in subordination to that of the clergy. Wrong. According to Warren, "There are no laypeople in a biblical church; there are only ministers. The idea of two classes of Christians, clergy and laity, is the creation of Roman Catholic Tradition" (391). According to traditional teaching, the distinction between laity and clergy is "of divine institution," by which it was meant, for all practical purposes, that one is superior to the other; Vatican II did not explicitly repudiate this teaching, and hence, it lingers on. (3) A church is only as strong as the number of its people in the pews. Wrong again. "Your church will never be any stronger than its core lay ministers who carry out the various ministries of the church. Every church needs an intentional, well-planned system for uncovering, mobilizing, and supporting the giftedness of its members" (367). There are about 1,500 recognized ministers at Saddleback for a Sunday attendance of about 10,000, or one minister for 10 attenders. Many parishes have 10 to

---

"Money spent on evangelism is never an expense, it's always an investment." (p. 201)
When finances get tight in a church, often the first thing cut is the evangelism and advertising budget. That is the *last thing* you should cut. It is the source of new blood and life for your church. (p. 202)

---

20 paid or unpaid lay ministers, instead of the 300 they would need for a Sunday attendance of 3,000, according to the Saddleback ratio. How can such a ratio be achieved?

At Saddleback, all ministers are likely to have spent years in daily prayer, biblical meditation, tithing, and membership in small groups in their journey to spiritual maturity; now they are ready to give back what they received. They need first to attend the monthly ministry classes—from 4:00 to 8:30 p.m.—and sign a Ministry Covenant that spells out their new commitments. They will discover their talents in another seminar, have an interview with someone in their area of interest, be integrated into a team, and finally be publicly commissioned to their ministry at one of the monthly fellowships they will henceforth attend. This is a lengthy process. "Most churches get in a hurry and try to do too much. Instead, pray and wait for God to bring you the person best shaped to lead a particular ministry" (385). Prayer is of paramount importance at all levels, from membership to maturity to ministry.

Ministry for what? Ultimately, for mission. In his first sermon, Warren expressed his dream of sending hundreds of missionaries around the world. His dream has been fulfilled beyond measure. "Saddleback Church started our first daughter church when our church was just one year old … By our fifteenth anniversary we had started twenty-five other churches" (181). By 2008, Sunday attendance has climbed to 23,000; about 1,700 volunteers have traveled to Rwanda, and 10,000 baptisms have been recorded there.[190]

There are great similarities between Saddleback and the Bayville Community Church. Both list the same goals in their mission statements: worship, spiritual growth, and evangelization; Saddleback also mentions discipleship and service, which are implicit at Bayville. In both churches, there is a distinction between regular attenders and members (800 members at Bayville versus 5,000 at Saddleback). In both cases, water baptism and a special class lead to full membership. Missions at home and abroad are important in both churches; it has been so at Bayville since its inception in 1955. There is no special service for the unchurched there; yet newcomers get special care in an introductory class. On the other hand, tithing is expected from the beginning of membership at Bayville, not just at a more advanced level. At Bayville, there is no hierarchy of courses, from the 100 to the 400 levels, as at Saddleback; all courses are open to all. Moreover, at Bayville, the journey to maturity and discipleship is undertaken informally, by attending classes and becoming involved, as Bayville is much smaller than Saddleback. Rick Warren has visited Bayville, and his influence is noticeable there. Both churches have strategies for quantitative and qualitative growth.

7. The Willow Creek Surveys

The Willow Creek Community Church started as modestly as Saddleback when, in 1975, a twenty-year-old with a Bible-studies degree and little prior experience began an unconventional Sunday service at the Willow Creek Theater in a Chicago suburb. It grew quickly, and by 1981, a 1,600-seat worship center had been built. Continuing to grow, the church expanded into a 150-acre campus, with a new 7,200-seat worship place. It now attracts about 20,000 worshippers every week. Its founder and senior pastor is Bill Hybels.

While Rick Warren's pastoral strategies can be described as "from above," rooted in reflection and prayer, Hybels's strategies are mainly "from below"—that is, empirically grounded (which does not exclude prayer and reflection). Since 1992 his church has taken surveys of the whole congregation every three years. In 1995 it was found that one-third of the attenders drove more than half an hour to church; hence, it was decided to create local campuses closer to people's home. So far, four campuses have been created, serving about 5,000 people. Recent research findings have been published in two slim volumes, *Reveal* (2007) and *Follow Me* (2008). It is through this research that Hybels has made and continues to make an important contribution. The findings are disseminated through the Willow Creek Association, which links together churches of a similar vision. The association currently has more than 12,000 member churches from 90 denominations and 45 countries.[191] The association runs yearly training conferences, the largest of which was the Leadership Summit of 2003, which attracted 100,000 participants thanks to the use of numerous satellite sites. The research published in *Reveal* is based on 6,000 questionnaires filled out at Willow Creek in 2004, plus 5,000 in 2007 from Willow Creek and six other churches of various denominations across the United States. Hence, this research has a solid quantitative basis.

How do people grow spiritually? Obviously—according to traditional wisdom—it is by coming to church, and the more often the better. In the Catholic view, spiritual growth is seen as related to the frequency of receiving the sacraments—again, the more often the better. People also grow by being involved in small groups and church activities. Over the last sixteen years, attendance at Willow Creek has increased by 50 percent, participation in small groups has increased by 500 percent, and service to the poor has also increased dramatically.[192] In the Willow Creek survey, spiritual growth is measured by two variables: spiritual behaviors (Sunday giving, serving others through the church, and evangelism) and spiritual attitudes (love of God and neighbors). The expectation is that improved behaviors and attitudes will be strongly related to church involvement (attendance and activities). But *this is not so*, according to the 2004 survey!

6.1 Christ-Centeredness and Spiritual Growth

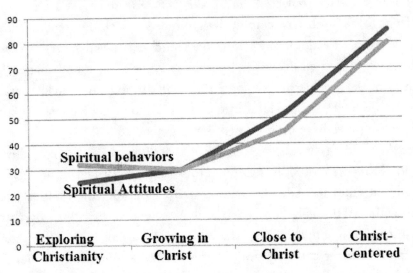

This finding was unexpected. It threw into question all traditional pastoral strategies. Does this finding apply to Catholics, in which case spiritual growth is *not* related (or only weakly related) to the frequent reception of sacraments? How could involvement in small Christian communities (like at St. Mary's) have no effect on spiritual growth? This zero relationship is hard to believe, yet we have seen that Sunday offerings at St. Mary's have not increased (they have remained at a flat 1 percent of annual income) in spite of the bourgeoning of SCCs over the last twenty years. So what is the role of the church (i.e., the clergy), and what is the point of church involvements?

The researchers stumbled into an unexpected answer: all measurements of spiritual behaviors and attitudes correlate strongly with closeness to Christ, as shown in graph 6.1 above.[193] There is a Lickert scale of four items in the questionnaire:

1. "I believe in God, but I'm not sure about Christ. My faith is not a significant part of my life." This level is called Exploring Christianity.
2. "I believe in Jesus, and I am working on what it means to get to know him." This is the level of Growing in Christ.
3. "I feel really close to Christ and depend on him daily for guidance." This is being Close to Christ.
4. And finally, there is the Christ-Centered level: "God is all I need in my life. He is enough. Everything I do is a reflection of Christ."

These four levels form a continuum of closeness to Christ. All spiritual variables are strongly related to this continuum.

According to traditional wisdom, spiritual growth is related to frequency of church attendance—to church-centeredness rather than Christ-centeredness. From this perspective, all pastoral strategies should encourage frequent church attendance. This traditional wisdom, however, was *not* confirmed by the data. As seen in the graph 6.1 above, spiritual behaviors (tithing, evangelism, serving) and spiritual attitudes (love for God, love for people) increase not with attendance, but with increased closeness to Christ. It is Christ-centeredness that is the key to spiritual growth: "Our research experts told us this was one of the *most highly predictive* models they had seen [emphasis in the text]" (36). If this finding applies to Catholics, it would mean that it is closeness to Christ, not the frequency of the sacraments, that explains spiritual behavior, because one may go to church every Sunday out of habit (which may be the case for many) and receive communion out of conformity (when the faithful go to communion pew after pew). Church attendance and communion may be habits, not necessarily signs of closeness to God. High levels of closeness to Christ, however, are likely to translate into high levels of spiritual behaviors and attitudes (e.g., the frequent reception of the sacraments). This finding throws into question many traditional pastoral practices.

The 2004–2007 research is summarized in six basic findings. The first is that "Involvement in church activities does not predict or drive long-term spiritual growth" (33), but closeness to Christ does. Thus the percent of people who say they pray increases from about 30 percent at level one (Exploring Christianity) to 75 percent at level 4 (Christ-Centered); Scripture reading increases from 10 percent to 45 percent; and "setting aside time to listen to God" from 10 percent to 30 percent (43). Giving ten percent or more of one's income increases from 12 percent at level 1 to 50 percent at level 4; serving at least once a week goes from 15 percent to 40 percent; and evangelizing ("I have six or more meaningful spiritual conversations per year with non-Christians") from 9 percent to 39 percent (46). Not just spiritual behaviors (i.e., prayer, giving, and evangelization) change; spiritual attitudes change as well. The centrality of prayer moves from about15 percent at level 1 to 65 percent at level 4; prayer as "continuous conversation with God all day long" moves from 5 percent to 60 percent; and the importance of Scripture ("If I don't read my Bible, something is missing in my day") increases from 5 percent to 45 percent at level 4 (98). In summary, as one moves closer to Christ in one's spiritual life, one is very likely to show increased spiritual attitudes and behaviors, as stated in finding two: "Spiritual growth is all about increasing relational closeness to Christ." This finding is likely to apply to Catholics, although some of the spiritual behaviors and attitudes may be different. This finding also contradicts the traditional Catholic expectation that spiritual growth happens nearly automatically through greater closeness to church and sacraments. In chapter 2, I stated that church-centeredness, rather than Christ-centeredness, was a major Catholic trait, and also a factor of decline; the findings of the Willow Creek study indirectly corroborate this thesis.

Third, "the Church is most important in the early stages of spiritual growth. Its role then shifts from being the primary influence to a secondary influence" (41). The same can be said about education. At the college freshman level, teachers are more important than textbooks, as students tend to rely mostly on teachers, while at the graduate level, students become more critical-minded and rely more on personal readings. At the early stages of spiritual development, the Sunday sermon or homily, the quality of the music, and the vibrancy of the liturgy are of paramount importance for newcomers; if dissatisfied they will not come back. Spiritual infants are not much involved in personal prayer, Scripture readings, community service, sacrificial giving, or small-group activities; they tend to be mainly on the receiving side. Then, in church as in higher education, attendance is primordial; equally important is engaging these freshmen in activities and small groups. As these freshmen move up, sermons and lectures become less important, while small groups gain in importance. The primacy of groups in turn fades away as personal prayer, Scripture reading, and personal devotions become the driving force. Finally, at the Christ-centered level, what is needed is mentoring, spiritual direction, and spiritual companionship with others who are equally Christ-centered; at that stage, service to others becomes the expression of (rather than one's means toward) one's relationship with Christ. Over time the image and function of the church change: at the beginning, it is the church as an institution of knowledge and resources that is valued; at the highest level, it is the church as a communion of saints.

Fourth, "personal spiritual practices are the building blocks for a Christ-centered life" (44). This principle states that, in the strong correlation between spiritual practices and Christ-centeredness, it is the practices that are the driving force for growth. The importance of personal devotions is well-known and accepted in Catholic spirituality. One could object that it is the sacraments, not the devotions, that are the prime movers of spiritual growth. This is a limited view, as daily Mass attendance cannot replace personal prayer and spiritual readings. One could then say that daily Mass, in addition to personal devotions, propels growth—but is the Mass a private devotion? Is the Eucharistic celebration a devotion? This question will be discussed in the next chapter.

Fifth, "a church's most active evangelists, volunteers and donors come from the most spiritually advanced segments" (45). According to the Willow Creek findings, "the evidence is consistent and compelling: the more one grows, the more one serves, tithes and evangelizes." (45). Rick Warren came to the same conclusion intuitively: "Your church will never be any stronger than its core lay ministers who carry out the various ministries of the church." Isn't this obvious? If it is, then it is the lack of Christ-centeredness at the highest levels that explains the poor financial contribution of Catholics, and their lack of involvement in parish activities and evangelism. Apparently the finding that the most active evangelists are the most advanced spiritually is not obvious; as the leaders of Willow Creek concluded, "this is one of the most significant findings we discovered" (45). There is good reason to take this finding seriously, as some of the most spiritually advanced members are most likely to be dissatisfied and leave the church.

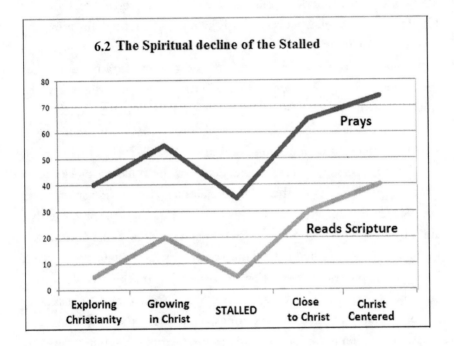

finally, "more than 25 percent of those surveyed described themselves as spiritually 'stalled' or 'dissatisfied' with the role of the church in their spiritual growth" (47). This, too, is a very important finding. Let us first look at the stalled and next at the dissatisfied.

Those who checked "I believe in Christ, but I have stalled and haven't grown much lately" are classified as stalled. If at Willow Creek, 25 percent are stalled or dissatisfied, what is the percent of Catholics who have not grown over the last five or ten years? How much food for growth can one find in ten-minute homilies, especially if they are uninspiring? Those stalled are found mainly at the first two levels of spiritual growth, while the dissatisfied are more common among the advanced. The effect of being stalled is catastrophic: all spiritual practices drop to their lowest level, and all the previous gains are lost, as shown in the graph 6.2 above. Personal prayer remains high, but only at the level of beginners. Scripture reading and personal time with God disappear—traits that also likely to characterize many Catholics attending Mass out of habit. Twenty-five percent of the stalled are considering leaving the church; hence, it is important to listen to them seriously.

The majority of those stalled are *satisfied* with the church services; hence the factors of their spiritual arrest come from the outside. The main factors are: 1) low priority of spirituality in daily living for 89% of them (more time is spent on TV, Internet, email, movies, shopping); 2) emotional problems for 48% of them (depression, anger, negative affects); 3) addictions (alcohol, gambling, pornography, shopping addiction); and finally 4) inappropriate relationships for 16% (e.g. affairs) (page 49). Thus stalling has nothing to do with poor sermons, but maybe with the absence of guidance on these issues which are practically ignored in most churches.

6.3 The complaints of the dissatisfied

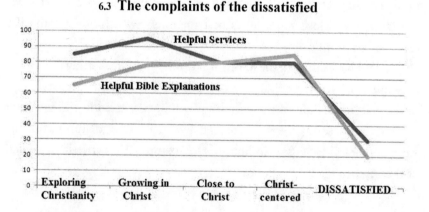

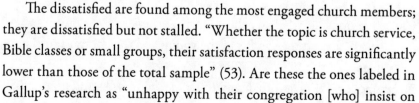

The dissatisfied are found among the most engaged church members; they are dissatisfied but not stalled. "Whether the topic is church service, Bible classes or small groups, their satisfaction responses are significantly lower than those of the total sample" (53). Are these the ones labeled in Gallup's research as "unhappy with their congregation [who] insist on sharing that unhappiness with just about everyone?" Even if they are, one cannot ignore them, because they are the most financially, socially, and spiritually active members of the congregation, and 63 percent of them are considering leaving. Actually, they want change rather than exit: 60 percent want more in-depth Bible teaching, and 56 percent want more challenge (53). Their level of dissatisfaction is extreme; as seen in the graph 6.3 above,[194] they are two to three times more dissatisfied than beginners who are not even "sure about Christ." A similar finding was made by the 2006 Pew survey: 90 percent of the Hispanic Catholics who converted to Protestantism did so because they wanted a more personal relationship with God, not because they were dissatisfied with Catholic teaching (see my chapter 1, page 26). Similarly, according to a recent study, the members of Voice of the Faithful are among the most dedicated Catholics (70 percent attended Catholic grade school, 62 percent Catholic high school, 57 percent Catholic college; 65 percent attend Mass weekly, and 79 percent pray daily), yet the proportion of those who might leave the church is double that of the national average (23 percent versus 14 percent).[195] The stalled are likely to stay, but by doing so, they tend to stall the whole church; but if the dissatisfied leave, the church will lose some of its best members, which will be another factor of church decline.

So far I have outlined the findings of the Willow Creek study that throw into question many traditional assumptions. The new pastoral strategies developed in the light of these findings will be presented in the course of my own proposal in the next chapter. It is now time to summarize the various renewal proposals in light of the six evaluation criteria presented at the beginning of this chapter.

8. Evaluation of Reform Proposals

Church reform should satisfy the following criteria:
1. Bring to an end the exodus of the young and the nontransmission of values;
2. Propose paths of spiritual growth rather than ideological programs;

3. Have concrete proposals in relationship to the world, more specifically:

    —devise forms of renunciation, as the church is in the world but not of the world

    —propose a critique of the consumer society to promote the spiritual growth of all, Christians and non-Christians, along Maslow's self-actualization model

    —emphasize community beyond conformity and cultural Christianity;

4. Appear as a servant church, rather than a power structure;
5. Support a moral culture, not just a moral theology from above;
6. Overcome the dichotomy of teaching versus listening by supporting a sacramentality from below, rather than romanization from above.

In broad terms, the US bishops' proposal *Go and Make Disciples* tends to fail. The exodus of the young is not acknowledged. Ideologically, their proposal espouses John Paul II's conservatism on sexual morality, ecclesiology, and dissent in the church, and his liberalism on social justice—and, in opposition to the US Lefebverites and ultraconservatives, his ecumenism and liturgical renewal. Bishops obviously favor spiritual growth for their flock, but they have little to say about it. The relationship between the church and the world is not touched, as it tends to be seen as a private papal domain involving world diplomacy and the relationship between the Vatican and sovereign states. On morality and sacramentality, they necessarily uphold the morality and sacramentality from above, according to the existing power structure of canon law. Their position can be understood in light of their dual role as both pastors of their flock and papal representatives accountable only to the papal administration.

RENEW and other forms of SCC propose a path for spiritual growth. In many cases, their development was due to the initiative of local bishops; when this support stopped (e.g., when the bishops were replaced or retired), their growth stopped as well. Most parish priests tend to see SCCs as a form of spiritual growth among many others, not as a major tool for parish revitalization, as has been the case at St. Mary's. Baranowski in 1988 had envisioned the parish as a community of small communities, thus making the latter a major tool for parish renewal, but his proposal was not followed. When the church is seen as a community, it is less likely to appear as a power structure. Moreover, SCCs tend to foster a popular moral culture and a broad sacramentality, rather than follow moral theologies from above. In short, SCCs have great potential, especially if seen as central to parish life.

The Gallup research divides the faithful into engaged, not-engaged, and actively disengaged. This is new. However, the hierarchy finds no place in this scheme, which is more appropriate for congregational denominations. There is great emphasis on community, a traditionally Catholic trait, yet engagement tends to be seen as belongingness, as in cultural Christianity or Fowler's stage 3. There is no real prophetic vision in this perspective, nor is there any implicit or explicit proposal for spiritual growth. With this tool, a parish may become a more engaged community, but without vision beyond that.

The Congregational Life surveys are tools of exceptional value. The nine major variables are conveniently synthesized into three major dimensions: inward qualities (faith, worship, and community), outward qualities (service, faith sharing, and inclusion), and managerial qualities (vision, leadership, and innovation). By taking the survey, a parish will gain overall and detailed knowledge of its strengths and weaknesses. The surveys are offered as a service, not for profit. They provide information on spiritual qualities and leadership well beyond what is provided by Gallup. Thus a pastor will learn about the levels of faith commitment and practices of his parishioners; their strength of belongingness; their understanding and acceptance of his vision or lack of it; his flexibility and openness to change; the inspirational value of the worship services; and the parish's inclusiveness, evangelism, and outreach activities. But once this knowledge is gained, all remains to be done: knowledge does not necessarily lead to action.

This is not the case of Warren's *Purpose-Driven Church*, which is action oriented. There is little sociological information but lots of wise pastoral strategies. At both the Saddleback and the Creek Willow churches, there appears to be no exodus of the young, as youth ministries are of prime importance. Many Catholic parishes have primary schools for children before their age of critical decision making, while Saddleback and Creek Willow target high schoolers and young adults, rather than children. At a public high school near Willow Creek, I attended a "praise and worship" service totally run by students (with the assistance of a Willow Creek youth minister) at the early hour of 6:30 to 7:15 a.m. The music was lively, and the singing loud. It was full room with about one hundred students, including some Catholics. Both Saddleback and Willow Creek propose paths of spiritual growth, with specific requirements at the various levels. Because they recognize various degrees of growth, their teaching is level-appropriate. Thus no financial contribution is expected at the lowest level, and there is little critique of the consumer society and few moral requirements at that stage. At the middle level, there is no tithing requirement, either—only the expectation of steady growth through prayer, Scripture reading, and involvement in small groups. At the highest level, the demands are comparable to those of secular religious institutes in the Catholic Church. Yet neither Saddleback nor Willow Creek are "churches," as they resisted the temptation of becoming new denominations; instead, they are a powerful social movement within Protestantism. Not being "churches," however, they have no theology on church and society; being nonhierarchical and nonsacramental, they have nothing to offer Catholics at the theological level on ecclesiology, moral theology, and sacramentality. Their contributions are pastoral, not theological.

While Warren's pastoral suggestions rest on their intrinsic wisdom, the findings of Willow Creek are based on solid empirical research. To the extent that these findings are applicable to Catholicism, they cannot be ignored by renewal proposals. At least two of their findings must be considered seriously. First, it is Christ-centeredness rather than church-centeredness (church activities) that promotes long-term spiritual growth, in contrast to the taken-for-granted Catholic tendency. Second, the stalled and dissatisfied must be taken seriously—the stalled because they are satisfied with the church's low requirements, and the dissatisfied, often the most valuable parish members, because they may leave, possibly taking with them the seeds of renewal.

It is now time to move on to renewal proposals in the next chapter.

CHAPTER 7

⌒

RENEWAL FOR HORIZON 2030

Long-term renewal requires planning and vision. Even if one falls short of one's goals, having goals is preferable to making limited improvements year after year. Every business or church should have a ten-year plan or vision. What will the church look like in 2030? Our task is to prepare for it.

Any vision for 2030 must begin with a sociological assessment of the current situation. We will begin with an overview of two deep cultural changes that have taken place over the last two generations (since about the time of Vatican II), namely the decline of devotions and the generalization of relationships. Traditional devotions were patterned after the social relations of piety toward parents, priests, and God. For the younger generation, however, it is equality, informality, and emotional closeness that characterize social relations; hence their alienation from church practices. After these two introductory discussions (of piety, on the one hand, and relationships, on the other), we come to the main point of this chapter—namely, the sociology of religious practices, and various proposals for Horizon 2030.

1. Sociology of Piety and Devotions

People relate to God and their church the way they relate to their parents. The type of relationship is experienced in the family early in life and then extended to God and the church throughout life. Family relations in turn depend on the economic system of their society. Thus, in societies with no retirement system and no employment for the young, the parents in old age are totally dependent on their children, and the children are made totally dependent on their parents until marriage; because of their mutual dependency, they form a strong bond of obedience and loyalty throughout life. Loyalty to parents was called *pietas* in the Roman culture and *filial piety* in Confucianism[196] (e.g., in China, Japan, and Korea), still prevalent today. Filial piety requires loyalty to the parents and also to their gods in Rome, their ancestors in the Far East, and to the church in the West. Filial piety is also central in Judeo-Christianity, as it is one of the Ten Commandments:

"Honor thy father and mother." This commandment has been the bedrock of social relations within the family for centuries. The crude little picture to the left clearly shows the pyramid of power: the father is seated, as he has full authority; the mother is standing next to him in support; the child is kneeling as a sign of deference and submission.

Family relations in the West followed this pattern, but with less rigidity. Things changed with the introduction of pension funds and social security in most Western countries in the 1930s; as a consequence, parents became less dependent on their children. The latter, in turn, became much less dependent on parents as they left home for school, could earn money, and could marry without parental approval once they had turned eighteen or so. As a consequence, obedience and loyalty have increasingly become somewhat meaningless in family relations (except in the case of small children); they are also less meaningful in relationships with God and the church, to the great harm of churches who continue to rely on these traditional values. In the pages to come, I will consider various characteristics of the traditional family system, their projection to God and the church, and their rejection by the young (and not so young) today. First, let's take a brief look at obedience in the pre-Vatican II church.

The general principle that people have the same relationship with God as with their parents was repeated many times in my 2002 interviews of parish leaders, then in their fifties. "I think of God as father because of my own father. He was a very loving, very generous person ... so I guess my image of God was that of a father." A more negative view: "What we call physical abuse today was normal parenting then. For example, my father's method of teaching spelling was to sit across from me with a wooden spoon in his hand, and each time I misspelled a word, I would get a whack. That was fairly normal. Most of the kids I grew up with had some physical discipline as part of their growing up." His childhood church was characterized by "distance of God, awesomeness of God; my grandmother always in black, always saying the rosary ... the pastor acting as if he were infallible ... the church teaching with an aura of infallibility about anything." In these interviews, the mother was seldom mentioned for the obvious reason that both church and society were mainly patriarchal. Women, like children, were to be seen, not heard, and God was a male figure.

Authority was a major characteristic of the pre-Vatican II family, church, and parochial school. This authority was asserted with various tools—namely, discipline, physical punishment, fear, guilt, shame, and silencing. The few people born in the 1930s that I interviewed had internalized these values; hence, they voiced few complaints. Those who grew up at the end of the pre-Vatican II era were often brutal in their comments. Here are a few. "As a child, they [parents, parochial school, and church] were more like a dictator, a power, you know. I guess controlling, too: they were very controlling as to everything you were going to do. Power is that *they* were everything. Everything kind of revolved around the church; the dictatorship and the power was that you had to do it their way. There was no other way to do it. And the controlling part was, in order to feel part of it, you did exactly what they said." Authoritarianism before WWII was part of the prevailing culture. "All authority figures were stern. Cops were stern. And doctors yelled at you if you didn't do what they told you." At that time, cops, priests, parents, and teachers were stern. Moreover, parents, nuns, and priests reinforced each other's authority: "My parents would support anything the school said or did. Overall, you wouldn't dare not do your homework. You wouldn't dare come late." In many cases, punishment at school was automatically followed by punishment at home. For the younger generation, however, these are totally unacceptable behaviors. It is revolting to hear adults say, "As a child, God was just there with that big stick, waiting for me to do something wrong, which is probably why I was such a good kid, you see. Because I wasn't going to let him hit me with that." While the authority of the church has greatly softened since then, has it changed much in substance? For many outsider Catholics, the church remains a structure of obedience and power.

The major tools of authority were discipline, guilt, shame, and fear. Here are a few extreme cases. At school, "they would hit with a ruler. That was commonly accepted in those days. They would just pick up an eraser and just fling it at you. ... They would ask you to kneel on a floor. I've seen boys smacked with a ruler. At the parochial school, with Dominican sisters, you know, hair pulled, ear pulled ... that's the discipline that was common. It was obedience, 100 percent. All the time. Obedience was the most important virtue. Obedience to God, to your family, to school." On guilt: "They did a good job at [guilt] in religious ed. They would keep track on charts of who went to Mass and who went to Communion, and the children who didn't get to Mass for whatever reason didn't get their sticker [of good behavior]. That was each week; and if it was the same children, they were made to feel terrible about that." On shame: "Humiliation, not at home, but at the parochial school, yes. The bad student would be called a name. You were always constantly told you were never gonna get anywhere, you were never gonna amount to anything, God doesn't love you, you were gonna go be in hell, and all that stuff." Fear was ever-present: excessive fear, constant fear, fear of God, fear of priests, fear of nuns. "I remember the pastor of the parish; you didn't go near him ... always damnation and hell, no matter what you did. You know, you were going to hell, there was always that fear. God was fear. ... My mom and dad would say 'God will punish you' if you didn't do the right thing, or something like that." Confession often invoked fear: "I remember my first confession. I was scared to death. ... At another time, I was the next in line, and the priest actually yelled in the confessional, 'It's been how long since you've been to confession? And you did what?' Everybody stood up and moved to the other side [to another priest]. Fear, that was a major thing." In that family, confession was mandatory for children every two weeks. Here is more on fear: "The nuns, we were scared of to death. I distinctly remember ... [physical abuse]." Here is a more humorous description of a CCD class in the post-Vatican II era: "I remember the religious education: we all had the fear of Sister Two Ton; she was like a really big lady, she was huge, and she was just overbearing. She was dominant. My view of religious education, what I remember, is that it was very strict. I didn't learn much." These are extreme but not isolated cases: I could give similar personal examples that took place thousands of miles away, as if the church of power, discipline, guilt, and shame were the same universally in the pre-Vatican II days. Although the Catholic Church has become more civil in its teaching methods since then, it has not changed substantially: obedience and loyalty remain the main virtues expected of priests and bishops, and canon law discipline remains the norm of church government at all levels.

This apparent digression on authoritarianism, guilt, and shame was necessary to understand the nature of Catholic piety and devotions in the Tridentine church. In the authoritarian civil and religious societies of the past, there was only one possible form of filial piety: *external* conformity to the demands and wishes of the authority figures. In the examples given above, external submission was the only option: when Mass attendance and Communion were recorded on a chart by the school nuns every week, obviously everyone attended (not surprisingly, attendance was close to 80 percent in the 1950s). When one's childhood image of God was "Don't mess with God: he could be an angry God; he could be a punishing God," then one was likely to be "a good kid" like everybody else. In the Tridentine church, piety was behavioral in the form of physical Mass *attendance* (arriving no later than the Offertory, to be accurate), and devotions were behavioral *practices*, the more the better. This emphasis on external conformity is best understood in light of the family system of the past.

In 1900, about 70 to 80 percent of the population lived in rural villages in the United States, Canada, Germany, and France. The Great Depression and WWII brought massive social changes, but the traditional mores endured throughout the Eisenhower presidency (1953–1961) and came to an end only with the counterculture of the 1960s.[197] Structurally, the traditional families were units of production with hierarchical social relations; the authority of the father was quasi-absolute; obedience to authority was necessary for survival, with little room for personal choice in career and marriage; and religion was central to family and community life, with no room for dissent or personal choice. All of these characteristics started to change in the United States and the West in the 1960s, but not in Catholicism; these changes have been slow to spread, but tend to be universal among the young, which explains their disaffection from traditional religion in most Western nations.

In preindustrial societies (and until very recent times) religion was ascribed, with children accepting for life the religion of their parents. Today parents often let their children select their religion by the age of thirteen or fourteen. While a career change is possible at age thirty, forty, or fifty, most churches expect their believers to be "confirmed" for life in their adolescent beliefs, without the help of a special ministry serving the needs of adolescents until marriage and childbirth. The results are usually disastrous for the transmission of faith, because today religion, like career and parenthood, is an achieved, not ascribed, status. While young people can find clear guidelines about college majors and career choices, no such help is available in the field of religion. Religious identity is increasingly personal; two brothers and sisters will often find different religious identities—as is also the case in professional identity, sexual orientation, and spouse selection. While in the choice of a career and a mate, individuals can find guidance in peers and adults, there is no such help in making religious choices. Again, the values found at school and work are not found in the church.

One of the major characteristics of traditional social relations was *behavioral* respect for those of a higher rank, which brings us back to devotions. In the old days, "wives [were] the first servants in the household"; they spoke to their husbands as to a superior person.[198]

Signs of respect were expected toward church and God, not just parents. Church representatives were to be greeted with the respect due to their rank, according to a hierarchy equivalent to nobility ranks in royalty. Giving honor and glory to the church was always seen as a way to give glory to God. Thus at his "enthronement," the new pope would appear in all the majesty of his office, wearing a triple crown more glorious than that of any king and riding on a *sedia gestatoria* (portable throne) carried by twelve footmen in red uniforms, in a more grandiose pageantry than in any empire. This custom of reverence and glory has been followed for more than a thousand years, was used for the last time under Pope John XXIII (1958–1963), and may still be remembered. In church, respect to God required absolute silence, as in the presence of a king.

In the village community, the requirement of weekly Mass attendance was mainly behavioral. Then, more than today, the church could use all its tools of shaming, guilt, social pressure, and excommunication—and even jailing, in the distant past—to enforce conformity. In the 1917 code of canon law, the obligation of Sunday Mass attendance is described as external conformity: "On days of obligations, the faithful must hear Mass; they must also abstain from menial work, from legal contracts, as well as from public markets, fairs, and other public auctions" (canon 1248).[199] All shops and stores (except bakeries for a few hours) were to remain closed on Sundays; gas stations were closed on Sundays in the South throughout the 1960s. In the 1917 code, Mass attendance is described as a behavior similar to the secular behaviors of shopping, writing contracts, and attending a village fair or a public auction, as if the level of interiority were the same in all of them. There is no reason given for the Sunday obligation: then, as today in the military, superiors give no reasons for their commands. Half a century later, to "hear Mass" was changed to "participate in Mass" in the 1983 code (canon 1247); but the requirement remains mainly behavioral. As explained in the canon that follows, "the precept of participating in the Mass is satisfied by assistance at a Mass which is celebrated anywhere in a Catholic rite" (canon 1248). Mass participation in the spirit of Vatican II is "satisfied," we are told, by attendance. Is it surprising, then, that in many parishes, singing at Mass is not encouraged very strongly, so that many Catholics today remain passive during the Eucharistic celebration? A major proposal for Horizon 2030 will be to move the inactive into the active category of Mass attenders.

Mass attendance is a behavioral requirement that can be controlled, individually and collectively, but there are many spiritual practices that are neither required nor necessarily behavioral, and these are usually called "devotions." Mass itself can be a devotion if attended beyond the level of obligation. Daily Mass attendance has always been recommended—even two Masses on Sundays, as was the custom for the pious of old. The revised canon law of 1983 even allows receiving Communion twice a day, which is strange (canon 917). The daily celebration of the Eucharist by priests is "strongly recommended ... even if the faithful cannot be present" (canon 904). Sunday Mass is an obligation. Daily Mass is *encouraged;* it is a devotion.

Neither canon law nor the *Catechism of the Catholic Church* deal with devotions, public or private, except to say that they must be regulated by the ecclesiastical authorities (canons 392 and 839). Public devotions belong to the local church and are found in diocesan or national catechisms. Thus the *Baltimore Catechism* taught children that "Prayer is necessary for salvation, and without it no one having the use of reason can be saved" (Q 1104). One should pray, not only on Sundays, but "every morning and night, in all dangers, temptations, and afflictions" (Q. 1105). Children had to memorize the "most recommended" prayers—namely, the Lord's Prayer, the Hail Mary, the Apostles' Creed, the Confiteor, and the Acts of Faith, Hope, Love, and Contrition (Q 1112). Diocesan catechisms do not deal with private devotions, which belong to the parish and individuals.

Most private devotions have been the specialty of religious orders. One wave of devotional practices occurred in the thirteenth century under the influence of the Franciscans, especially through their tertiary societies; a proliferation of home altars and private prayer books occurred shortly after St. Francis of Assisi's death. The rosary has been spread by Dominicans and Franciscans; the devotion to the Sacred Heart by Jesuits; the use of scapulars by Carmelites; and the liturgy of the hours by Benedictines. Most of the traditional devotions (the rosary, the First Friday Mass, the Forty Hours, perpetual adoration, the miraculous medal, private retreats, devotion to saints and their relics, and novenas of all kinds) were spread by religious congregations. Another wave of private devotion, the *devotio moderna,* started in the fifteenth century, influenced by both the Reformation and humanism, emphasizing the use of Scripture, private meditation, and a personal connection to God. Devotions, both individually or in parish associations, were widespread in the pre-Vatican II church.

Devotions are *practices* that one performs on a regular basis. They belong to the universe of *pietas* and are quite foreign to the universe of Christian discipleship that emphasizes a personal relationship with Christ. *Pietas* requires the practice of respect and dedication to one's parents, especially in their old days, and respect to church and God. Some religious practices are to be performed weekly (Mass attendance), others yearly (reception of Communion and confession of sins), or daily (recitation of morning and evening prayers), or several times a times a day (Office of the Hours); in all cases, they are behavioral, as indicated by the very terms of attendance, reception, confession, and recitation. One is said to *practice* Catholicism (as a practicing Catholic) or mainline Protestantism (as a practicing Protestant). Both *pietas* and practices are based on social relations that are disappearing in the West. The new order is that of relationships.

2. Sociology of "Relationships"

The notion of "relationship" is a modern concept that appeared as an outgrowth of "going steady" in the dating process. Dating itself became generalized only in the 1930s and '40s; before that, courting was the normal process of mate selection. St. Alphonsus of Liguori (1696–1787) would allow couples to meet no more than once or twice before having to decide about marriage; this was actually common practice. In the 1950s, a new phenomenon appeared on the dating scene: "going steady." Before the 1950s, it was common for boys and girls to come separately to public dances, to dance once or twice with the same person, and then return to their separate worlds. Moral theologians viewed going steady with suspicion. According to a stricter view, "going steady is always sinful; generally a mortal sin; sometimes only venial."[200] John Connery, SJ, in his "Notes on Moral Theology" tried to strike a middle course: "I am inclined to consider it [going steady] a passing fad, about as stable as the teen-agers who engage in it. But while it is with us, it does present a problem."[201] What happens when going steady breaks down? What do we call a second or third "going steady"? What among adults was called "an affair" came to be called "a relationship" among teenagers. While having affairs was and is not looked upon favorably among adults, having sequential relationships was considered part of growing up, and *being* in a relationship was normal and desirable. The term "relationship," applied to male-female steady encounters, appeared in the 1960s or 1970s, according to Giddens.[202] Since then, "relationships" have become a standard way of relating to others, to one's spouse, and to friends, colleagues, and relatives.

Several new characteristics make relationships different from traditional romantic love. According to Giddens,[203] a relationship is entered "for its own sake"—that is, without reference to marriage; besides dating, friendships and associations with family members can also be relationships. Second, the traditional gender roles of male conquest and female passivity are abolished; today's relationships tend to be egalitarian. Third, while romantic love was goal oriented (namely, toward marriage or male conquest), a relationship is a psychological *process* that pursues no other goal than individual and mutual gratification. Finally, while in romantic love success was most often measured in terms of "they lived happily ever after," in a relationship, gratification is psychic, emotional, and oriented to the present, rather than future. In the past, romantic love was mainly male initiated; in today's relationships, it is more often women who set the agenda in terms

of emotional and psychological closeness. Today relationships as a way of relating to others with emotional and psychological closeness have become standard in the United States, and increasingly the rest of the world, because of Hollywood movies.

Dating adolescents can now be seen in any high school in the United States and the West. Yet in the picture to the left,[204] there is nothing that suggests a learning environment, as if schools were places for dating rather than learning. There is no room for authority in this picture, in sharp contrast to the image of filial piety shown above (page 209). The kneeling son listening to this seated father can symbolize the Catholic laity of the past receiving obediently the teachings of the church, in childlike simplicity of heart and mind. In the world of dating adolescents, however, there is no room for authoritative teaching. The church has to learn to speak the language of the day and speak of relationships, as in Hosea and the letter to the Ephesians, rather than quote Romans 13:1 ("All authority comes from God …"). The church must teach relationships—with God and others—rather than obedience.

A relationship "refers to a situation where a social relation is entered for its own sake … and which is continued by both parties to deliver enough satisfaction" (ibid). Marriages are supposed to be relationships that provide mutual satisfaction; a loveless marital relationship is a contradiction in terms and will end as soon as one of the partners deems it appropriate. This attitude toward marriage is applied to all institutions: as soon as a major in college, a job, a career, or an involvement in a church ceases being gratifying—that is, the contribution to the institution in question becomes unsatisfying—the relationship is deemed over, and one will look for another involvement.

The family itself becomes a web of relationships when parents realize that "Children have rights … to be cared for emotionally, to have their feelings respected and their views and feelings taken into account."[205] Now it is parents who must show respect for their children when they reach the age of reason; the time of behavioral respect for superiors and abuse of inferiors (so clearly shown in cases of sexual abuse by priests) is over. The authority of the parents is transformed from coercive and disciplinary to moral and educational. Fear of parents—and of God and church—is of another age; now it is parents who may fear losing their children via excessive authoritarianism and emotional distance. The ideal family now is one of mutual respect and emotional closeness, not behavioral respect, submission, and emotional repression, as in the past. With time, family members become close to one another,

sharing a mutual presence wherever they go, as suggested by the picture to the left.[206] This mutual presence is comforting, not oppressive.

Relationships with authority figures (parents, teachers, churches, and so on) will be democratic to the extent that the latter recognize the "principle of autonomy" according to which "individuals should be free and equal in the determination of the conditions of their own lives."[207] The principle of autonomy requires open discussion based on mutual trust and accountability. The principle of autonomy prevails in schools (and families) when students can discuss their course preferences and negotiate special arrangements for special circumstances; on the other hand, students must be accountable to both parents and teachers to allow for mutual respect. Discussions in the classroom and home are gratifying to the extent that authority figures respect views and feelings, even those contrary to their own.

In relationships, identity is based on reflexivity and self-actualization. "Reflexivity of the self is continuous, as well as all pervasive. At each moment, or at least at regular intervals, the individual is asked to conduct a self-interrogation in terms of what is happening."[208] "What I am gaining from this? Where is this leading me? Will I gain greater self-fulfillment in this?" Questions may also be positive, in search of improving the relationship and the fulfillment of self and others. Reflexivity makes relationships unstable: they will seek constant improvement, and they will be terminated if that improvement does not occur. There is no room for stale relationships at home, school, or church. As in Maslow's pyramid of development, in relationships there must be constant self-actualization.

The type of social relations found at home also prevails in religion. Today people seek a "personal relationship" with God and Jesus Christ. Closeness to God has always been the ultimate goal of Christian spirituality, and such closeness is found in the lives of all deeply religious people. Yet the language of a "personal relationship" is modern; it was absent as much in Luther as in the Catholic Counter-Reformation. Wesley and the holiness movement are credited for having introduced it, and evangelical Protestants for having disseminated it. Now it is prevalent in all churches, including the Catholic Church. But if a personal relationship with God, rather than behavioral submission, is the basis of Catholic life, the church itself will be transformed.

Conclusion: The Church as Communion in Discipleship

It is now time to summarize what we have covered so far by asking what the church would look like as a web of relationships, a community of communities, or communion in discipleship. If we applied to the church the principles of individual autonomy, respect for the opinions of others, constant reflexivity, and discussion that are dear to the new generation, we would expect to find—in the distant future of 2030 or even later—freedom of speech, freedom of association, and freedom of the diocesan press; these are minimum conditions for communion in discipleship.

To the extent that reflexivity is the core of any quest—relational or professional, as well as spiritual—open discussion must be the core of any religious institution. In the postmodern frame of mind of the new generation, there are no absolutes, only partial truths; hence, all voices must be heard, especially the dissenting ones. In this perspective, the practice of silencing theologians appears as repulsive and counterproductive; disciplinary actions like excommunication are as obsolete as the disownment of one's own children when they do not conform to parental expectations. Not much was gained from excommunicating Luther and the ideals the Reformers stood for; it took four hundred years for Catholicism to appropriate some of their ideas.

A Postmodern View
"I believe in responsible dissent from the church's teachings. Infallibility is a very difficult concept even to raise in a postmodern era. I don't know what it could possibly mean, even. I think that it would be very, very difficult to be an adult Catholic not have some areas in which you dissent."
—Interview with religious education director and PhD

There is no freedom of association in the Catholic Church when any bishop can excommunicate or forbid organizations like Call to Action or

Voices of the Faithful and receive Vatican approval for it. Dissent should not be repressed, but valued. It would be of great benefit if, following the example of Paul dissenting with Peter, bishops were to form informal groups to discuss burning issues like celibacy, the ordination of women, or greater subsidiarity in worship, inviting bishops from around the world to join them in their reflection. A central authority that is respectful of the opinions of all should not feel threatened by dissenting voices, but on the contrary, should see them as an opportunity for renewal in a church *semper reformanda* (always in need of reform).

If equality is seen a main characteristic of friendship from Aristotle to today, then communion in discipleship requires first-name relationships at all levels. Increasingly parish priests want to be called by their first (and baptismal) names. Jesus is seen today as "first among equals,"[209] first among his disciples, while popes and bishops appear as first among unequals. Bishop are less available than senators; they are more like state governors, except that they are not elected. They appear more like CEOs than shepherds; they use secrecy rather than public disclosure. Catholicism cannot be a communion of communions when papal nuncios write secret reports on local churches, their institutions, and their leaders. The bishops should appear as brothers, from brother pope to brother bishop X or bishop Y or Z, and be as open as brothers, within the limits of their responsibilities.

In short, the de facto pluralism of the laity should be a Christian right, not a consequence of the lack of hierarchical power over them; the monolithic papalism of the hierarchy is a counterproductive anachronism, and the declining number of priests a sad consequence of the present state of affairs. For Christians, freedom of speech was granted by the spirit of Pentecost, the right of dissent was a common practice in the early church, and the right to assembly was first practiced by Jesus when he associated with sinners and social outcasts. In other words, for Christians, basic human rights emerge from the practice of discipleship, rather than from written constitutions. The practice of discipleship inevitably leads to a new understanding of church and Christian life. But where does the notion of discipleship come from, and how important is it in the Catholic Church today?

Bonhoeffer was probably the first in recent times to bring the concept of discipleship to the center of Christian life. He was best known during his lifetime for his 1937 book titled *Discipleship* (translated as *The Cost of Discipleship* in the first English translation). Of course, discipleship has always been central in Christian life, and Bonhoeffer, Kolbe, and Romero and many others paid with their lives being faithful to it. In the Tridentine Catholic Church, however, only religious orders were expected to follow the ideals of discipleship—that is, the evangelical counsels of the beatitudes—while the demands of the Ten Commandments were deemed sufficient for the laity. For Bonhoeffer, discipleship is at the heart of Christian life for all.

His call for "costly grace" is well-known: "Cheap grace is the deadly enemy of our Church. We are fighting today for costly grace. Cheap grace means grace sold on the market like cheapjack's wares. The sacraments, the forgiveness of sin, and the consolation of religion are thrown away at cut price." This critique was directed at Bonhoeffer's Lutheran Church, but it can equally be applied to Catholicism. "Cheap grace means grace as doctrine, a principle, a system. ... An intellectual assent to that idea is held to be sufficient. ... The Church which holds the correct doctrine of grace has, it is supposed, *ipso facto* a part in that grace." Costly grace, on the other hand, "is the call of Jesus Christ at which the disciple leaves his nets and follows him."[210] While there will always be a great difference between the ordinary faithful and the religious elite, Sunday attendance easily becomes "cheap grace" without constant reminder of the demands of discipleship.

Discipleship is now the major theme of church teaching in Latin America. The General Conference of Latin American bishops meets every ten years or so, and their conclusions often are of world significance. The Medellin conference of 1968 shook the Catholic world with its emphasis on the preferential option for the poor[211] and the liberation theology that emerged from it and made it possible. The methodology of Medellin was new: it began "from below" with a sociological analysis of the current situation, not "from above"—that is, from theological premises. This is also the methodology of liberation theology and all the theologies "from below" that have emerged since then and have brought a new dynamism to theology.

The central theme and title of the Fifth General Conference of 2007, which took place in Aparecida (Brazil), was Discipleship and Mission. This central theme is best summarized by the picture on the cover page of the Aparecida document (shown below)—a picture which, in the words of Pope Benedict XVI, "represents the Lord shortly before ascending into heaven, giving his followers the mission to make disciples of all nations. The pictures [of the triptych] suggest the close relationship of Jesus Christ with his disciples and missionaries for the life of the world."[212] This triptych from the school of Cuzco (probably from the Vatican Museum) was a personal gift of Pope Benedict to the conference as "a souvenir for continuous inspiration." This picture of the risen Christ contrasts sharply with that of the suffering Christ that has dominated Latin American piety for centuries. This change suggests a paradigmatic revolution from *pietas* to relationships, as outlined above.

Also on the cover page at the top is the icon for the evangelization for all of Latin America: a red cross next to the sphere of the world, surrounded by two half circles. This is the icon of the "Continental Mission" to be developed by all national conferences and to be discussed by the next General Conference in about ten years—to take place, significantly, in Havana, Cuba. This Continental Mission "will endeavor to put the church in a state of permanent mission."[213]

To summarize my conclusion about relationships (and discipleship), let us recall that the traditional image for the relationship between Christ and the church is that of husband and wife (Ephesians 4:21–33). Today the family relations are no longer based on the ancient model of family *pietas*, but on egalitarian *relationships*. From that perspective, the church appears in a new light. Four of the six evaluative criteria described at the beginning of the previous chapter apply here. The church does not appear as a structure of power to the extent that it incorporates the egalitarian ideal of husbands and wives. Having given up conservative or liberal ideologies, it stands as "in the world but not of the world," promoting the ideal of growth in discipleship (as in Maslow) rather than obedience and submission. The fuzziness of morality should fade when Christian life is conceived as the concrete practice of discipleship, rather than obedience to abstract deontological principles. Finally, to the extent that the church is communion in discipleship, the split between upper and lower levels of the church will progressively disappear. Some criteria still do not apply: the disaffection of the young and the fuzziness of sacraments. However, if church teaching is adapted to the various Catholic audiences, from the nonpracticing to those totally committed, the young will again find their place in the church, and then sacraments will appear as analogical.

Let us turn to the various Catholic audiences.

3. Sociology of Religious Practices

In his letters, St. Paul directs different messages toward different audiences. He offers different advice to men and women, the married and the single, the old and the young, and the slaves and their masters. Within any parish, one is likely to find different audiences, and each may require an adapted message.

It is traditional in the sociology of religion to distinguish between different levels of religious practice—that is, the frequency of Sunday church attendance. This distinction is more important than ever, as the differences in attendance have greatly increased since the 1950s, when religious practice in the United States was most homogeneous. The graph below shows the various levels of religious practice of Catholics and the various audiences for the years 2002 to 2008, according to GSS data.

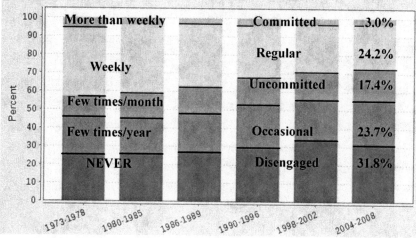

HOW OFTEN R ATTENDS RELIGIOUS SERVICES BY GSS YEAR FOR THIS RESPONDENT

1. At the bottom of the chart are those who never or practically never attend church. They constitute the biggest religious group (31.8 percent in 2004–2008). What shall we call them? The term "unchurched" suggests that they only need to come back to become "good Christians" again. This view is myopic, unless one believes that Christianity is only a matter of church attendance. If one looks at Christians as the "followers of the way," Christianity is a subculture, and those who have no contact whatsoever with the "followers of the way" seem to be no different from gentiles. I will call them "disengaged," because for them, attendance and sacraments have little or no meaning. For parents who have not attended church in years, what meaning can the baptism of a child have? What are the chances that they will "come home"? Very small. Only some kind of conversion experience (e.g., marriage to a religious spouse; an abysmal failure in marriage, work, or health; and/or exposure to an evangelical-minded Christian) will change their life course. They may have their children baptized, but the latter, growing up in a home without religion, will progressively drift into the "no religion" category. A totally new pastoral strategy is necessary to bring them back.

2. The disengaged (31.8 percent) are more numerous than the regular church attenders (24.2 percent in 2004–2008). Hence, the disengaged

are likely to have a greater gravitational force for the occasional attenders (a few times per month, 23.7 percent in 2004–2008) than the regular attenders (24.2 percent). If Christianity is a true subculture, the occasional attendance a few times a year will have little or no impact on one's life. These sporadic attenders are like students who attend a course a few times a year. Very little is gained in such a short time, yet they themselves have not given up: they continue coming back. Because they have become strangers to their childhood religious subculture, they are not ready to come back to regular church services. Like students who have missed years of education, they need some easy introductory classes. Many evangelical churches have special services for these potential members. Hence, there is a need for a special pastoral strategy for them.

3.   Next on the chart come the monthly attenders (17.4 percent, several times a month). They are regular Sunday attenders, yet unwilling or unable to attend weekly. Some may be prevented by family, business, or practical matters, while others may be content to stay at the fringes of weekly attendance. I call them "uncommitted," with the understanding that a nod or set of circumstances may push them up into regular practice or down into religious disengagement. A general encouragement of more frequent practice is likely to have little effect; what may be needed is a personal invitation or push by a friend, relative, or committed fellow Christian.

4.   The regular weekly attenders (24.2 percent) stand in the middle, between the totally committed and the uncommitted, yet in a church dominated by disengaged and occasional believers, they are more likely to be influenced by the secular culture than by magisterial teaching. This is documented by empirical research. The Gallup research presented in the previous chapter divides church attenders into three groups: the engaged (29 percent), the not-engaged (54 percent), and the actively disengaged (17 percent). In the Gallup parish surveys, however, the category of the disengaged is dropped. We are left with only two groups, the engaged and the not-engaged; I will call the former "active" and the latter "passive" church attenders. The main point of the Gallup research here is that

together, the not-engaged and actively disengaged (or passive attenders) are far more numerous (about three times) than the engaged (or active attenders).

In Gallup, the engaged are defined as those who have "strong psychological and emotional connections to their church or parish. They are *more* spiritually committed, they are *more* likely to invite friends, family members, and coworkers to congregational events, and they give *more*, both financially and in commitment in time [emphasis added]."[214] This definition is vague, as suggested by the repeated use of "more." The not-engaged are similarly defined vaguely by their lesser emotional and spiritual connection and their minimal contribution in time and money. Gallup does not reveal how these variables are measured, yet these data lead to an important conclusion: the engaged are a minority of less than one third (or even less in Catholic parishes), while the nonactive members are the majority. It is likely, then, that in Catholic parishes, the passive attenders constitute the majority or even the vast majority (maybe two-thirds) of Sunday attenders.

Gallup found that the not-engaged Sunday attenders "are just as likely as the engaged to be completely 'satisfied' with the congregation. ... I can show up at church once a month or so, put $2 in the offering, sleep through the sermon, and actually be 'extremely satisfied.'"[215] Is this true of all not-engaged or only a fraction of them? In the Willow Creek research, only those "stalled" in their faith are mentioned as also satisfied with the services. It is likely that many Catholics, among both the active and the passive attenders, are stalled in their faith but satisfied; hence, they are likely to oppose any change toward higher standards.

Although there are no quantitative measurements to distinguish active from passive attenders, participant observation leaves little doubt that these are two different audiences. I will offer further description of both groups in the presentation of pastoral strategies for renewal.

5. A small minority of people attend Mass more than weekly. Their number has declined by half, from 5.5 percent to 2.9 percent, between 1972–1974 and 2004–2006. One may consider this small group as marginal, but Rick

Warren has warned us about the importance of the core ministers: "Your church will never be any stronger than its core lay ministers who carry out the various ministries of the church." This was true in the pre-Vatican II church, when the staff of most parishes consisted of several priests and numerous religious sisters. With 10.2 sisters per parish and 3.3 priests in 1965,[216] Catholic parishes were led by a core group of religiously trained leaders that remains unmatched today. Members of religious congregations usually go through a religious training more demanding than that of priests, since it includes one year or more of postulancy and novitiate, and is followed by vows of poverty, chastity, and obedience. They also receive some theological training that is not as easily available to lay ministers today. The rules of religious congregations usually require daily prayer, often of an hour or so, and usually a yearly retreat. Members of a given congregation also share a common spirituality and a common way of life that predisposes them toward joint ministerial work in schools, hospitals, or parishes—all of which cannot easily be replicated by lay ministers today. As religious orders were the main propagators of religious devotions, one may say that religious sisters were the backbone of the parish of the past.

Among the religiously committed are two different audiences, the "totally committed" (consisting of the leaders of the church ministries) and those, quite numerous, willing to be "involved" in devotions and parish activities yet do not achieve total commitment. These two different audiences need different spiritual support.

6.   So far we have analyzed the various Catholic audiences, leaving out the ex-Catholics. The latter should not be ignored, as they constitute about 25–30 percent of those raised in the Catholic Church. More precisely, according to the General Social Surveys for the period of 2002–2006, 27 percent of those raised in the Catholic Church no longer belong to it. These percentages have steadily increased over the years, from 16 percent in 1973, to 25 percent in the year 2000, to 30 percent in 2008; the percentage of ex-Catholics will increase to 35 or even 40 percent as new defections are added to the previous ones. A steady 45 to 50 percent of ex-Catholics converted to Protestantism, while 37 to 40 percent switched to "no religion."

The level of religiosity among ex-Catholics who converted to Protestantism seems higher than that of Catholics: from 1972 to 2008, three times more ex-Catholic Protestants attended church more than weekly: 14.4 percent versus 3.9 of Catholics. This statistic suggests that some dedicated Catholics are leaving. Thus Catholicism is facing losses on two fronts: the loss of some uncommitted to "no religion" (about 40 percent) and the loss of some committed Catholics to Protestantism (about 50 percent).

If we include ex-Catholics to the table of church attendance, we get a new vision of reality that is much more disturbing than the one from the previous graph. In the next two graphs, I combined into one category weekly and more than weekly attendance (on the right). I also combined into one category ex-Catholics and never-attending Catholics (on the left). In 1972–1975, as seen in the first graph, weekly practicing Catholics clearly held the majority with 41.2 percent; hence, the church could hope to influence noncommitted and seasonal Catholics to come back to regular practices. Quite different is the situation in the four surveys of 2002 to 2008, seen in the second graph. Now, ex-Catholics and nonpracticing Catholics are the majority by a proportion of two to one in reference to practicing Catholics (46.1 versus 21.2 percent). Now, only one adult in four practices weekly. This means that in every Catholic family, children see that half of the adult Catholics have either left the church or never attend, and another 3 out of 10 attend seasonally or without commitment.

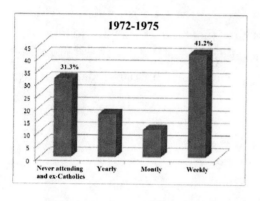

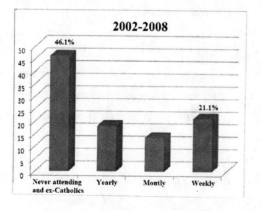

What is the future of the new generation, and what is being done to help them? This raises again the question of pastoral strategies.

Many Catholics tend to take these defections lightly, on the conviction that "the gates of Hades will not overpower" the rock of the church (Matthew 16:18). Sociologists may agree on secular grounds: judging from the last three or four millennia, it is unlikely that either Christianity, Hinduism, Buddhism, or Islam will disappear in the foreseeable future, yet the relative importance of each faith is likely to shift.

If church authorities tend to take these statistics lightly, church historians cannot. During its first thousand years, Christianity was prevalent in most of North Africa, Egypt, Israel, Jordan, Iraq, Turkey, and the Balkan States. Here are the percentages of Christians today, according to the CIA "World Factbook":[217]

Algeria	:	1% Christians and Jews
Morocco	:	1.1%
Tunisia	:	1%
Libya	:	0%
Egypt	:	9% Coptic; 1% other Christians
Israel	:	1.7% Arab Christians
Jordan	:	6% Christian, mainly Orthodox
Iraq	:	3% Christians and other non-Muslims
Turkey	:	2% Christians and Jews

Given the catastrophic Catholic decline in Europe, Canada, Australia, several Latin American countries, and increasingly in the United States, it is likely that in a few centuries, the religious map of these countries will appear significantly different. Today there are already more Muslims than Catholics in the world, and evangelical Protestants are growing at a much faster rate all over the world, as will be discussed below (see data on page 272). No business organization would look passively at losses of this magnitude without instituting drastic new policies. So far the Catholic Church has done little to nothing.

In summary, I have distinguished five different audiences with different needs (leaving aside the ex-Catholics, who are now out of reach): the disengaged, who practically never attend church (31.8 percent); the occasional attenders, who attend a few times per year (23.7 percent); the uncommitted, who attend on various occasions during the month (17.4 percent); the regular weekly attenders (24.2 percent), subdivided into passive and active participants; and the committed (3 percent, for whom more than weekly attendance is not a good indicator). Those committed can in turn be subdivided into those totally committed (discipleship) and those involved (doing more than just Sunday Mass attendance). What are the pastoral strategies for these various audiences? As a general principle, pastoral strategies must endeavor to move each group to a higher level. There are also specialized audiences, like the children, the young adults, the divorced and remarried, the sick, and people in prison; I will not consider these specialized ministries, but concentrate on the pastoral strategies needed for the various parish audiences distinguished above.

I will concentrate on three strategies:
- Moving Sunday attenders from passive to active Mass participation
- Helping active attenders become involved
- Leading the involved to totally committed discipleship

4. Moving from Passive to Active Mass Participation

According to Gallup's research, only 19 percent of Catholics, nationwide are "engaged" parishioners. We cannot conclude from this statistic that only 19 percent actively participate in Mass while 81 percent attend passively, as the criteria of Gallup's measurements are not known. Let it suffice to say that the majority of Sunday attenders are not actively involved in the liturgy. Is this true?

One gets a totally different impression when looking at the faithful from the front and from the back of the

> **Maslow and Spiritual Growth**
> A weekly visit to a therapist for fifty weeks is likely to lead to growth as understood in Maslow, Piaget, or Erikson, but weekly Mass attendance for fifty weeks may not lead to growth if there is no path for development. Spiritual growth is more likely to happen if there is a developmental path from passive attendance to discipleship.

church. In the front pews, most people sing and participate; this is what priests see from the altar. Totally different is the view from the last pews. I have attended services in both the first and the last pews. Here are field notes from a parish that was singled out to me as one of the most dynamic in the diocese. At a 5:00 p.m. Saturday Mass, the church was full; arriving late, I could only get a seat in the last pew.

In front of me was a young mother with three children. She spent the whole time keeping her younger one quiet, having brought a bag of toys (e.g., crayons) for him to color in a book, at all times speaking to him, putting her hand on his mouth each time he talked too loud, then giving him a soft drink, putting a straw in his mouth to keep it shut, but at no avail. They left at Communion; actually, the whole pew left.

The participation of the faithful was weak. Most people responded to the *Kyrie*, because the priest allowed them to say their line, but for the recitation of the Gloria, Credo, or the Our Father, the priest spoke more loudly into his microphone than anyone else. I could not see a choir from the back of the church, nor could I hear it, except at brief intervals.

The cantor acted as song leader, as apparently there was no choir. She had a beautiful voice but did not articulate the words, so I could only hear vowels separated by silences. I could not guess what language she was singing in. She extended her right arm to the assembly to invite people to sing, but only the organ responded, and she sang louder. At times I could only hear the organ, unable to hear whether anybody was singing at all.

On this day of the feast of Saint Paul, the homily summarized his life and concluded with the invitation of bringing the message of Christ to the whole world, but with no specific suggestions about it. The lady next to me said the rosary during the homily; she continued saying the rosary during the rest of the Mass.

About one-third of the assembly left during or after Communion. The last song was as silent as the rest.

a. **Small children** are often disruptive. Often parents bring toys or electronic games for them to play with, which draws the immediate attention of all those around them. Often the service is disrupted by the crying of small children. Usually nothing is done about it. In some churches, children under a given age are not admitted or must attend in a separate room with video facilities. I personally would not allow students to bring children to class if they were disruptive: the good of the class is more important than the physical attendance of students. What is more important in church, physical presence or participation? From observation, it seems that for most Catholics, attendance trumps participation. Something should be done about it.

b. In many churches, the quality of **the readings and the sound system** are not conducive to active participation. Gothic churches have tunnel-like naves, with low sound quality at the end of the tunnel. In famous churches like the Westminster Abbey, the Westminster Catholic cathedral in London, the Notre-Dame cathedral in Paris, and the Episcopalian church of St. John the Divine in New York (supposed to be the biggest gothic structure in the world when completed), as well as in ordinary Catholic churches, I found the sound to be poor in the back but quite good in the first pews. The same can be said about the quality of the readings, which may be acceptable for those in front but inaudible at times for those in the back. This holds for priests, especially those foreign-born. For people in the back who appear to be bored and absentminded, the Mass may seem like the purring and humming of words, sound, tones, and tunes, without much to focus on or keep their attention alive. And not much is done about it.

c. Merely having the song leader symbolically extend his or her arms as an **invitation to sing** is not sufficient to get the faithful to join. Usually the immediate response is overwhelming organ music, loud solo singing by the presiding priest or the song leader, and a few voices in the first rows. If we took as a rule of thumb that one should be able to hear distinctively the music of the organ, the voices of the choir, and the singing of those near oneself, the music quality in most parishes would be considered poor. This is not what I observed at the Bayville services, and to a lesser degree at St. Mary's. At a public concert, most people would expect to hear distinctively the singing and the orchestra; if disappointed, they may simply not come back. What can be done? First of all, such churches should not *discourage* participation.

d.   Active participation is implicitly discouraged **when priests themselves do not participate** in the singing. In solemn Masses shown on television, one can see in close-ups the faces of the celebrant and other participants. At the funeral Mass of John Paul II, broadcast throughout the world, one could see rows of cardinals and bishops and witness the fact that most of them did not participate in the singing. During the Great Litany, when the assembly was to repeat numerous times *"libera nos Domine"* and *"te rogamus audi nos,"* the cardinals and bishops could be seen as remaining silent, although they were the few who understood Latin. Close-up pictures of faces can reveal inner devotion or the absence of it. In local parishes, priests may sing in a loud voice to invite others to join, as if, at that time, inviting others to sing were part of their pastoral duty; at other times, they may be seen as waiting for the singing to come to an end, as if singing were the role of the choir or the assembly, and not their own. Totally different is singing from the altar with fervor and conviction, which is likely to draw others in.

e.   Active **participation of the laity is discouraged by the very structure of the liturgy.** Since the first centuries, the liturgies of the churches of Jerusalem, Antioch, Rome, and of other major cathedrals have been role models for the rest of the Christian world. Today one can easily watch papal Masses broadcast from Rome and pontifical Masses in one's own diocese of the local bishop in his cathedral. Let us compare the participation in three 2009 Easter Masses: that of Pope Benedict, that of a Pontifical Mass in a US cathedral, and that of a local Easter Mass within that diocese. The time spent in singing, reading, praying, and listening to the homily was recorded in minutes and converted into percentages. Here are the results.

	Papal Mass	Pontifical Mass	Parish Mass
Active singing of laity	0%	20%	24%
Choir, cantor, organ	81%	31%	33%
Readings, prayer, Canon	14%	29%	19%
Homily	5%	20%	24%
Total time	140 min.	80 min.	79 min.

As the solemnity of the Mass increases, the participation of the laity decreases. At the Easter 2009 papal Mass, all the singing was done by the various choirs (half a dozen of them). The laity (about 100,000 strong that day) was practically excluded, since most of the singing was done in Latin. Even the Gloria, Credo, and the Pater Noster were in Latin; the members of the choirs did not seem to know the Pater Noster, either, as they constantly had to look at their music sheets.

Pope Benedict's homily was short (seven minutes), but he had given a long homily at the Easter Vigil (more than three hours long), and he was going to deliver a second homily from his balcony, *Urbi and Orbi*, straight after the Easter Mass. The first reading was in Spanish, the second in English, and the Gospel in Italian, but the canon of the Mass was all in Latin. Pope Benedict could be seen reading the canon from the missal throughout the Mass, although one would expect that after fifty years in the priesthood and saying Mass in Latin, he would have memorized it.

The papal Easter Mass could have been celebrated without the faithful, but not without the cameras to broadcast it throughout the world to about sixty countries. The presence of the faithful was not necessary, because their participation was replaced by that of the choirs. Why is music so important? Is sacred music a prayer or a performance? In most cases, sacred music is a pageantry well suited for public celebrations like Christmas and Easter, and for high officials of church and state. All royal courts of the past, secular and clerical, had their paid musicians (e.g., Bach and Palestrina). Queen Elizabeth II of England entertains a choir of twenty-four boys and twelve men at her Windsor Castle, where she usually attends services on weekends. Courtly musicians were deemed as important as the royal guard, or the Swiss Guard in Renaissance Rome. So is sacred music mainly a performance? It does not need to be, as this is not the case at either the Bayville church or St. Mary Star of Hope. I will present below suggestions for singing that is both a prayerful and practical model for the faithful to follow.

The Easter Mass at the local parish—let us call it St. Barnabas—was special in more than one way, particularly in the recitation of the canon, the delivery of the homily, and the participation of the laity, points to be touched upon shortly. St. Barnabas is a suburban parish of 1,800 families, too big for its pastor to know his sheep. In any such big parish, thieves may come and steal sheep at will; the pastor will not even notice it. St. Barnabas has many devotions, but they are treated as private matters, as no devotional group plays an active role in the parish pastoral strategy. As a consequence, St. Barnabas is essentially a sacramental service station characterized by maintenance (education of children, baptisms, weddings, funerals, and Sunday services) rather than growth or mission. There is, however, a latent dynamism that comes from the dedication and imagination of its priests, as will be seen below.

e.   There are many instances of **great willingness on the part of the faithful to participate,** although in unexpected ways. At otherwise silent Masses, I have witnessed the faithful recite in one voice the Gloria, the Credo and the Agnus Dei, as already noticed at St. Mary's. The recitation of the Our Father is very popular in many churches, often with hands raised, leading to the enthusiastic proclamations, both hands raised high, "For the kingdom, the power and the glory are yours, now and forever." The recitation of the Hail Mary is usually also very fervent. In short, the faithful tend to participate more eagerly in vocal prayers than in songs, and they pray loudest when the choir and the organ are silent, as if the latter were obstacles to prayer. At the end of the Holy Thursday Spanish Mass in front of the Blessed Sacrament at St. Barnabas, when the priest started reciting the rosary first in English, and then in Spanish, and finally … in Latin, the people's answer was a loud roaring of prayer, as if the institutional dam retaining their power of prayer had been broken down, giving them permission to pray in their own way. Their prayer was a mixture of English, Spanish, and Latin, all praying fervently in their own language. Is it surprising, then, that people say the rosary during Mass rather than singing hymns they never had a chance to learn while the choir is likely to take over anyway?

f. **Repeated appeals to participate are the key.** Every teacher knows that most students will not participate in class unless constantly pressed to do so. Even in small classes of twenty or thirty students, teachers must constantly work the crowd, walk throughout the classroom, and address students individually by their first name. Some students persistently select the back seats in order not to participate. These students require special attention, without which they will be absentminded most of the time. If high-school classes were run the way priests run Masses, most classrooms would be empty, at least in elective courses. Because song leaders have no pastoral responsibility toward the faithful, it is the pastor who must encourage the singing, not from the altar or the first pews, but from the middle of the assembly or even the last pews. Several parishes could share a priest or deacon to encourage participation at the various Masses. At the Bayville church, all associate pastors attend and participate in all three Sunday services, from 8:30 a.m. to 1:30 p.m. Catholic Masses are organized in shifts, with one priest responsible for each shift, with no involvement when their shift is over. It is exceptional to see a priest actively join the faithful while another priest is celebrating Mass. It is not edifying to see noncelebrating priests and deacons come and go during a Mass as if they had no part in it because it is not their shift.

Most schools and universities have class visitations and student evaluations. The purpose of these evaluations is, at least in theory, teaching improvement. Liturgical services could be greatly improved through the use of feedback. There has been no resistance to filling out Gallup and other surveys before or after Mass. More practical questionnaires could prove very useful for improvement. Discussions in focus groups would bring up many of the issues raised in these pages. Let us review the major parts of the Mass.

g.   Mass usually begins with a **processional** of the priest(s), the deacon(s) and the acolytes marching in hierarchical order, while the faithful sing an entrance song. This hierarchical procession is most obvious in papal and pontifical Masses. Which of the following entrances, we may ask, is the Mass procession most like? Is it that of Pontius Pilate entering Jerusalem before Passover, preceded by his court and army with all the attires of their ranks, all marching in hierarchical order? Is it the entrance of Jesus in a tumultuous crowd cheering cheerfully and walking in total disorder? Or is it the entrance of Pope Benedict at public audiences on Wednesdays in the Audience Hall, shaking numerous hands on his way to the platform to deliver his address in five to ten different languages? At the Easter 2009 Mass, Pope Benedict shook a few hands and blessed a few babies on his way to the altar on St. Peter's Square. In most parishes, priests shake hands at the end of Mass; what prevents them from shaking hands at the entrance, like the pope, rather than marching with self-righteousness as Christ's representative? Here is the processional entrance of the New York's new archbishop:

Processional entrance of New York's new Archbishop: pomp and power

With the choir in full throat and the organ at high pitch, the opening procession filled up a full hour: white-robed priests followed by miter-topped bishops and sashed cardinals in red, marching solemnly in single file through the cathedral's front doors on Fifth Avenue, as the smiling archbishop stood outside, greeting them nonstop.

About 3,000 people filled the pews, including Gov. David A. Paterson, Mayor Michael R. Bloomberg and the state's two United States senators.

—*New York Times*, April 16, 2009

---

h. **The Confiteor** is probably the only prayer the laity is allowed to recite, because neither the priest nor the choir are likely to do it for them; at solemn Masses, the choir is likely to take over the Gloria, the Credo, the Sanctus, and the Agnus Dei, but not the Confiteor. Moreover, the Confession of Sins is always in English, while the other prayers may be in Latin, although fewer people know Latin than know Spanish, Italian, or Polish. Latin has a nostalgic quality that Spanish and Polish do not have. But is the liturgy about nostalgia? The liturgy of the Easter Mass calls for the singing of *Victimae paschali laudes*, written in the eleventh century. Because very few know Latin, in the diocese of St. Barnabas it was sung in English, but to the tune of the original Gregorian music. If people do not know Latin, how likely is it that they will know the original Gregorian music of that hymn? At St. Barnabas, this singing was a total flop. Because many parts of the Catholic liturgy are venerably old, nostalgia prompts liturgists to want to keep them; unfortunately only scholars, not the iPod generation, can appreciate their value.

i. It is customary to **proclaim the Gospel ceremoniously**, by first holding it high like a monstrance, showing it in various directions, and then reading it in a clear and loud voice. These practices are reminiscent of the predigital age when church ceremonies were major Sunday entertainments in village life. When people could not read, it was imperative to read to them, and in predigital times, all teaching was magisterial. Only fifty years ago in French universities, students would rise at the entrance of their professor before he delivered his lecture of the day. Today magisterial lectures are obsolete; they only lead to absentmindedness due the shortness of people's attention span. As to the "monstrance" of the gospel in all directions, it is impressive only the first few times it is performed; it easily becomes one more customary ritual.

It is increasingly common in Catholic churches to find Bibles in the pews. Rather than read the Gospel ceremoniously, it is more beneficial for the faithful to invite them to open their Bibles and have them cursively read the preceding and following chapter(s) before reading aloud the Gospel of the day or part of it; in some churches, the pastor or priest has the assembly repeat after him the main lines he wants to draw attention to. In schools and churches, people remember what they read themselves better than what is read to them.

Education is increasingly digital. While in the past, teachers wrote on the blackboard, today they use video clips and PowerPoint presentations. Innovative evangelical churches follow this trend. Catholics may resist these secular innovations, but at St. Barnabas, there was no resistance to using a big screen for the purpose of … money! On the occasion of the bishop's fund drive, a publicity video was produced by the diocese, and the clergy was encouraged to show it in lieu of a homily to drive in money. The following Sunday, the homily was a commentary on the video, with the additional sales pitch that 20 percent of the proceeds would revert to the parish. If money is not too secular as a homily, why would a screen be, as a teaching tool in the church? At St. Mary's, a big screen is used for all singing. At most churches, a screen could also be used advantageously during the homily or the announcements.

At solemn Masses the celebrant kisses the Gospel. On Good Friday, the faithful are invited to kiss the cross. Could a few faithful also be occasionally invited to kiss the Gospel before or after the reading? In some synagogues, the Torah is ceremoniously carried throughout the temple to allow the assembly to kiss it or at least touch it, and many people do so. Could Catholics do the same with the Gospel? Nothing says the rubrics are to be followed mechanically: one step to the right, one step to the left, bow, kneel, sit … Is the liturgy merely a ritual performance or also, if not mainly, a prayerful creation?

> **Homily as Monologue**
> "In most Catholic churches worldwide, the homily is one of the last forms of public discourse in which no feedback is expected.
> "In a world of increasingly educated hearers brought up amid democratic discourse, the one-way street of the monologue homily risks becoming a cultural curiosity or an alien, authoritarian symbol."
> —*America*, May 25, 2009

j.   How can **homilies** increase the active participation of the faithful? Let us compare the homilies at the three Easter Masses of 2009. Pope Benedict lectured by reading his notes, seated on the papal throne in homage to his role as universal teacher. His homilies are usually available in the specialized press and are probably intended for specialized audiences, as the faithful are not likely to follow his lectures more than a few sentences at a time. At both the US cathedral and St. Barnabas, the homilies consisted of recounting the stories of the Passion and the Resurrection. Most homilies recount the stories of the Gospel of the day, together with other stories from the Gospels and the Old Testament. Scripture is seen mainly as a book of stories. Catholics may not know Scripture as much as Protestants, I was told in an interview, but they know the stories. Storytelling is a lively literary genre; Aristotle believed that good stories (as in the Greek tragedies) have a cathartic or therapeutic effect. But is Scripture mainly a book of stories, except maybe for children? Pope Benedict's homilies are mainly exegetical and theological. Parish homilies often include theological teachings, but usually at the level of catechism. Theology is a reflection on the deposit of the faith, while catechism is a theological summary for the purpose of memorization. A summary of seminary courses is not theology, but catechism. Theology treats people as active participants, catechism as passive recipients. Is catechism the purpose of homilies?

If the church is a communion in discipleship, as concluded above, homilies should deal primarily with spirituality and Christian discipleship. Priests should be able to say, "I have been crucified with Christ and I no longer live, but Christ lives in me. The life I live in the body, I live by faith in the Son of God, who loved me and gave himself for me" (Galatians 2:20). Of course most would be too modest to say "Christ lives in me," but all could say they strive to live with the crucified Christ. Paul often writes about his own spiritual life, but priests seldom speak about theirs in their homilies. This absence reflects the privatization of faith in the Catholic Church, illustrated by the dispersion of the faithful throughout the church, with only a few people in each pew, and as separate from one another as possible. It is this privatization of faith in megaparishes that is overcome in small Christian communities in which faith again becomes shared. If priests do not share their faith, how can they expect the faithful to do so?

Interactive homilies are common in the Catholic Church, but only with children, not adults. At the 2009 Easter Mass at St. Barnabas, the homily was tentatively interactive, as indicated by this transcript.

At the beginning of Mass:

—Good morning, everyone!

—Good morning, Father!

—It is customary when two Orthodox Christians meet on Easter Sunday to say to one another, "He has risen!" and the answer is "He has truly risen." So I say to you, "He has risen!"

—He has truly risen!

—Oh, that sounds so good!

During the homily:

—Jesus was talking about the temple of his ... what?

—Body

—The stone was rolled away, and the tomb was ...

—Empty.

—Louder!

—EMPTY!

Later:

—Do you believe this?

—Yes.

—Do you really believe it?

—YES!

This assistant pastor of about sixty walked the aisle during his homily, while in his cathedral, the local bishop read his notes from behind the pulpit. The spontaneous response of the crowd at St. Barnabas shows once more that the faithful are eager to participate if given the opportunity.

Preaching the homily is to be "reserved to a priest or deacon" (canon 767), but other forms of talk are not excluded; they are actually quite common when it comes to ... again, money. Many parishes have laypeople report about parish finances and promote fund drives. At the 2009 pontifical Easter Mass, the song leader interjected—quite out of place—that the bishop's fund drive mentioned previously was below expectations. In one parish of this diocese, parishioners give a witness talk on stewardship on several occasions during the year. At first, people had to be invited; now people volunteer to do so. In short, although only priests can deliver the homily, the faithful can give witness talks. The topics for testimonials are endless: the parish outreach program; devotional groups; small Christian communities; home and foreign missions; singing in the choir; individual prayer and meditation; and so on. In any parish there are professionals who would feel honored to give a small talk about matters of interest to the faithful. Doctors, nurses, financial advisors, teachers, police officers, and so forth could all make the Christian faith less introverted and less privatized. In summary, good homilies and witness talks can substantially increase the active participation of the laity.

k. **Responsorials and singing**. During the Middle Ages, polyphony progressively replaced Gregorian chant—first of the proper, but later also of the ordinary of the Mass. For some time, the Kyrie, Gloria, Sanctus, and Agnus Dei were left to the faithful to sing, but later (and today) even the ordinary (or order) of the Mass was and is taken over by the polyphonic choir, at least in solemn occasions. According to a historian of the Eucharistic practices, "As polyphonic composition overtook the *Sanctus*, the assembly's voice was excluded from what could be considered their last integral liturgical chant. From this point on ... their musical role could be considered both peripheral and expendable, more occurring 'in' the liturgy than actually a voice 'of' the liturgy."[218] At the papal Easter Mass, as noted above, the presence of the laity was actually unnecessary. What can be done? It may be tempting to go back and prefer "Low Masses" for devotion rather than "High Masses" for public performance, but more radical solutions are necessary.

First, it has to be stated again that the purpose of choir singing is prayer, not artistic performance. Ideally the choir should be a small Christian community, an SCC, whose function is to assist in the collective prayer of the faithful, as is the case at Bayville and St. Mary's, described previously. The "concerts for an audience of One" idea illustrates the point. At Bayville, the pastor of music conceived the project of an additional musical service to be given on Sunday evening, but who would come, considering that the prospective audience had already spent several hours at church in the morning? He then decided that the musical service would be only for the glory of God ("for an audience of One"), even in the total absence of a public. How wrong he was! People flocked into the church to listen and sing along. Since then, the concerts for an audience of One, but in the presence of hundreds, have become regular events. The same can be said about the yearly Passion plays. In 2009, as in previous years, five or six performances had to be scheduled during the holy week, all filled to capacity (600 to 800 people). They are not mainly artistic performances, as the senior pastor invites the audience to prayer on two or three occasions during the performance. The performances are both prayerful and of high professional quality, which both require work and numerous rehearsals.

Singing belongs to the assembly, but rehearsals are needed. In times past, people could learn the hymns through yearly repetitions, because the music did not change much. Today the parish missalettes may contain a new musical edition every year, with additions, deletions, and a new pagination. Now rehearsals are imperative. The responsorial psalms after the first reading change every Sunday and hence must be rehearsed. The cantor or choir sings the verses, and the assembly repeats the response. Very little participation usually occurs, because the faithful are passive recipients throughout the liturgy of the Word, during the first reading, and throughout the Gospel and the homily. The response to the responsorial psalm should be rehearsed and repeated several times, with the invitation to sing LOUDER! A more actively creative participation in the liturgy of the Word and a less mechanical following of the rubrics would also be helpful.

Historically, as the choir progressively took over all the singing, usually in Latin, the trend emerged to sing hymns in the vernacular. In the pre-Vatican II days, the music of these hymns reflected the basic trends of the secular music, in the tradition of Bach and Palestrina. High-culture music changed substantially with Debussy and Stravinsky, but popular music changed even more drastically with rock and roll. Evangelical churches clearly saw that the Gospel message should be expressed in the language of the people. They welcomed unknown artists and groups, who have created a full-fledged industry of songs, videos, tapes, and books. Over the last twenty-five years, the Vineyard music has provided inspiring worship material that has become widely accepted in the youth culture. On the

Catholic side, young, talented artists emerged around Spirit and Song, a youth-culture division of OCP (Oregon Catholic Press), a publisher of liturgical music. Unfortunately they received much less support from the hierarchy and the clergy than the Eternal Word Television Network, whose content and music fall within the Tridentine tradition. Is religious music *qua music* different from secular music? Or is it the content and the emotions that make music religious or secular? There is a tendency to define religious music according to a nostalgic past, that of Bach and Handel. Unfortunately oratorios (even Handel's Messiah) are as foreign to the youth culture of today as operas. Church music must always comprise contemporary songs, not museum pieces for aficionados.

In short, the singing of the choir must serve, not replace, the prayer of the assembly. This, however, is generally not the case. The choir should be a musical community of prayer, not a community of musicians, as will be developed below.

1. **Prayers of the Mass and the canon.** Each Sunday, Mass begins with an opening prayer, which summarizes the theme of the day. In this prayer, the priest is supposed to invite the assembly to private prayer, and after a moment of silence, he is supposed to "collect" these prayers according to the theme of the day. This is seldom done. The words "Let us pray" are seldom an invitation to pray, but rather the occasion for the celebrant to *read* a preconceived prayer from the missal. This gives the Sunday celebration a poor start: how would students react if their teachers were to begin class by reading from a book a few lines summarizing the lesson of the day, and without looking at them, just invite them to say "amen"?

This does not have to be so. At the pontifical Easter celebration described above, the bishop improvised or recited from memory the opening prayer, looking at the audience, with a voice inspired by the text rather than focusing on the recitation of the text. Something similar happened at St. Barnabas, with the introductory "Good morning" and "He is risen" mentioned above. The opening prayer is only a few lines long and can easily be memorized, so that the presider of the Mass can be its animator, rather than its reciter.

The canon has not changed substantially for the last few centuries, yet many priests still need to read it from the missal, and people may see that they seem to concentrate on the missal rather than God. Quite different is a canon recited from the heart, so that the priest's inner gaze can concentrate on the content rather than the printed page. When the priests said Mass facing the high altar, in a soft voice in Latin, it might have conveyed a sense of mystery; now that the canon is said (and more often read) in English for all to hear, the faithful can read the priest's face and may have little sense of mystery. The active participation of the faith receives its first cue from the participation of the celebrant in the sacred mysteries. There is nothing unusual about this suggestion: on Easter Sunday at both the cathedral and St. Barnabas, the celebrants celebrated the canon from memory—that is, from the heart.

m. Communion and dismissal. The "real presence" of Christ has been a question of debate since Beranger took a controversial position in the eleventh century. Later, the debate shifted to the exact timing of the "transubstantiation." By the end of the thirteenth century, it was commonly accepted that it is at the consecration that the bread and wine become the body of Christ. It also became customary in the Middle Ages to lift up the host at the time of the consecration.[219] The dramatization of this moment increased when incense and the chiming of bells were added,

---

Pre-Vatican II Communion Preparation

"Central to everything was the Mass, not daily but Sunday Mass. Around Mass and Communion there was an atmosphere of awe, mystery and a sense of unworthiness. … To receive the body and blood of Jesus Christ into a sinful soul was an offence of wellnigh unlimited proportions against God's majesty. To avoid that possibility, [Mr. Molony (1897-1958)] received communion only at Easter and Christmas. Beforehand, he went to Confession, sent his best suit to the dry-cleaners, had a haircut and, if required, bought new shoes. Only then was he ready to welcome his Lord, but on every occasion it was clear that he still felt utterly unworthy.

—*The Australian Catholic Record* 85, no. 2 (April 2008): 136–137.

---

while an acolyte lifted the chasuble, or outer vestment, of the priest as a sign of reverence. From then on, the elevation became the high point of the Mass: the faithful came to church not only to attend Mass but also to see the consecration. This pattern was set at the time of the Council of Trent and has prevailed down to us.

Any outsider can see that the consecration and elevation are the central part of the Mass. From that perspective, Communion becomes anticlimactic. In a "church" that emphasizes mandatory attendance, people may wonder when the Mass is over. Theoretically the Mass ends with the *Ite missa est*, but the latter conveys a double message. It is translated (in the missalettes) as "The Mass is ended, go in peace," but it conveys the implicit and repeated injunction, "Don't leave yet!" Often people make their own decision and leave at various times at the end of the canon—for example, at Communion, or straight after Communion, as if Communion were an exit ritual. Many priests may consider this tendency to be deplorable but do little about it.

The importance of the consecration and the devaluation of Communion reflect the implicit theology of sacraments as rites of passage, as behavioral *practices* rather than rites of transformation. As behaviors, sacraments are classified as either repeatable or nonrepeatable, and if repeatable, the more often the better. Pope Pius X introduced early Communion for children, with the hope that frequent Communion will preserve their innocence. The age of reason was defined according to Aristotelian logic as taking place at about age seven, while today's psychologists would refuse to set it at any age, considering that most people achieve adulthood at various stages during or after high school or college. When frequent Communion is emphasized at the early age of First Communion, sacraments come to be experienced as rites of passage rather than rites of transformation. According to the logic of "the more, the better," Catholics are implicitly expected to receive Communion at all Masses. One may even receive Communion twice a day, as stated in canon 917; moreover, in case of danger of death, Catholics "are strongly urged to receive again" (canon 921, no. 2). In that perspective, one may leave church upon receiving Communion with the feeling of "job done!" The ceremonial exit of the priest and his acolytes at the end of the Mass seems to have little meaning, as people tend to rush to the door in a smoothly chaotic disorder. The end of the Mass tends to be experienced as the end of an obligation, rather than the beginning of a religious mission (one of the meanings of *Ite Missa est*).

The Catholic Church also has a venerable tradition of adoration of the Blessed Sacrament, but this adoration is somewhat divorced from Communion. Priests do not stay after Mass in adoration, and nocturnal adoration is usually divorced from the Eucharistic celebration. Moreover, perpetual adoration is often divorced from the meditation of the Word. Finally, Eucharistic adoration is often associated with traditional hymns in Latin rather than folk music: on Holy Thursday at St. Barnabas, the adoration was celebrated by singing *Pange lingua gloriosi / Tantum ergo* (as suggested in the official missalette), and later the recitation of rosary in English, Spanish and ... Latin, as described above; both practices imply that the Blessed Sacrament is not related to either Scripture or the Mass.

A more active participation of the faithful in the meaning of Communion is needed to make them less passive attenders. This complex task involves a sacramentality of inner transformation rather than the one of behavioral practices prevalent today. Also needed is a deeper understanding of the Mass as Eucharistic celebration and as concelebration of all participants, the living and the dead, the saints and the sinners. This challenging topic will be picked up in my section on discipleship.

In summary, a pastoral strategy for renewal implies, as a first step, an invitation to passive attenders to become active participants in the liturgy. This is an urgent first step, as the church is hemorrhaging due to the loss of so many of its members, the majority of which are passive attenders turned into nonattenders (and, later, into nonmembers). Satisfied passive attenders may continue coming to church, but their children are not likely to follow in their footsteps. Too often the liturgy itself is a show of ritual pomp and music, with little retention power. It is imperative to have a choir that involves the faithful, not just enhance the liturgy. The homily is a teaching opportunity that would gain from becoming more interactive, as is the norm in secular teaching. Finally, priests are role models: their active participation in prayer and adoration will translate into a more active participation of the faithful. We also come to a clearer understanding of active attendance as including joyful, even enthusiastic participation. As good students attend class because of satisfaction and not obligation, so do active churchgoers because of inner satisfaction, not tradition or requirement.

Sociologists commonly distinguish between religious dwellers and seekers; the first like the comfort of the *status quo*, the second the excitement of discovery.[220] The Willow Creek study further distinguished between those who are stalled, and often satisfied, and those who are dissatisfied and want change. One cannot easily please both the seekers and the dwellers, or both the happy stalled and the dissatisfied who want change. The tendency of catering mainly to the satisfied is shortsighted, because the seekers will leave if not attended to. Hence, our next strategy is to invite the active Sunday attenders to become involved rather than leaving.

5. Helping Active Attenders Become Involved

Gallup's general thesis that involvement in any organization leads to greater satisfaction is well-founded: involvement brings greater social consciousness and relatedness, hence greater subjective appreciation of togetherness. This principle holds for churches, yet togetherness and subjective relatedness are only intermediary steps toward higher goals.

The first move toward involvement may well be active engagement in social and cultural activities. In the Tridentine ghetto church, most parishes endeavored to serve all the social, educational, recreational, and cultural needs of their parishioners. According to Herberg, in the 1950s and 1960s, American churches served as cradles for ethnic and religious identification for immigrants: the melting pot of Protestants, Catholics, and Jews is what made the integration into the American society possible. At the same time, "American religion and American society would seem to be so closely interrelated" that religion became somewhat secularized as religious togetherness, having lost "much of its authentic Christian (or Jewish) content."[221] With the disappearance of the ethnic church and the competing attraction of the counterculture of the 1970s and consumerism today, the churches have lost their function of social and cultural carriers; they are no more communities, except at a reduced level; today's megaparishes are not communities much more than neighborhood libraries. Not much is left of the traditional Catholic moral culture, with little sense of community.

A sense of community can be achieved at the micro level through the creation of small Christian communities, and at the macro level through general meetings. The Bayville church and St. Mary's use both strategies. At Bayville, people interact through their numerous ministries, weekly classes, and prayer groups, and at the corporate level through the biyearly meetings in which registered members vote on church policies and elect officers. At St. Mary's, parish integration is achieved through the small Christian communities (which involve about one-third of Sunday attenders) and the monthly cafés, in which parishioners are invited to a free lunch after Mass. The Knights of Columbus, 170 members strong, make it one of their priorities to create a sense of parish community through parish picnics and lunches in which they invite strangers to become acquainted and make friends around a lunch table. After most Sunday Masses, coffee is served to foster interaction; most parish groups and the SCCs have a summer BBQ or potluck dinner for all members. In the fall, there is a weekend of festivities. Hence, both Bayville and St. Mary's have re-created a sense of community to replace the parish ethnic community of the past.

Most Catholic parishes have social events like dances, dinners, sports activities, senior clubs, or bingo nights, but these may serve fragmented interest groups rather than parish unity. There is more to collective consciousness than social and emotional togetherness; it requires a common vision, ideology, purpose, or ideal. In lieu of small Christian communities, many parishes have ministries bringing together small teams of volunteers. Thus at St. Barnabas there is an outreach program consisting of a thrift shop and a food pantry; a full-fledged religious education program; a lively music ministry; and schedules of perpetual adoration. Many of these programs, however, consist of parallel activities that do not create communities. Thus the food pantry is a place where one can donate food, and the thrift shop a place to take used clothes and furniture. The choirs enlist schoolchildren, and perpetual adoration attracts unconnected volunteers to staff the various hours of the day and night. Only the parish core ministers may have a sense of community to the extent that all ministries emanate from them and gravitate around them.

How can the active Sunday attenders become engaged in discipleship? How can the parish create a sense of community that is more than togetherness? I will suggest three strategies: first, develop ministries that are small Christian communities; second, actively promote traditional devotions as forms of discipleship; and third, and more generally, develop a vital and integrated Eucharistic spirituality.

a.   Ministry communities. Among the many ministries of today, one can distinguish four types: 1) worship ministries that cater to the needs of the liturgy; 2) service or maintenance ministries necessary for the well-being of the organization; 3) formation ministries geared toward spiritual growth; and 4) mission ministries for evangelization. Most parishes have worship and service ministries; few have programs of spiritual formation, and practically none promote evangelization. Moreover, ministries are public functions within the church, while devotions are considered private; as a consequence, ministries usually do not include devotions, while the latter often do not lead to public ministries. This situation is conducive neither to community formation nor to Christian discipleship.

Worship ministers (altar servers, lectors, Eucharistic ministers, ushers, sacristans, organists, music directors, singers, cantors, song leaders, greeters, and so on) serve the needs of the liturgy and the house of God. In the past, many of these functions were taken care of by deacons and subdeacons. With the decline of the number of priests and the concomitant recognition of the priesthood of the laity, these roles have been taken over by the laity. How are volunteers selected? Any volunteer may be accepted as an usher or an altar server, but public reading, singing, or playing an instrument requires talent. Eucharistic ministers are usually selected by the clergy; hence, volunteers are not welcome. Moreover, at any time, the worship needs may already be filled, requiring no further involvement; hence, little room remains for active Sunday attenders to become involved in worship, except in the less socially desirable ministries.

Service ministries always need volunteers: receptionists; bookkeepers; accountants; coaches for the Boy and Girl Scouts and sports; craftsmen for building maintenance; bulletin editors; parish webmasters; and so on. In an interview, a priest gave the following examples of involvement: "We need to paint the pews, we need to put windows in, and we need to stuff mailings." Church buildings need to be vacuumed; the liturgy requires flowers and altar decorations; the food pantry and the thrift shop need volunteer staff. These programs involve mostly maintenance work of a low level of engagement, which may not be attractive enough for Sunday attenders to become involved. These jobs are more service than ministry; they are more draining than nourishing spiritually, but they would look different if combined with programs of spiritual growth. The same can be said about religious education and choir singing to the extent that they involve giving rather than receiving, spiritually. Religious education teachers are asked to teach from the bottom of their hearts, but often without receiving much food for their souls. Choir singing requires a good voice and numerous rehearsals; in the absence of volunteers, professional singers can be hired. Service ministries mainly require free labor, without much nourishment to the soul to motivate such labor.

Spiritual growth through *formation ministries* is a primary church goal at both Bayville and St. Mary's. At Bayville, all ministries are paths of spiritual growth, as all are based on prayer. I have previous listed their numerous prayer groups (intercessory prayer meetings, prayer walking, evangelism explosion prayer, missions prayer partners, men's and women's groups, Christian school prayer meetings, and so on), all of which are animated by laypeople. Two cycles of thirteen-week classes offer instruction on a great variety of subjects. Yearly retreats for men and women draw about one hundred people each. The examples of prominent church members suggest a path for personal growth. One begins with prayer, serves in various ministries, and becomes proficient in biblical wisdom; and later, one may lead others in prayer and ministry, and even in classes and retreats. At St. Mary's, the path of spiritual growth is not as clearly marked. The normal path begins with involvement in an SCC, discussing together the Sunday Gospel and attending a few classes; with time, SCC members learn to become biblically literate and more Gospel-centered in their lives, sharing their faith more openly while being involved in numerous ministries. A few may start their own prayer groups or initiate their own ministries. No similar opportunities exist at St. Barnabas or other local parishes, although there may be numerous devotions.

There are no *mission ministries* at St. Mary's, which may explain its numerical decline, while Bayville has monthly water baptisms to integrate new members. The vast majority of Bayville members are converts, mainly from the Catholic population. Missionary work is its major ministerial focus at the local, the national, and the international levels. One Sunday service every month is dedicated to missionary work through prayer, the commissioning of new missionaries, and information about missionary progress. There are two missions' conventions every year with numerous exhibitions, public talks, and round-table conferences. Most Catholic parishes exhibit little or no such missionary effort. If salvation can be found outside the church, as most Catholics believe, why become a Christian? Even theologians find it difficult to answer this question, I found out in my interviews. They have come to appreciate the positive contribution of the various world religions, but increasingly find it difficult to justify missionary work. On the other hand, the official position of *Dominus Iesus*, the 2000 declaration of the Congregation for the Doctrine of the Faith about exclusive salvation through Jesus Christ, finds few advocates.

Ideally, the four types of ministries—of worship, service, growth, and missions—should be interrelated. I believe this is possible as a long-term goal for 2030. In short, it is *not ministries* but ministry-oriented *communities* that should be the ultimate goal of parish life. Ministries may be performed individually; hence, they do not create communities. Ministry-oriented communities, on the other hand, have growth and evangelization as their primary function and from these, ministries naturally derive. Let us look again at SCCs.

Base communities originated in Latin America with an emphasis on social justice, in the spirit of the Latin American bishops' conference of Medellin in 1968. Although social justice is a major emphasis of the postconciliar church, it has not become the major focus of SCCs in the

United States. The emphasis of RENEW International of the archdiocese of Newark, New Jersey, is different: it, according to its web page, "fosters spiritual renewal in the Catholic tradition by empowering individuals and communities to encounter God in everyday life, deepen and share faith, and connect faith with action." This organization has been quite successful, thanks to the support of American bishops. RENEW creates small Christian communities that coexist with other parish groups; hence, parishes may have one or several SCCs, which together may only have a marginal influence on the parish; the latter often looks like a supermarket of ministries and devotions. Totally different is Art Baranowski's proposal, outlined in his *Creating Small Faith Communities: A Plan for Restructuring the Parish and Renewing Catholic Life.*[222] This plan calls for restructuring the parish along two strategies: establishing small communities of faith and transforming existing parish programs into prayer communities. Nationwide, this effort is supported by the National Alliance of Parishes Restructuring into Communities (NPRC). This plan offers a global vision for parish life as at St. Mary's, developed independently of Baranowski's proposal.

To show the integration of the four types of ministries (worship, service, growth, and evangelization), I will describe two ministries found in all parishes, music and religious education. In the Middle Ages, *scholas* of music developed in the cathedral churches to serve the needs of the Latin liturgy and increase the pomp of episcopal Masses, both of which decreased faithful participation. Among the Protestant Reformers, many banned church polyphony, while Luther innovated by creating biblically based hymns in German to the tunes of secular songs. No major change took place in the Catholic Church: "The active participation of the congregation was not highly valued in Roman Catholic Eucharist after Trent."[223] In spite of the recommendations of Vatican II, the active participation of the faithful in the liturgy is still low.

The purpose of a choir is prayer, not performance; its function is to increase worship participation, not to replace it. These goals will be achieved to the extent that the emphasis is on spiritual growth and evangelization; hence, the four types of ministries come into one. At St. Mary's, the choir is an SCC whose rehearsals begin or end in prayer. This is not the case in the vast majority of parishes. How can change be brought about? In many cases, change and reform breed division and conflict, as in the case of the Protestant Reformation. Megaparishes have options that small denominations do not have: they can create an additional service open to change; it is always possible to create one more choir and have one innovative Mass, scheduled at a time unlikely to spur conflict, like 8:00 a.m. on Sunday morning.

> **Can Organs Pray?**
> If God listens to the heart rather than to the music, polyphony adds little to prayer, and the pomp of a ritual adds nothing if it does not express the merriness of the participants. Pipe organs can play; they cannot pray.

The purpose of a choir is to pray by singing, as in Benedictine abbeys, for God alone and not for an audience. A new choir may begin with only a couple of members who commit themselves to praying and singing daily if possible (e.g., with a digital music player or CD player). Music is pervasive in today's youth culture; hence, praying and singing with an iPod or CDs, at home or in one's car, are quite natural. The new choir would pray and sing liturgical hymns and popular songs to be used at church. They could meet once a week to sing for an audience of One, for God alone. After a few weeks, they would be ready to sing these hymns and songs at a Mass, from memory—not together as a choir, but dispersed throughout the assembly. Their ministry is not only to worship in singing, but also to encourage others to do so in an evangelical outreach, in church and outside the church. People are much more likely to join in singing when their immediate neighbor does so than when they are invited by a song leader twenty or thirty feet away. A praying choir of only two or three can make a difference—small at first, but likely to grow. It is their ministry of evangelization to recruit others, so that they will grow from three to five, from five to ten, and ten to twenty. Change cannot be imposed; it must grow through its own inner dynamism, which emanates from its vision. Singing for worship and evangelical outreach offer such a vision, which is likely to grow if nurtured.

How realistic is the above? Taizé is an ecumenical monastery in the east of France, founded by a Protestant minister. It attracts a weekly average of 2,000 to 3,000 visitors (mostly Catholics) who come to sing and pray for a whole week. Obviously there is no permanent choir, since participants change every week. Every day includes about three hours of singing and prayer by an invisible choir—which is dispersed throughout the assembly. The quality of that singing is such that a CD of songs is published nearly every year, and some of these songs have been adopted throughout Europe. Taizé offers a simple model of prayerful singing. This model can be adapted to a great variety of settings. There are also quite a few vibrant parishes throughout the United States. These vibrant parishes should be seen as the norm, not the exception, and as models that can that realistically be emulated.

Religious education can equally be transformed when spiritual growth and outreach are integrated into its program. Spirituality should be the first priority of all pastors. Volunteer catechists have already moved one step above the level of active Mass attenders, since they volunteered to teach CCD. Hence, they may be ready for another step: Christian discipleship.

Is religious education a service like that of the ushers or altar servers—jobs any person of goodwill can do? Or is a ministry of formation requiring personal growth? Are children taught mechanical prayers and rites of passage, or prayerfulness through rites of transformation? It is a question of priorities. Community formation should be the first step. All catechists, even if in the hundreds, can communicate by phone, e-mail, or texting, if they cannot meet physically. A Listserv (which is a list of names to whom an email can be sent) can create a community easily and nearly instantaneously if a leader engages members into a creative dialogue. Collective prayer requires a sense of community, and the latter *can* emerge from e-mail interaction. At one time or another, it may be appropriate to introduce the great variety of Christian prayers, beginning with *lectio divina* and Scripture reading. The World Wide Web can be of great help, as it offers a thesaurus of information. Common prayer does not require a common physical presence; there will be common prayer if there is a sense of community, even if people pray individually.

Again, how realistic is this form of catechesis based on personal growth rather than teaching doctrine? I have seen it at work at Bayville and St. Mary's. Recently I visited a neocatechumenal group of about hundred members dedicated to religious teaching. They meet once a week for fellowship, celebrate the Sunday liturgy for two hours, and attend a monthly one-day retreat. I was told that a few thousand such members can be found in Guatemala City. Moreover, several parishes have three-year training programs for catechists. These are models to follow, because they work. In the United States, too, there are diocesan programs of faith formation and theological training for catechists. They should be seen as the norm, not the exception.

Spiritual growth has occurred, according to the Willow Creek surveys, if one can indicate some spiritual change or innovation in the last six months or so. By that criterion, most practicing Catholics are stalled, and stalled people are often satisfied, if not complacent, in their mediocrity. It is the job of the pastor to provide impetus for growth on a regular basis through information and teaching. What is centering prayer? What is meditation? What is the Jesus prayer? What is the prayer of the hours? What are the mysteries of the rosary? How can one pray in a busy occupation? What is special about the various liturgical seasons? What are some of the classics of spirituality? Besides information available on the Internet, a small parish library would be welcome. People need theology and spirituality that are reflections on the life of faith; they do not want catechism, which often is no much more than religious indoctrination for children. A pastor should be a specialist in theology and spirituality, as his parishioners are specialists—often at the graduate level—in their own fields; for all other matters, he should rely on others, as parishioners rely on electricians and plumbers when the matter at hand is not in their field. Pastors will help others to grow only if they grow spiritually themselves. Parish catechists are a privileged group of volunteers ready to move into a spirituality of discipleship if invited to. By creating a sense of community, through a Listserv or otherwise, and then inviting the group into prayer through example and information, and finally bringing them into a closer relationship with Jesus Christ, the pastor will create a small community of disciples. Only masters have disciples, and the quality of the disciples reflects the quality of the master. Priests must be in discipleship, leading others to become disciples.

The parish will become a community of communities by creating many small Christian communities. How can this be achieved? By personal invitation as well as membership drives. If the shepherd knows his flock, a pastor is likely to know intuitively who can do what. A personal invitation to join a group is by far the most effective method of recruitment. Every pastor should seek a personal relationship with all or most of his parishioners. He may greet people individually *before* Mass, as they arrive slowly one by one. At the solemn entrance at the beginning of the Mass, he could shake hands on both sides of the aisle, as Pope Benedict does on many occasions, rather than entering like a king into his kingdom, without even making eye contact. As systematic house visits have become nearly impossible, he can send endless e-mails and leave innumerable phone messages. Most people respond positively to a personal invitation, feeling honored for having been singled out. Regular membership drives are also necessary, not as impersonal announcements at the end of the Mass, but as pencil-and-paper answers, as is done at St. Mary's, each person indicating what group they could join and at what time. Two yearly membership drives are likely to leads to the creation of new SCCs and are a strong impetus for spiritual growth. The only step left is to make the whole parish a community—that is, a community of communities—through general assemblies and/or socials.

b. Devotions as forms of discipleship. In the Catholic Church, devotions are seen as private; in the post-Vatican II church, they have often become invisible. Some of the most popular devotions are the first Friday and first Saturday Masses; novenas to St. Anthony or St. Jude; the miraculous medal; and, for the old-timers, the blessing of the throat on St. Blaise's Day. What exactly are these devotions? Little information is gained from announcements in parish bulletins, such as the following item, in reference to the first Saturday of every month: "In 1917 Our Lady of Fatima requested 1st Saturday Devotion to Her Immaculate Heart. Her message is to Pray,

Pray, Pray for Reparation for Sin and especially Eucharistic Reparation. COME!!! *Pray for Peace throughout the World!!!* [in italics in the text]" In this ad, we have some of the clichés and practices ("Immaculate Heart," "Pray," "Reparation," "Eucharistic Reparation," "Peace") of a vanishing religious culture that is of little appeal in our postmodern world.

No, in the Catholic Church, devotions are not private: they represent specific forms of discipleship propagated by religious orders. The magisterium does not support some in preference to others, but, in the absence of spiritual support from spiritual leaders in the post-Vatican II church, these forms have in fact often become privatized. Devotions are *structured forms of discipleship* (as in third orders, confraternities, solidalities, congregations, and so on) that follow forms of spirituality propagated most often by religious orders. Thus the Franciscans, the Dominicans, and the Carmelites have third orders that follow in the world the way of life of these religious orders. The Benedictines were probably the first to welcome secular members (oblates), who recite the liturgy of the hours without living in celibate communities. Third orders flourished in the thirteenth century as lay associations that wanted to pursue in the world the specific ideals (Franciscan, Dominican, or Carmelite) of religious life. At that time also originated what we call lay ecclesial movements or lay associations, like the Vaudois of Lyon or the *Fratres Humiliati*, both evangelical organizations for preaching and charity work. Two dimensions are found in all these organizations: an institutionalized form of discipleship and, secondly, an organizational chart defining the structure of the organization, the devotions to be engaged in, and the frequency of meetings. These two dimensions correspond to two felt needs: the need for clearly defined practices leading to spiritual growth and the need for mutual support in a social structure. Devotions conceived as isolated individual practices satisfy neither of these two needs.

Athletes Train with Coaches, not Alone
The first athletes of Christ in the deserts of Egypt in the third century discovered the need to train through spiritual exercises, first alone and later in communities. Asceticism (from Greek *askeo,* to exercise) refers to these exercises. Devotions as structured forms of discipleship outline paths of growth through regular exercises in a community of like-minded disciples.

Renewal in the Catholic Church is more likely to happen with a renaissance of devotional associations, the most appropriate today being the SCCs, which meet once a week to read Scripture, pray, and share their faith. The national survey mentioned in the previous chapter puts their number in 2000 to at least 37,000, involving over a million members, the majority being connected to a parish.[224] SCCs have an organizational structure, but often no clear path of growth. Without continuous support, they become isolated cenacles without a growth program, service ministry, or evangelical outreach. The minimum outreach of any religious organization is to attract new members, which obviously presupposes a strong spirituality on the part of its members. The most effective organizational growth is achieved through cell division: every three to five years, a group divides into two and starts new growth, in order to divide again a few years later. When this is the case, as in some evangelical churches, the growth is phenomenal.[225]

Let us look at two of the most popular devotional associations found in many parishes, the Knights of Columbus and the Legion of Mary. The Knights of Columbus, with about 1.7 million members, are probably the largest Catholic lay organization. They are an American creation (founded in 1881) that does what Americans often do best: namely, raising money, but for charitable causes (with about $145 million raised yearly). They are both a social structure defining the various ranks and obligations and a devotional association emphasizing prayer and spiritual growth. They can be seen as the rear guard of the church because of their relatively conservative agenda of charity work, Marian devotion (rosary), and liturgical pomp. They can easily find their place in any parish; at St. Mary's, they are 170 strong. The same can be said about the Legion of Mary, which involves a structure of weekly meetings and a program of daily prayer. It is another Anglo-Saxon creation that originated in Dublin in 1921. It was founded and propagated by laypeople, not members of a religious order; yet it emphasizes collective spiritual growth, as in religious congregations, not individual piety in isolation.

Devotion to the saints is often an individualist practice today, but it mustn't necessarily be so. The saints are the departed members whom the church remembers for their exemplary lives; hence, they are role models as much as intercessors. Every organization must celebrate its most prominent members because of the legacy of their example. What would the United States be without the memory of George Washington, Abraham Lincoln, and even Kennedy, Johnson, and Reagan? The memory of saints and heroes is based on familiarity with their lives, so that daily living can become an encounter with them as companions and an intercessor, as in J. Martin's *My Life with the Saints.*[226] When the church is seen as a communion in discipleship, as in Bonheoffer, the vision of the church as a *communio sanctorum* is not a "sleeping symbol" anymore, because the saints become friends of God and prophets of his kingdom, as in E. Johnson.[227] The devotion to the saints is not the individual veneration of their relics, but the collective appropriation of their cherished examples.

Who can lead individuals to community-mindedness—for example, in the adoration of the Blessed Sacrament and their individual recitation of the rosary? Clearly, every parish needs leaders, and the quality of the parish depends on the quality of its leaders. Training for leadership is the topic of the next section, which deals with those totally committed—a group different from the active members considered in this section. For active members to learn discipleship, the parish must first become a community of communities rather than a devotional service station, as is often the case. A spirituality of Eucharistic celebration should foster such community-mindedness.

From this...

Mass as private devotion with an assembly of one or two children

c.   A spirituality of Eucharistic/ thanksgiving celebration. A strategy for renewal must be aware of the paradigm shift taking place today. I describe it first; next I will briefly outline the various forms of Eucharistic celebrations.

The paradigm shift at work today implies a move from the traditional conception of truth as propositional, according to which two opposite propositions cannot be equally true, to the more inclusive conception that predominates in the social sciences and everyday wisdom. According to this inclusive view, two opposite statements (e.g., by Catholics and Protestants) may both contain partial truths, while according to the official Catholic position, they are mutually exclusive. The traditional Catholic view espouses an Aristotelian epistemology, while the pluralistic perspective is closer to Hegel and phenomenology. This distinction is very important for evangelization and ecumenism. In the inclusive view, the Tridentine and the post-Vatican II paradigms are *not* mutually exclusive, although one may prefer one rather the other. In a sociological perspective, it seems that the first is likely to fade away to be replaced by the second. (See references of pictures in endnote.[228])

The paradigm shift at work today was already described in the chapter about St. Mary's (pages 129-130). Here is another take on it. Scholastic theologians raised three major questions about the Eucharist. First, at what time does the host become the body of Christ during Mass?

... to this:

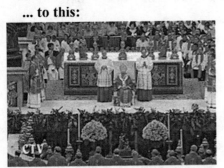

15,000 priests concelebrate with Benedict XVI
at the end of the "Year of the Priests"

Answer: at the exact time of the consecration, but today's vision of the manifold forms of Christ's presence makes this first question obsolete. Second question: how does the host become the body of Christ? Answer: through transubstantiation. This view is based on the Aristotelian theory of hylomorphism, according to which in transubstantiation the substance changes but not the accidents; this metaphysical view of matter as substance and accidents makes little sense in our Einsteinian understanding of the universe. Finally, in what sense is the Eucharist a sacrament? According to Medieval/Tridentine theology, the Mass is a visible sign of the Passion of Christ—that is, a sacrifice—and as with all repeatable sacraments, the more the better, as each Mass is an additional source of grace. This mechanical view of the sacraments as rites of passage rather than rites of transformation is equally obsolete, although still prevalent. These three questions were never raised in Orthodox theology, which does not hold the theories of transubstantiation, consecration, and sacraments as efficacious by themselves. These three positions were also rejected by most of the Reformers; Catholicism is slowly moving away from the medieval philosophico-theologies upheld by Trent.

The Mass as sacrifice is still prevalent today to the exclusion of all other views. This theology may lead to various forms of abuse. In the past, when Mass stipends were a major source of income for the clergy, this encouraged not only the selling of Masses but also their daily repetition. Moreover, it led to silent Masses with only one altar boy, as no assembly was required. As only attendance but not participation was mandatory on Sundays, the only way to enhance the solemnity of Masses, especially in cathedrals, was to entrust its solemnization to the creativity of music directors, choirs, and the organ, with little or no contribution from the faithful; this is still often the case today. Moreover, as the liturgical readings change every day, the celebration of the Mass becomes a reading or recitation from the missal that the faithful must come to "hear," to use the word of canon 1248 of the 1917 canon law. Finally, because the sacrifice of the Mass is seen as the highest glory to God, other forms of worship were devalued—the liturgy of the hours progressively disappeared outside monasteries. The notion of Mass as the highest glory to God also led to the "massification" of Masses: at any occasion of public prayer (anniversaries, pilgrimages, retreats, and so forth) priests will say/read a Mass rather than work together with the faithful to engage in spontaneous prayers appropriate to the circumstances. There is no Catholic equivalent of the praise and worship services that serve as the attraction of evangelical churches.

A primary insight of post-Vatican II theology is the awareness of the multiple presences of Christ in church, Scripture, the sacraments, the celebrating priests, and the sacred species (Constitution on the Sacred Liturgy, no. 7). To ask when Christ is "really present" as opposed to simply "present" reflects the anti-Protestant rhetoric of the Counter-Reformation. The contemporary recognition of the multiple forms of Christ's presence, not only during and after the consecration but throughout the celebration of the Eucharist, opens the way for a new understanding of the Eucharist as concelebrated thanksgiving (see concelebrations at St. Mary's, pages 124-129). Because various forms of Christ's presence are possible, various forms of Eucharistic celebrations are also possible; hence, concelebrations can take place even outside the parameters of the Mass—that is, without a priest, collectively and individually. I will distinguish two basic types of Eucharistic celebrations.

(1) *The Sunday Eucharist* consists of three moments of particularly high intensity: the liturgy of the word, the Eucharistic prayer, and Communion. The liturgy of the word may involve expressions of adoration and thanksgiving, leading to an interactive homily in which both the faithful and the homilist reach a deeper understanding of the Gospel and intellectual nourishment for the coming week. According to canon law, only the priest says the Eucharistic prayer, but to assume that the faithful are to be passive would be against the spirit of the law. In the pre-Vatican days, it was common for the faithful to follow in their own missal, and even recite in a soft voice, the prayers of the canon. The high moment of the Eucharistic prayer should be one of high-intensity silent adoration instead of empty silence. This takes place when the faithful know the Eucharistic prayers by heart, which will happen naturally over the years if the priest says them aloud prayerfully. Of course, the priest should pray from the heart, not just read from the missal. Communion should be another high-intensity moment. Instead of initiating singing to keep people busy until the end of the distribution of the hosts, it would be appropriate to use the time for a litanic song endlessly repeated, beginning with the traditional *Agnus Dei*. The liturgy should not end with the triumphalist exit of the clergy or a last performance of the choir followed by applause, as in a concert. The multiple forms of Christ's presence will become acknowledged when Christ is seen as present in the assembly, not only in the host and the clergy. This may be fostered through the practice of individual Eucharistic prayer, to be considered next. Any Eucharistic or thanksgiving celebration consists of Trinitarian prayers through Jesus Christ in the Holy Spirit. Any doxology is such a Trinitarian prayer.

(2) Individually or collectively, *Eucharistic celebrations without bread and wine* are as natural and normal as doxologies. The *Didache* (from the first or second century) suggests to "eucharistize [Greek: *eucharistate*] thus: We give you thanks, our Father, for the holy vine of your servant David which you revealed to us through your servant Jesus. To you the glory for ever." And further, "We give you thanks, our Father, for the life and knowledge which you revealed to us through your servant Jesus. To you the glory for ever." After sharing the meal, the community should likewise "eucharistize thus: We give you thanks, holy Father, for your holy name ... Come Lord [Aramaic-Greek: *marana tha*]! Amen!"[229] There is no explicit reference to bread and wine here (obviously there was), but explicit thanksgiving. This is also the spirit of the "Mass on the world" of Teilhard de Chardin, a priest-anthropologist doing research in the steppes of Asia in the 1920s. "[Having] neither bread, nor wine, nor altar ... I, your priest, will make the whole earth my altar and on it will offer you all the labours and suffering of the world ..." This *messe sur le monde*[230] or Mass on the world was inaccurately translated in English as *hymn of the universe*.[231] Yet this individual "Mass" was a concelebration in union with all the Eucharistic celebrations of the world. The 1988 Roman directory actually "urge[s] the assembly [the Sunday assembly without a priest] to unite itself in spirit"[232] with the Eucharistic celebrations over bread and wine, thus making it a concelebration in spirit. All the Masses celebrated through time and space are concelebrations of the eternal celebration of the Lamb described in the book of Revelation. Any individual Eucharistic celebration is a spiritual concelebration that "eucharistizes" the celebration of the Lamb.

Today many committed Catholics have adopted—as I learned from interviews—a form of interactive prayer of praise, either at appointed times or throughout the day. This form of prayer is quite different from the Eucharist as sacrifice of traditional theology. To "eucharistize" the celebration of the Lamb opens an eschatological and Trinitarian perspective missing in the traditional devotions. Many Protestant praise and worship services can be seen as Eucharistic celebrations without bread and wine.

This spirituality of Eucharistic thanksgiving is well suited for our times. One may hope that such a Eucharistic spirituality will foster community-mindedness and relate individual piety (e.g., in individual adoration of the Blessed Sacrament) to local and global community awareness, a sense of "church" (or *sensus fidelium*) in the adoration of the Lamb. In a post-Vatican II perspective, individual "praise and worship" is always a concelebration, a participation in the collective celebration of the Lamb of the communion of saints. While in the Tridentine tradition, the Mass is mostly seen as individual participation in the re-enactment of the sacrifice of the cross, from the post-Vatican II perspective, a personal relationship with God will foster the awareness of God's universal relationship with all believers and unbelievers; a relational theology will lead to a personal relationship not only with God, but also with others, as community.

Let me summarize the various characteristics of involvement beyond the level of active Sunday participation: involvement consists of a wide range of activities, from low to high participation, leading to increasing growth over the years. Involvement may begin with volunteer work in a ministry (e.g., a service ministry requiring little time) and progress to more emphasis on prayer and devotion, either alone or later in an SCC, while also fostering the need for greater religious knowledge through personal readings or classes and lectures. Finally, church involvement is likely to lead to greater financial participation, above and beyond the mere 1 percent of one's income, which is the pittance given to the church by the average Catholic. Involvement thus includes at least four dimensions: ministry, prayer, community, and financial participation. But these dimensions are likely to be discovered progressively. Involvement is not a dichotomous variable, but a continuum over a lifetime.

6. Leading the Involved to Totally Committed Discipleship

Any church is often only as good as its leaders, as mentioned earlier. The average pre-Vatican II parish was led by about ten to fifteen *totally committed* sisters and priests, plus a halo of dedicated laypeople without official church position. To show the importance of this leadership group, I turn to financial contributions.

The chart below indicates what percent of the total amount of money is donated by church attenders, in groups of five percentiles, in all US churches.[233] Thus the highest 5 percent of contributors gives 51.1 percent of the total amount, and the next five percentiles 14.6 percent. This pattern makes the churches very dependent on their best contributors, and very vulnerable in case of their leaving. The bottom 30 percent contributes as little as nothing (0.85 percent). Of the bottom churchgoers, 60 percent contributes 7 percent, while the top 40 percent gives 83 percent. This seems to be the pattern of all activities based on voluntary contributions, from politics to public broadcasting (e.g., PBS, the Public Broadcasting Services, which sponsor non commercial channels like the channel thirteen). We can now see the importance of community leaders: for a church to lose its top 5 percent of financial contributors is to lose half of its income. Similarly for a church to lose its top 5 percent ministry leaders is like losing half its spiritual resources. Most Catholic parishes have lost over the years their top 5 percent leaders, in terms of sisters and assistant pastors; thus they may have lost half of their spiritual power. If a church is only as good as its leaders, an evangelical church with many totally committed leaders will be far superior to an equally good Catholic parish without such leaders.

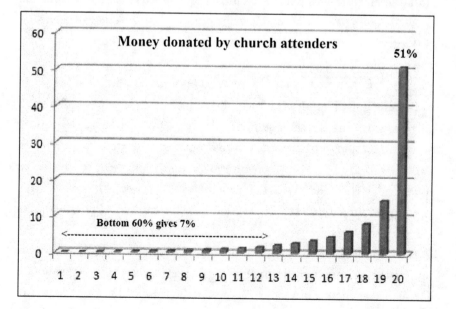

It is often believed that the rich contribute most while the poor cannot afford to give. This is not true: those in the highest income group contribute 1.2 percent of their income, while those in the lowest give 2.3 percent; the second-highest income group gives 0.91 percent, while the second-lowest contributes 1.7 percent; average earners contribute about 1 percent of their income.[234] These data also explain a very common complaint that the churches are always asking for money. This is subjectively true: for the bottom 40 percent, which contributes only 1.25 percent of the total church money, any second collection is unbearable, and any request for money is an irritant that turns them off. Yet these noncontributors still come to church. What they expect is a good homily. The major responsibilities of the clergy thus seem to be good sermons for the passive attenders, and spiritual direction for the committed.

Do the churches practice what they preach? Not when it comes to giving. On average, US churches use 71 percent of their income for operating expenses, but only 1.4 percent to help the poor, while investing 13 percent in property improvement and acquisitions, and 4 percent in savings.[235] From informal information, I learned that most priests do not seem to contribute financially on the belief that they already consecrate most of their time—which is what most professionals do. Stewardship and sacrificial giving are common Catholic phrases, but they seem ineffective, as Protestants contribute twice as much without these theological justifications. The standards for tipping followed by most people are those expected of them; thus, in US restaurants, most Americans give 13–14 percent but different amounts when in Canada or Mexico. "Give as much as you can" is a poor standard that yields poor results. Suggesting donations of about 10 percent for the totally committed, 5 percent for those involved, and nothing percentagewise for the passive attenders yields good results when put forth, assuming that the clergy contributes likewise. These standards rest on trust in God to provide, rather a vague rhetoric of universal stewardship.

The evangelical precepts have traditionally been the ideals of the totally committed, usually in the form of vows of poverty, chastity, and obedience. These ideals remain valid today and tend to be practiced by the majority of church leaders I have interviewed. Vowed poverty means renunciation of property ownership, but also, in most cases, the security of food, shelter, and care in old age. What is often lost in the institutionalization of poverty is dependency on God. It is this dependency on God that becomes a major spiritual experience for those who contribute 10 percent of their income. This is why tithing is seen by many evangelical churches as a norm for their members (but not for their nonmembers or visitors).

Chastity is a common topic in evangelical churches, at least among the committed—that is, chastity of the eyes and the heart. Those with pure hearts who will see God praised in the Sermon on the Mount are those without inordinate attachments to relationships, riches, careers, and sex. Only those with pure eyes can denounce the prevailing epidemic of pornography that has been spreading with the video and Internet revolutions. In a society saturated with eroticism, chastity of the eyes is needed as much by the married as the celibate—at least by those totally committed to a kingdom different from the prevailing one.

Obedience is due to God when there no clear chain of command; in that case, obedience is due to God rather than to humans. It is a common belief that God speaks through interaction with people and everyday events, through the laity as well as the papacy. Obeying God rather than waiting for orders from a superior is a very high standard well suited to the laity.

Prayer and Scripture reading are obvious daily expectations. The standard of one hour a day at Bayville seems a very high demand, but the ten to fifteen minutes a day suggested at St. Mary's seems low. Fasting as a discipline of the mind rather than the castigation of the body was common in the past and needs to be rediscovered; it will do little harm to the health of a population that is two-thirds overweight. Vegetarian abstinence can be seen as a form of stewardship in a world where the economy of cattle raising in the West leaves 800 million people suffering from hunger in the rest of the world.

How realistic are these ideals? They are quite realistic at Bayville's church (although not exactly in the terms used above), but not at St. Mary's. At Bayville one could buy a T-shirt showing "Pray Always" printed on the back; a few men would wear it at church, but many more at the annual retreat. From interviews I learned that the philosophy of "pray always" was part of their lives. No such thing at St. Mary's. At Bayville, members are encouraged to spend vacation time working in missions, at their own expense, and scores of youngsters are invited to perform evangelical mimes and short plays in prisons and nursing homes, also at their own expense. At St. Mary's, as in most Catholic parishes, such expectations would be seen as excessive. At Bayville, tithing is the norm, but not at St. Mary's. Finally any talk about chastity would have little credibility in a church rocked by sex scandals. In short, the ideals of the evangelical precepts seem to have retreated from common Catholic discourse with the withdrawal of religious priests and sisters from parish life. I must add, however, that I have found quite a few totally committed Catholics who practice these ideals on their own. Most parish leaders I interviewed draw inspiration from the evangelical precepts of the beatitudes, but not belonging to a group of like-minded disciples, they do not speak a common language about prayer, obedience to God in daily life, poverty through giving, and chastity of the eyes and heart in a sex-oriented society. They may have learned the language of the beatitude in silence, but not having practiced that language in a core group, they are not good at witnessing, which is the heart of evangelization.

At Bayville there are eight pastors for a church of 2,700, while at St. Mary's, there is one priest and no deacon for about 12,000 people (3,800 registered families). Is the church mainly a sacramental service station? Statistics leave little doubt about the answer: with 1.5 diocesan priests, .85 deacons, and 1.6 lay ecclesial ministers in 2008,[236] the average parish of 760 resembles a school with 1.5 teachers, .85 assistant teachers, and 1.6 helpers for 760 students. In such a structure, students are likely to drop out or go elsewhere. Sacramental ministers are likely to only produce sacramental practitioners, while well-staffed churches teaching discipleship can produce disciples. Although the two are not mutually exclusive, renewal calls more of the latter and less of former.

The special role of the totally committed is service—service to others rather than just service to the parish, as in worship and service ministries.

Their mission is missionary. They must animate ministries rather than perform them. They are the immediate source of inspiration of those involved in the ministries which they direct. In these ministries, not only is it their job to attract new volunteers, they must also encourage those involved toward an ever-greater involvement. They are the ones who will encourage the most committed to become totally committed to an ever-higher degree. Ultimately, they will turn the emotional energies of spirituality to the outside world, *ad extra*, not only in charity outreach to the less fortunate, but also in evangelization. They are the ones who will allow the church to grow, not just by attracting parishioners from other parishes, but through genuine conversions.

8. Catering to Nonsacramental Christians

Why is the Catholic Church so little involved in missionary work? The church is losing ground in the West and Latin America, while Islam is expanding. There are more Muslims than Catholics in the world today, as seen in the table below. Muslims and evangelicals are growing at a rate double that of Catholics. In the United States, there are already more evangelicals than Catholics. Worldwide, within one or two generations, Catholicism has moved from the number-one world religion to second place, after Islam. Catholicism may even take third place if and when the non-Catholics Christians (the Orthodox, Protestant, and other Christian churches) outnumber Catholics. According to the table below, there are already more non-Catholics Christians than Catholics, but there is some disagreement about these statistics; if not today, then by 2030, non-Catholics Christians will outnumber Catholics, because of the latter's greater growth rate.

There are theological reasons for this lack of Catholic evangelism, more specifically in the areas of sacramentality, ecclesiology, soteriology, exegetical hermeneutics, and even pastoral sociology. Sacramental churches preach salvation through the sacraments, with special emphasis in Tridentine theology on the Eucharist and the priesthood. The post-Vatican II insight that the evangelical mission belongs by baptism to all has not yet been put into practice. The ecclesiology of the church as an unequal society is still in effect, as only priests can do missionary work: "The supreme direction and coordination of endeavors and activities which deal with missionary work and missionary cooperation belong to the Roman Pontiff

Changes in membership (in millions):				
	1970	2009	Increase	2025
World population	3,699	6,828	84%	8,010
Christians	1,235	2,271	84%	2,714
Muslims	550	1,450	164%	1,880
Catholics	665	1,135	70%	1,317
Evangelicals	98	259	164%	347
Non-Catholics	570	1,137		1,397
http://www.worldreligiondatabase.org/wrd_default.asp				

and the college of bishops" (canon 782). In order to do missionary work, one must be sent "by the competent ecclesiastical authority" (canon 784), which, in most cases, includes only clerics. In fact, in my cursory survey of the reports of US lay missionary societies, I found that *all* dedicate themselves exclusively to work of charity, not evangelization. Moreover, many missionary congregations of priests emphasize in their pamphlets their charity work, seldom highlighting their missionary accomplishments, as if missionary work were mainly charity work abroad. Parish outreach programs often offer soup kitchens, food pantries, and thrift shops, but this is not very different from what secular social agencies do; usually they do not offer spiritual help to any great extent.

While the traditional *extra ecclesiam nulla salus* (no salvation outside the church) is still upheld by most evangelicals—which gives them strong missionary incentives—no equally compelling missionary theory has replaced it in the mainline churches. Prominent Catholic theologians (e.g., Dupuis, Sobrino, Haight, and Waldenfels) have promoted an inclusive theology of inter-religious dialogue that recognizes the salvific dimension of non-Christian religions; whatever the value of inclusivity, there is little missionary imperative in such dialogue, which takes place mainly among highly specialized intellectuals.

Finally, the pastoral strategy at work in Catholicism is based on the expectation that the "inactive Catholics" will come back, as seen in previous chapter, and that the "separate brothers" (actually the excommunicated brothers) will come back to the fold recognizing their errors. A strategy based on the aphorism, "it is not the healthy who need a doctor but the sick" (Matthew 9:12), will make catering to the spiritually poor a high priority; it will cater to the unchurched, the alienated youth, and all the spiritually sick of society, rather than simply hoping for the return of inactive Catholics. The more alienated one is from God and the church, the more help one needs and the more one should get. This is the pastoral strategy of many evangelical churches.

Besides these theoretical reasons for the lack of Catholic evangelization, there is also a structural one: the absence in parishes of totally committed leaders in any great numbers promoting evangelization directly and indirectly. In the pastoral plan outlined here, a parish should be first of all a vibrant community of active participants with only a minority of passive attenders. Out of these enthusiastic members, 20 to 30 percent could be expected to become involved over a ten-year period, and out of these involved, maybe 5 percent could become totally committed leaders in the following years. Thus the average parish of 760 Sunday attenders could expect over 150 involved members, and at a later stage, maybe 7 or 8 totally committed leaders. This was approximately the structure of many pre-Vatican II parishes staffed with many priests, sisters, and devout members. This is also the structure of the churches at Bayville and Saddleback. In the absence of these totally committed leaders, a parish may be a tower built on sand. It is these evangelically minded leaders who will inspire the evangelization effort of the most enthusiastic parishioners. As shown in sociological research and illustrated in evangelical churches, local evangelization is usually the work of ordinary church members, rather than extraordinary preachers; abroad it is more often the work of missionaries supported by their religious congregation and prayer teams at home. The pastoral plan outlined here also explains the priestly decline: vocations are the natural outgrowth of the process that leads from active family participation in the liturgy to involvement in devotions and small groups to total commitment in discipleship. A vital parish is one that produces vocations to either religious or lay ministry, some of whom will be working abroad. Today the situation is reversed: instead of sending missionaries abroad from among its most committed members, the Catholic Church is importing priests who come not as missionaries but simply as sacramental subs, often foreign to their new culture, thus aggravating the problems of poor Sunday celebrations. Today the church has difficulty catering to its own people and is ill prepared to cater to the unchurched.

According to a *New York Times* poll, 63 percent of Catholics believed in 1994 that the bread and wine of the Eucharist only represent a "symbolic presence of Christ." A full 70 percent of the 18- to 29-year-olds, and 51 percent of regular Mass attenders believe so today.[237] This is not surprising since transubstantiation means little to those not versed in Aristotelian philosophy. Most nonpracticing Catholics do not seem to need sacraments, as they increasingly drop, first, Sunday attendance and confession, and years later, even the baptism and instruction of their children. Even regular practicing Catholics who join evangelical churches do not seem to need the sacraments, as they find Christ more "really present" in Scripture and their new church than in their past weekly Masses, according to what they say. Hence, the bottom line is that most nonpracticing Catholics are nonsacramental Christians requiring a pastoral strategy that treats them as such.

Much more could be said about evangelization. Rick Warren spends most of his book, *The Purpose-Driven Church*, on reaching the unchurched. I have spent more time on moving passive attenders into active participants. Logical steps in pastoral development need to be followed: there will be little evangelization in a parish without totally committed disciples, and there will be no disciples without the first step of active participation of all the faithful in the liturgy. The purpose of church life is spiritual growth: "The product of the church is changed lives, not quality worship," states a sociological study of church renewal. "Enhancing worship is only relevant in terms of the transformation effect it has on the people who attend."[238] When lives are changed, they become role models for others to follow—that is, a form of evangelization. Discipleship naturally leads to evangelization.

The lack of missionary work in the Catholic Church is very serious, not only because it leads to decline in membership, but also because it betrays serious evangelical and theological weaknesses. An evangelical life inevitably leads to evangelization and a compelling theology of missions. Catholicism has long taken pride in its superior theology. Maybe the age of superior theologies (e.g., Rahner, Schillebeeckx) is over; maybe superior forms of spirituality (e.g., Mother Teresa, Bishop Romero, Archbishop Tutu) is what is needed today and tomorrow. What is needed is renewal, not restoration. *Ecclesia semper reformanda.* The church always needs renewal. Luther believed so, but not the papacy of the time. When renewal finally came with Trent, it was a *Counter*-Reformation, a restoration.

In summary, this proposal is based on the organic growth model of ever-higher differentiation, in which lower levels must be achieved before higher levels can emerge. It is inspired by observation and traditional wisdom. This model expresses at the theoretical level what we have observed at Bayville and St. Mary's. These churches are Christ-centered rather than church-centered; they offer a sacramentality of transformation

> **In Short**
> "We bring them in as *members*,
> we build them up to *maturity*;
> we train them for *ministry*,
> and send them out on *mission*."
> *Purpose-Driven Church*, 108

rather than rites of passage; they suggest models of transcendence, as in Maslow's theory of development, and spiritual growth, as in the Christian tradition. These two churches are real communities, as seen in their weekly meetings, their Sunday worship, and their structures of governance, not just in their Sunday-morning assemblies. St. Mary's can be taken as a model of liturgical participation, having few passive attenders. Most parishes should achieve that level in order to stop losing members. The next level is best illustrated by Bayville, which can be seen as a school of discipleship leading to total commitment. The Catholic Church has a rich tradition of spirituality in its monasteries and convents, but they need to be rediscovered and propagated. These goals are achievable, as attested by both Bayville and St. Mary's. The year 2030 may be soon with us, but the challenges of church decline and renewal will remain with us for a long time.

LAZARUS, WAKE UP!

It happened in the past. It can happen again. *Marana-tha!*

References

Introduction

[1] See
http://www.Bible.ca/global_religion_statistics_world_christian_encyclopedia.htm
http://www.wholesomewords.org/missions/greatc.html#religions

[2] Paul Perl, Jennifer Z. Greeley, and Mark M. Gray, "How Many Hispanics are Catholic? Reviewing the Evidence," a paper presented at the annual meeting of the Association for the Sociology of Religion, August 2004, summarized as "Identifying U.S. Hispanic Catholics," *CARA Reports* 10, no. 2 (Fall 2004).

[3] http://cara.georgetown.edu/sacraments.html

Chapter 1: Inconvenient Statistics

[4] Quoted by Paul Lakeland, "Maturity and the Lay Vocation: From Ecclesiology to Ecclesiality," in *Catholic Identity and the Laity*, ed. Tim Muldoom (Orbis Books, 2009), 246.

[5] Dean M. Kelly, *Why Conservative Churches are Growing* (New York: Harper and Row, 1977).

[6] Ibid., 10.

[7] Barry A. Kosmin and Ariela Keysar, *Religion is a Free Market* (Ithaca, NY: Paramount Market Publishing, 2006), 60–61.

[8] "Faith in Flux: Changes in Religious Affiliation," in the US Pew Forum Report of April 27, 2009, http://pewforum.org/docs/?DocID=411.

[9] Joseph Fichter, *Social Relations in the Urban Parish* (University of Chicago Press, 1954), 85.

[10] William McCready and Andrew Greeley, "The End of American Catholicism?" *America* (October 28, 1972).

[11] Dean R. Hoge, *Converts, Dropouts, Returnees: A Study of Religious Change Among Catholics*, presented at the United States Catholic Conference in Washington DC (New York: The Pilgrim Press, 1981), 24.

[12] *CARA Reports* 10, no. 4: 10.

[13] Between 2000 and 2007, CARA administered twelve telephone (face-to-face) interviews and found an average weekly attendance of 34.25 percent, while in six self-administered (anonymous) surveys, the average attendance was only 22.7 percent. See http://cara.georgetown.edu/MarriageReport.pdf "Marriage in the Catholic Church: A Survey of U.S. Catholics" 2007, p. 32.

[14] See the 2008 CARA report "Sacraments Today: Belief and Practices among U.S. Catholics," found at http://cara.georgetown.edu/sacraments.html.

[15] Robert Wuthnow, "Recent Pattern of Secularization: A Problem of Generations," *American Sociological Review* 41 (October 1976).

[16] Alasdair Crockett, "Generations of Decline: Religious change in 20th-Century Britain," *Journal for the Scientific Study of Religion* (2006), 45(4): 567–584.

[17] Christian Smith with Patricia Snell, *Souls in Transition: The Religious and Spiritual Lives of Emerging Adults* (Oxford University Press, 2009), 99.

[18] Christian Smith, *Soul Searching: The Religious and Spiritual Lives of American Teenagers* (Oxford University Press, 2005), 216.

[19] Ibid., chapter 2.

[20] Data on priests and sisters in *CARA Report* 12 (Summer 2006): 7.

[21] Rodney Stark and Roger Finke, "Catholic Religious Vocation: Decline and Revival," in *Review of Religious Research* (December 2000).

[22] Data on Catholic schools from *CARA Report* 12, no. 2 (Fall 2006): 6.

[23] *CARA Report* 12, no. 3 (Winter 2007): 3.

[24] *CARA Report* 12, no.1 (Summer 2006): 1.

[25] *CARA Report* 12, no.3 (Winter 2007): 3.

[26] Ibid.

[27] Donald Dietrich, ed., *Priests for the 21st Century* (New York: Crossroad, 2006), 135.

[28] *CARA Report* 15, no.1 (Summer 2009), 6.

[29] James D. Davidson, "Fewer and Fewer: Is the Clergy Shortage Unique to the Catholic Church?" *America* (December 1, 2003), 10–13.

[30] http://www.christianpost.com/article/20070629/poll-americans-confidence-in-the-church-nears-all-time-low/

[31] Ibid., 96–100.

[32] This table is a summary of data presented on pages 96, 99, and 100 in William V. D'Antonio, James D. Davidson, Dean R. Hoge, and Mary L. Gautier, *American Catholics Today: New Realities of Their Faith and Their Church* (New York: Rowman and Littlefield, 2007).

[33] Cynthia Woolever and Deborah Bruce, *Beyond the Ordinary: 10 Strengths of U.S. Congregations*. (Louisville, KY: Westminster John Knox Press, 2004), 37–42.

[34] Ibid., 13–20.

[35] Ibid., 89.

[36] Ibid., 56–60.

[37] Ibid., 101–05.

[38] http://www.thearda.com/mapsReports/reports/US_2000.asp

[39] http://livinginliminality.files.wordpress.com/2009/03/aris_report_2008.pdf

[40] "Changing Faiths: Latinos and the Transformation of American Religion," http://pewhispanic.org/reports/report.php?ReportID=75, page 29 of printed report.

[41] Ibid., 31.

[42] Ibid., 31.

[43] Ibid., 44.

Chapter 2: Three Factors of Spiritual Decline

[44] For a quick introduction, see http://en.wikipedia.org/wiki/Maslow's_hierarchy_of_needs

[45] Jeffrey K. Hadden, 1987, "Towards Desacralizing the Secularization Theory," *Social Forces* 65: 587.

[46] Max Weber, *The Protestant Ethic and the Spirit of Capitalism*, trans. Talcott Parsons (New York: Charles Scribner's Sons, 1958), 181.

[47] Steve Bruce, *God Is Dead: Secularization in the West* (Malden, MA: Blackwell Publishers, 2002).

[48] Dobbelaere Karel, "Toward an Integrated Perspective of the Processes Related to the Descriptive Concept of Secularization," in Swatos William H. Jr. and Daniel V.A. Olson, *The Secularization Debate* (New York: Rowman and Littlefield, 2000), 24; italics in the text.

[49] *Le Monde*, January 20, 2007, and May 10, 2007.

[50] http://www.csun.edu/science/health/docs/tv&health.html

[51] http://en.wikipedia.org/wiki/Derivatives_market

[52] http://www.marketwatch.com/story/derivatives-are-the-new-ticking-time-bomb

[53] http://en.wikipedia.org/wiki/Subprime_mortgage_crisis

[54] Roger Finke and Rodney Stark, *The Churching of America 1776–1990: Winners and Losers in Our Religious Economy* (New Brunswick, NJ: Rutgers University Press, 1992), chapters 3, 5, and 7.

[55] Ibid., 255–274.

[56] Thomas Luckmann, *The Invisible Religion: The Problem of Religion in Modern Society* (New York: Macmillan, 1967), 94–106.

[57] Peter L. Berger, *The Sacred Canopy: Elements of a Sociological Theory of Religion* (Garden City, NY: Doubleday, 1967), 133.

[58] Dobbelaere Karel, "An Integrated Perspective," 25.

[59] Robert Bellah, *Habits of the Heart: Individualism and Commitment in American Life* (New York: Harper and Row, 1985), 221.

[60] Ibid., 235.

[61] Barry A. Kosin and Ariela Keysar, *Religion in a Free Market* (Ithaca, NY: Paramount Market Publications, 2006), 60–61.

[62] Sargeant, 1994, page 10, quoted in
http://religiousmovements.lib.virginia.edu/nrms/superch.html#mode
This page no longer available. Similar ideas are expressed by Kimon Howland Sargeant in *Seeker Churches. Promoting Traditional Religion in a Nontraditional Way*. Rutgers University Press, 2000.

[63] Report of the National Center on Addiction and Substance Abuse (CASA) at Columbia University at www.casacolumbia.org.

[64] Peter Berger, *Sacred Canopy*, 133.

[65] Ibid., 156.

[66] William V. D'Antonio, James D. Davidson, Dean R. Hoge, and Katherine Meyer, *American Catholics: Gender, Generation, and Commitment* (Walnut Creek, CA: AltaMira, 2001), 27.

[67] Erik Erikson, *Identity and the Life Cycle* (New York: International University Press, 1959).

———, *Identity, Youth and Crisis* (New Yolk: Norton and Co., 1968).

———, *The Life Cycle Completed* (New York: Norton and Co., 1982).

[68] James W. Fowler, *Stages of Faith: The Psychology of Human Development and the Quest for Meaning* (San Francisco: Harper and Row, 1981), 161.

Chapter 3. Three Factors of Catholic Decline

[69] *Baltimore Catechism*, No. 3 (Rockford, IL: Tan Books, 1974), question 490.

[70] Robert J. Miller, "Why Catholics Don't Attend Sunday Mass: An Action Research Approach," paper presented at the SSSR meeting, Tampa, 2007, page 13.

[71] Available at http://www.ppo.catholic.org.au/researcharts/researcharts.shtml#movingAway.

[72] http://www.ppo.catholic.org.au/pdf/DCReport.pdf, page 6.

[73] Jacques Dupuis, ed., *The Christian Faith in the Doctrinal Documents of the Catholic Church*, 6th ed. (New York: Alba House, 1995), 285.

[74] *Humanae Vitae*, no. 4 (available at www.vatican.va).

[75] All quotations from James A. Coriden, Thomas J. Green, and Donald E. Heintschel, eds., *The Code of Canon Law: A Text and Commentary* (Mahwah, NY: Paulist Press, 1985).

[76] Text published in the *National Catholic Reporter*, July 17, 1998.

[77] http://www.usccb.org/laity/marriage/MarriedLove.pdf

[78] *National Catholic Reporter*, November 24, 2006, 24.

[79] http://www.usccb.org/dpp/Ministry.pdf

[80] http://www.usccb.org/faithfulcitizenship/FCStatement.pdf, paragraph 44.

[81] *America*, January 7–14, 2008, 7.

82 *National Catholic Reporter*, December 29, 2006, and *New York Times*, January 5, 2007.

83 William D'Antonio, James D. Davidson, Dean R. Hoge, and Mary L. Gautier, *American Catholics Today: New Realities of Their Faith and Their Church* (New York: Rowman and Littlefield, 2007), 61.

84 *National Catholic Reporter*, September 30, 2005, 15.

85 *National Catholic Reporter*, March 9, 2005, 5.

86 James O'Toole, ed., *Habits of Devotion: Catholic Religious Practice in Twentieth Century America* (Cornell University Press, 2004) 60.

87 Ibid., 61.

88 C. Kirk Hadaway and Penny Long Marler, "Growth and Decline in the Mainline," paper presented at the SSSR convention in Tampa. Fl, 2007, pages 1–2.

89 Wade Clark Roof, *Spiritual Marketplace: Baby Boomers and the Remaking of American Religion* (Princeton University Press, 1999), chapter 6.

90 Christian Smith with Melinda Lundquist Denton, *Soul Searching: The Religious and Spiritual Lives of American Teenagers* (Oxford University Press, 2005), 68.

91 Jacques Dupuis, *The Christian Faith* (New York: Alba House, Sixth Revised Edition, 1998), 183–88.

92 Ibid., 170.

93 http://www.vatican.va/holy_father/john_paul_ii/audiences/1986/index_en.htm

94 Paragraph numbers are taken from the *Osservatore Romano*.

95 Roger Haight, *Jesus: Symbol of God* (Maryknoll, NY: Orbis Books, 2000), 225–26.

96 St. Anselm, *Proslogium, Monologium, Cur Deus Homo*, trans. from Latin by Sidney Norton Deane (Chicago: The Open Court Publishing Company, 1903), 230–31.

97 Trent, "Decree on Original Sin No. 512" in Jacques Dupuis, ed., *The Christian Faith in the Doctrinal Documents of the Catholic Church*, 6th ed. (New York: Alba House, 1995), 187.

98 Michael Finlan, *Options on Atonement in Christian Thought* (Collegeville, MN: The Liturgical Press, 2007).

99 Richard P. McBrien, *Catholicism* (New York: Winston Press, 1980), 732.

100 William M. Thompson, ed., *Bérulle and the French School: Selected Writings* (New York: Paulist Press, 1989), 184.

[101] Walter M. Abbott, ed., *The Documents of Vatican II* (New York: The America Press, 1966), 141, no. 7.

[102] "Leaving the Roman Catholic Church: An Empirical Enquiry Among Former Members," a random telephone survey (50 percent London, 25 percent York, 25 percent Exeter, with 1,604 questionnaires returned) by Leslie J. Francis, University of Warwick (paper presented at the SSSR convention of 2008).

[103] Antony Koch and Preuss Arthur, *A Handbook of Moral Theology*, vol. 1. (St. Louis, MO: Herder Book Co., 1918), 119.

[104] Ibid., 1:7.

[105] Ibid., 2:1.

[106] Ibid., 1:130.

[107] http://www.vatican.va/holy_father/pius_xii/encyclicals/documents/hf_p-xii_enc_12081950_humani-generis_en.html

[108] Joseph Fuchs, *Personal Responsibility and Christian Morality* (Washington DC: Georgetown University Press, 1983), 53.

[109] Ibid., 75.

[110] Ibid., 120.

[111] Joseph Fuchs, *Christian Ethics in the Secular Arena.* (Washington DC: Georgetown University Press, 1984), note 1, pages 63–64.

[112] Vincent MacNamara, *Faith and Ethics* (Washington DC: Georgetown University Press, 1985), 4.

[113] Ibid., no. 10, in Walter M Abbott, ed., *The Documents of Vatican II* (New York: The America Press, 1966).

[114] *Gaudium et Spres*, no. 27, in M. Abbott, ed., *The Documents of Vatican II* (New York: The America Press, 1966), 226.

[115] John Paul II, *The Splendor of Truth* (Washington DC: Office for Publishing and Promotion Services, USCC, 1993), no. 80.

[116] Ibid., no. 82.

[117] Charles E. Curran, *The Catholic Moral Tradition Today: A Synthesis* (Washington DC: Georgetown University Press, 1999), 73.

Chapter 4: The Missionary Church of Bayville

[118] Randall Collins, *Interaction Ritual Chains*. (Princeton University Press, 2004), 48.

[119] Victor Turner, *The Ritual Process: Structure and Anti-Structure* (Ithaca, NY: Cornell University Press, 1969), 144.

[120] On April 20, the day Pope Benedict XVI visited New York, the senior pastor briefly prayed for the spiritual success of the pope's visit.

[121] Victor Turner, *The Forest of Symbols: Aspects of Ndembu Ritual* (Ithaca, NY: Cornell University Press, 1967), chapter 4.

[122] Ibid., chapter 3.

[123] US Congregational Life Survey, 2001 (data available at http://www.thearda.com/Archive/Files/Downloads/USCLSRA_DL.asp).

[124] George Maloney, *Inward Stillness* (Starrucca, PA : Dimension books, 1974), 115–18.

[125] Piroska Nagy, *Le don des Larmes au Moyen-Âge* (Paris: Albin Michel, 2000), 140.

[126] On the gift of tears, see http://www.helpforchristians.co.uk/articles/a28.asp.

Chapter 5: The Community of Communities: St. Mary's

[127] Joachim Wach, *Sociology of Religion* (The University of Chicago Press, 1944), 173.

[128] Ibid., 173–86.

[129] *The Rule of St. Benedict*, trans. with introduction and notes by Anthony C. Meisel and M. L. del Mastro (Garden City, NY: Doubleday Image Books, 1975), 47.

[130] Patricia Wittberg, *The Rise and Fall of Catholic Religious Orders: A Social Movement Perspective* (Lexington Books, 2006).

[131] Ernst Troeltsch, *The Social Teaching of the Christian Churches*, trans. by Olive Wyon, with an introduction by H. Richard Niebuhr (Harper and Row, 1960), 691–805 and 1006–10.

[132] Roger Finke and Patricia Wittberg, "Organizational Revival from Within: Explaining Revivalism and Reform in the Roman Catholic Church," *Journal for the Scientific Study of Religion* 39 (2000): 154–70.

[133] Dogmatic Constitution of the Church (*Lumen Gentium*), no. 11, in Walter M. Abbott, ed., *The Documents of Vatican II* (The America Press, 1966), 29.

[134] http://cara.georgetown.edu/FreeResearch.html

[135] Ernst W. Burgess and Harvey J. Locke, *The Family From Institution to Companionship* (New York: American Book Company, 1945), 3.

[136] USCCB, *Follow the Way of Love* (1992). See also Florence Caffdrey Bourg, *Where Two or Three are Gathered: Christian Families as Domestic Churches* (University of Notre Dame Press, 2004), chapter 6.

[137] Maxwell E. Johnson, *The Rite of Christian Initiation*, 2nd ed. (Collegeville, MI: The Liturgical Press, 2007).

[138] References withheld, to avoid identification.

[139] Arnold Van Gennep, *The Rites of Passage* (University of Chicago Press, 1961).

[140] USCCB, *The Rites of the Catholic Church as Revised by the Second Ecumenical Council* (Collegeville: The Liturgical press, 1990) No 141.

[141] Maxwell E. Johnson, *The Rite of Christian Initiation*. (Collegeville, MI: The Liturgical Press, 1989) pp 369-373.

[142] Constitution on the Sacred Liturgy, no. 2 in Walter M. Abbott, S.J., ed., *The Documents of Vatican II* (The American Press, 1966).

[143] Ibid., no. 14.

[144] Ibid., no. 48.

[145] *Baltimore Catechism*, No. 3 (Rockford, IL: Tan Books, 1974), question 490, page 97.

[146] Constitution on the Sacred Liturgy, no. 48.

[147] The Latin text and the English translation can be found at http://www.catholicliturgy.com/index.cfm/FuseAction/TextContents/Index/4/SubIndex/67/TextIndex/9.

[148] The French text of the Roman Canon can be found at http://www.portstnicolas.org/Prieres_eucharistiques.html.

[149] In the *New Roman Missal* to be implemented the first Sunday of Advent of 2011, all the shortcomings mentioned here have been changed.

[150] These shortcomings are also changed in the *New Roman Missal*.

[151] Henri de Lubac, *Corpus Mysticum: L'Eucharistie et l'église au moyen âge* (Paris: Aubier, 1948).

[152] Louis-Marie Chauvet, *The Sacraments. The Word of God at the Mercy of the Body* (Collegeville, MN: Liturgical Press, 2001) 139–41.

[153] Joseph Martos, *Doors to the Sacred* (Garden City, NY: Doubleday, 1981), chapter 8.

[154] Edward Foley, Nathan D. Mitchell, and Joanne M Pierce, eds., *A Commentary of the General Instruction of the Roman Missal* (Collegeville, MI: The Liturgical Press, 2007), 171.

[155] Ibid., 173–80.

[156] http://blog.adw.org/tag/latin-mass/ Not copyrighted.

[157] Constitution on the Sacred Liturgy, no. 52.

[158] Catholic Encyclopedia, entry "homily."
See http://www.newadvent.org/cathen/07448a.htm.

[159] James A. Coriden, Thomas J. Green, and Donald E. Heinstschel, eds., *The Code of Canon Law: A Text and Commentary* (Paulist Press, 1985), 553.

[160] The text of the homilies is available in the weekly parish bulletin.

[161] Report available at http://cara.georgetown.edu/pdfs/FinancingCatholicParishes.pdf.

[162] http://www.christlife.org/evangelization/articles/C_newevan.html

Chapter 6: Planned Renewal

[163] Robert Wuthnow, "Recent Pattern of Secularization: A Problem of Generations," *American Sociological Review* 41 (October 1976).

[164] Erik H. Erikson, *Childhood and Society* (New York: Norton, 1950).

[165] James W. Fowler, *Stages of Faith: The Psychology of Human Development and the Quest for Meaning* (San Francisco: Harper and Row, 1981).

[166] http://www.census.gov/hhes/www/poverty/data/incpovhlth/2007/index.html

[167] http://ncadi.samhsa.gov/govpubs/prevalert/v5/5.aspx

[168] http://www.casacolumbia.org/absolutenm/articlefiles/380-Wasting%20the%20Best%20and%20the%20Brightest.pdf

[169] Text available at http://www.usccb.org/evangelization/goandmake/index.shtml.

[170] http://www.usccb.org/evangelization/programs.shtml#prayernet

[171] This quotation has been deleted from the PNCEA page on inactive Catholics found at http://www.pncea.org/ministries/inactive.aspx

172 William V. D'Antonio, James D. Davidson, Dean R. Hoge, and Mary Gautier, *American Catholics*: (Rowman and Littlefield, 2007), 27 and 43.

173 http://www.pepparish.org/best-practices/

174 Bernard J. Lee with William V. d'Antonio, *The Catholic Experience of Small Christian Communities* (New York, Paulist Press, 2000), p. 10

175 http://www.renewintl.org/RENEW/home.nsf/vLaunch/Home?OpenDocument &MainLink=/RENEW/home.nsf/vPages/WhyCathOV?OpenDocument

176 See James Kelley, "Does the RENEW Program Renew?" *America* (March 7, 1987), 197–99.

177 Albert L. Winseman, *Growing an Engaged Church: How to Stop "Doing Church" and Start Being the Church Again* (New York: Gallup Press, 2007), 63.

178 This graph illustrates what is found in Albert L. Winseman, *Growing an Engaged Church*, 151.

179 ARCS (Action Research—Church and Society), *Living Church in the Global City: Theology in Practice* research report (University of London: Pastoral and Social Studies Department, Heythrop College), 29.

180 Ibid., 70.

181 Seminar handout, page 10 (information withheld for the sake of the anonymity of participants).

182 See Joe McGinniss, *The Selling of the President* (1968).

183 Will Herberg, *Protestant, Catholic, Jew* (Garden City: Doubleday,1955, 1960), 260–61.

184 I follow the presentation of John Bellamy, Bryan Cussen, Sam Sterland, Keith Castle, Ruth Powell, and Peter Kaldor, *Enriching Church Life: A Practical Guide for Local Churches.* (Adelaide, South Australia: Openbook, 2006).

185 Cynthia Woolever and Deborah Bruce, *Beyond the Ordinary: Ten Strengths of U.S. Congregations* (Louisville, KY: Westminster John Knox Press, 2004), 136.

186 Christian A. Schwarz, *Natural Church Development: A Guide to Eight Essential Qualities of Healthy Churches* (Carol Stream, IL: ChurchSmart Resources, 1998), 23.

187 Ibid., 28.

188 Ibid., 33.

189 Rick Warren, *The Purpose-Driven Church: Growth Without Compromising Your Message and Mission* (Grand Rapids, MI: Zondervan, 1995), 32–33.

287

190 *Time*, August 18, 2008, 37–42.

191 See http://www.willowcreek.com/AboutUs.

192 Greg L. Hawkins and Cally Parkinson, *Reveal: Where are You?* (The Willow Creek Association, 2007), 14.

193 Ibid., 37.

194 Ibid., 52.

195 *National Catholic Reporter*, January 9, 2009, 15.

Chapter 7: Renewal for Horizon 2030

196 Reference to picture of filial piety: http://www.sgpolitics.net/?p=3529 (August 2009). Not copyrighted. Also at http://4en.veduchina.com/attachments/2008/09/1_200809061053551wHXD.jpg.

197 James Coleman, "The Rational Reconstruction of Society," 1992 Presidential Address, *American Sociological Review* 58: 1–15.

198 Edward Shorter, *The Making of the Modern Family* (New York: Basic Books, 1975), 55–57.

199 The English translation has been removed from the web; see the Latin text at: http://www.jgray.org/codes/1917CIC.txt

200 *Theological Studies*, December 1955 p. 583

201 Ibid., 590.

202 Anthony Giddens, *The Transformation of Intimacy* (Stanford, CA: Stanford University Press, 1992), 58.

203 Ibid., chapter 3.

204 See http://bradley.chattablogs.com/archives/2009/02/. Not copyrighted.

205 Anthony Giddens, *The Transformation of Intimacy*, p. 109.

206 Photo courtesy of Ann Parry, www.AnnParryPhotography.com.

207 Anthony Giddens, *The Transformation of Intimacy*, p.185–86.

208 Anthony Giddens, *Modernity and Self-Identity: Self and Society in the Late Modern Age* (Stanford, CA: Stanford University Press. 1991), 76.

[209] Terrence W. Tilley, *The Disciples' Jesus: Christology as Reconciling Practice* (New York: Orbis Books, 2008), chapter 4.

[210] Dietrich Bonheoffer, *The Cost of Discipleship* (New York: The Macmillan Company, 1959), 35–36.

[211] Segunda Conferencia General del Episcopado Latinoanmericano, *Documentos Finales de Medellín* (Buenos Aires: Ediciones Paulinas, 1968).

[212] V Conferencia General del Episcopado Latinoamericano y del caribe, Documento Conclusivo, Aparecida, 4th ed. (Mixco, Guatemala), 21.

[213] Ibid., 223, no. 551.

[214] Albert L. Winseman, *Growing an Engaged Church* (New York: The Gallup Press, 2007), 67.

[215] Ibid., 68.

[216] http://cara.georgetown.edu/CARAServices/requestedchurchstats.html

[217] https://www.cia.gov/library/publications/the-world-factbook/appendix/appendix-d.html

[218] Edward Foley, *From Age to Age: How Christians Have Celebrated the Eucharist* (Collegeville, MN : Liturgical Press, 2008), 207.

[219] Ibid., 195–96.

[220] Robert Wuthnow, *After Heaven: Spirituality in America Since the 1950s* (University of California Press, 2000).

[221] Will Herberg, *Protestant, Catholic, Jew: An Essay in American Religious Sociology* (Garden City, NY: Doubleday and Co., 1955, 1960), 3.

[222] Arthur R. Baranowski, *Creating Small Church Communities: A Plan for Restructuring the Parish and Renewing Catholic Life,* 3rd ed. (Cincinnati, OH: St. Anthony Messenger Press, 1996).

[223] Foley, *From Age to Age,* 265.

[224] Bernard J. Lee, S.M., *The Catholic Experience of Small Christian Communities* (New York: Paulist Press, 2000), 10.

[225] Christian A. Schwarz, *Natural Church Development* (Carol Stream, IL: ChurchSmart Resources), 33.

[226] James Martin et al., *My Life with the Saints* (Loyola Press, 2007).

[227] Elizabeth A. Johnson, *Friends of God and Prophets: A Feminist Theological Reading of the Communion of Saints* (New York: Continuum, 1999).

228 Tridentine Mass at http://blog.adw.org/tag/latin-mass. Not copyrighted. Also at http://groups.yahoo.com/group/tlmarlington. The Picture of Pope Benedict XVI concelebrating Mass with fifteen thousand priests (of public domain) was posted by Canal JesusTV in the second half of July 2010.

229 Aaron Milavec, *The Didache: Faith, Hope, and Life of the Earliest Christian Communities, 50–70 CE* (The Newman Press, 2003), 30–33.

230 See French text at http://rmitte.free.fr/suivre/teilhard/teilhard4.htm

231 Pierre Teilhard de Chardin, *Hymn of the Universe* (New York: Harper and Row, 1965), 19–37.

232 1988 Directory for "Sunday Celebrations in the Absence of a Priest," no. 42.

233 Christian Smith and Michael O. Emerson with Patricia Snell, *Passing the Plate: Why American Christians Don't Give Away More Money* (New York: Oxford Press, 2008), 42.

234 Ibid., 44.

235 Ibid., 53.

236 Computed from CARA's Frequently Requested Statistics at http://cara.georgetown.edu/CARAServices/requestedchurchstats.html

237 *National Catholic Reporter*, January 28, 2000, and *America*, December 23–30, 2000, 14.

238 C. Kirk Hadaway, *Behold I Do a New Thing: Transforming Communities of Faith* (Cleveland, OH: Pilgrim Press, 2001), 34.

INDEX

Durkheim, 70

negative (apophatic) way of relating to
God, 172
neoscholasticism and "perfect society,"
169
never-attending Catholics, 229
New Jersey archdiocese of Newark,
RENEW International at, 254
New Roman Missal (2011), 128
New York Times
poll on symbolic presence of Christ
in Eucharist, 273
on processional entrance for new
archbishop, 238
on trend towards personal religion,
54
Newark New Jersey, archdiocese of,
RENEW International at, 254
newcomers to churches, 23
Nicaea (325), Council of, 105
no religion group, 3, 11–13, 33, 244,
247
nocturnal adoration, 53
non-Catholic Christians
changes in membership in, 272
number of, 2
view of Catholic morality, 172
nonmarital sexuality, surveys on, 20
nonpracticing Catholics, 229, 274
nonsacramental Christians, catering to,
271–275
Notre Dame study of Catholic parish
life, and parish dynamics, 21
novenas, 53, 215, 258
Novo Ordo (1969), 129
NOW (National Organization for
Women), 69

O
obedience
in pre-Vatican II, 38
as virtue, 63
object relations theory, 37
objectivism, 51–52, 65
OCP (Oregon Catholic Press), 245

"operation Lazarus," launching of, v
Orange (529), Council of, 56
Oratory, development of, 59–60
Order of Catechumens, 119
ordinations
of lesbians and gays, 35
of women, 26, 35
Origen, 135
original sin, 56–58, 63, 118, 163–164
Our Lady of Fatima, 258–259
outsiders in Catholic Church
description of church as power
structure, 46, 50
make up of, 41
moral vacuum and, 66
obstacles to, 165–169
ritualism and, 54
on sex reparations, 49–50
view of canon laws, 46–49
view of John Paul II, 65
view of sacraments, 44

P
PADS, 122
papacy
authority of, 46, 63, 65
custom of reverence and glory in,
214
Grand Theologian of church, 107
influence of Vatican II on, 106
religious respect for teachings of, 48
paradigm shift from traditional
conception of truth to a
inclusive conception, 261–262
parental relationship to God and
church, 208–209
parish kits, 176
Parish Mission, 175
Parish Renewal Project, 175
parishes
as communities of communities,
258
effect of declining number of priests
on, 18–19

truth, traditional *vs.* inclusive view of, 262

Turner, Victor, 70–71, 91

TV commercials, exposure to, 31

U

unchurched, 225

uncommitted Christians, 226

United States (US)

  bishops on homosexuality, 49

  Catholic Church as percent of US population, 10

  churches as melting pots, 249

  clergy supply of all churches in, 19

  declining number of priests in, 19

  evangelicals as religious force in, 2

  factors of decline of Catholic Church in, 42–43

  Latinos (Hispanics) religious identification in, 25–26

  loss of Catholic membership in, 7

  number of evangelical Christians and Catholics, 24

  prevalent social ideology in, 30

  rates of church attendance in, 2–3

  religious identification in, 11–12

  religiousness characteristic of, 185

United States Conference of Catholic Bishops (USCCB)

  Go and Make Disciples, 174–178, 205

  renewal programs, 165–174

universal priesthood of Christ, 111

US Congregational Life Survey

  about, 186–190, 206

  categories respondents could identify themselves as, 24

  parish dynamics and, 21–23

US Religious Landscape Survey (2008), 43, 55

"us" *vs.* "them," in church, 170

V

values

  fear of transmission of, 35

  nontransmission of, 34, 39

Van Gennep, Arnold, 117–118

  Les rites de passage, 117–118

Vatican II. *See also* pre-Vatican II

  creation of episcopal conferences, 106

  devotions in post, 258

  on homilies at Sunday readings, 135

  on idea of two classes of Christians, 195

  on multiple presences of Christ in churches, 263

  on participation in Mass, 214, 254

  priests and nuns in parishes post, 228

  privatization of devotions, 259

  on revelation, 51

  on sharing priesthood of Christ, 17–18

  surveys on moral issues pre- and post-, 20–21

  on theological pluralism, 64

  vision of Mass, 130–131

vegetarian abstinence, 269

virtues, obedience, 63

Voices of the Faithful, 221

W

Wach, Joachim, 103, 104, 110

Waldenfels (catholic theologian), 272

Warren, Rick

  on core lay ministers, 201

  on core ministers, 201, 228

  The Purpose-Driven Church (Warren), 176, 190–196, 206, 274–275

Weber, Max, 28–29, 30

websites, posting sins on, 137–138

Wesley, John, 55, 220

Western Europe, church attendance in, 29

CPSIA information can be obtained at www.ICGtesting.com
Printed in the USA
LVOW060957180911

246781LV00004B/13/P